BEST PLACES®
DESTINATIONS

NORTHERN CALIFORNIA COAST

2ND EDITION

EDITED BY MATTHEW POOLE

SASQUATCH BOOKS
SEATTLE

Matthew R. Poole, a native Californian, has authored and contributed to more than 20 travel guides to California and Hawaii. A graduate of the University of California, Santa Barbara, Matthew has managed to combine three of his stronger passions—writing, photography, and traveling—to his advantage. Before becoming a full-time travel writer/photographer, Matthew worked as an English tutor in Prague, ski instructor in the Swiss Alps, and scuba instructor in Maui. Addicted to a life of chronic freedom, he spends most of his time on the road doing research and avoiding commitments. He currently lives in San Francisco and can be reached at mrpoole@sirius.com.

Copyright ©1999 by Sasquatch Books.

Printed in the United States of America.
Published in the United States by Sasquatch Books
Distributed in Canada by Raincoast Books
Second edition

Series editor: Kate Rogers
Assistant editor: Novella Carpenter
Copy editor: Cynthia Rubin
Cover design: Nancy Gellos
Cover photo: Werner Dieterich/The Image Bank
Foldout map: Dave Berger
Interior design adaptation and composition: Fay Bartels,
Kate Basart, and Millie Beard

ISSN: 1095-9769
ISBN: 1-57061-173-4

SASQUATCH BOOKS
615 Second Avenue
Seattle, WA 98104
(206)467-4300
books@SasquatchBooks.com
http://www.SasquatchBooks.com

Sasquatch Books publishes high-quality adult nonfiction as well as children's books, all related to the Northwest (San Francisco to Alaska). For information about our books, contact us at the above address, or view our site on the World Wide Web.

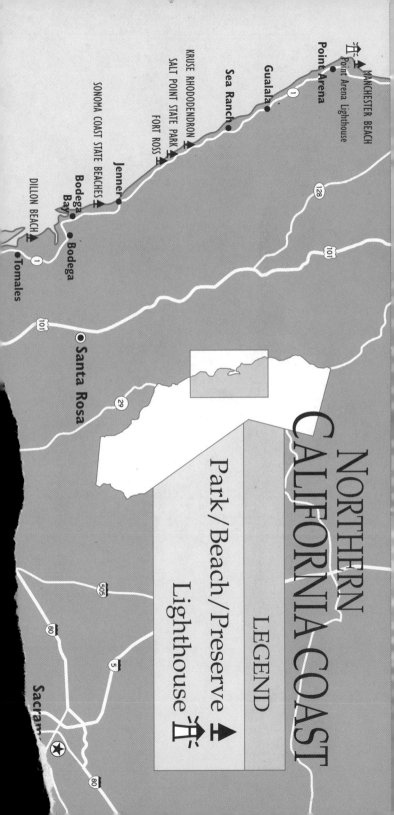

NORTHERN CALIFORNIA COAST

LEGEND

Park/Beach/Preserve ▲

Lighthouse 🔦

MANCHESTER BEACH

Point Arena Lighthouse

Point Arena

Gualala

Sea Ranch

KRUSE RHODODENDRON

SALT POINT STATE PARK

FORT ROSS

SONOMA COAST STATE BEACHES

Jenner

Bodega Bay

Bodega

DILLON BEACH

Tomales

Santa Rosa

Sacram...

128

101

101

29

505

80

5

80

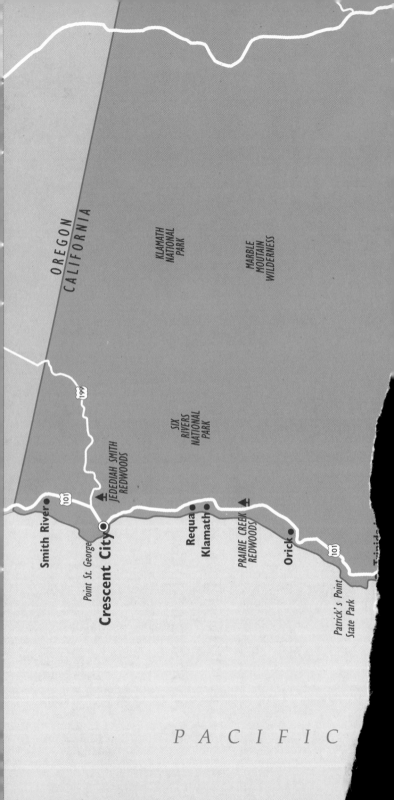

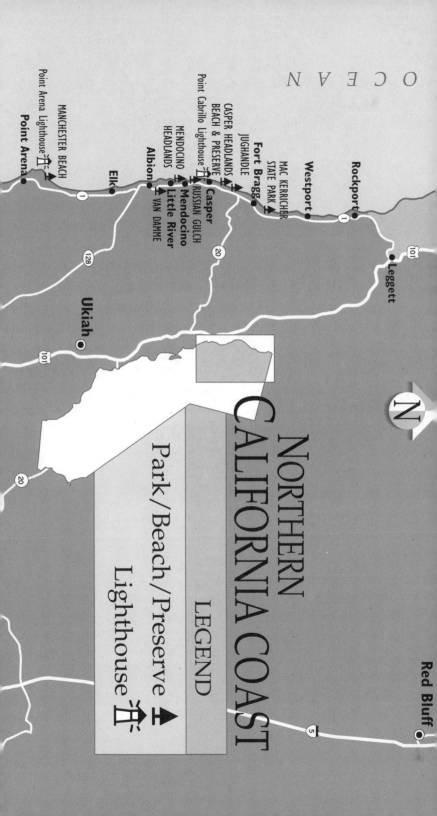

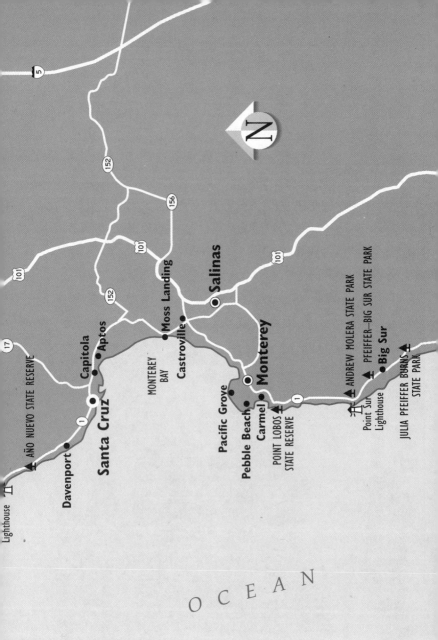

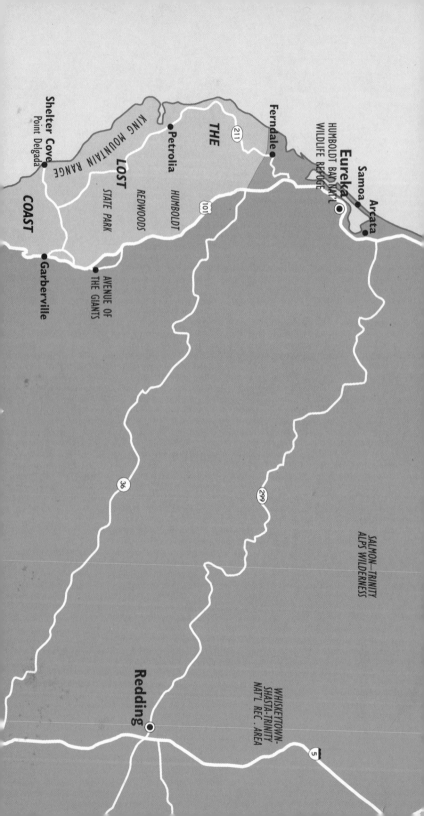

CONTENTS

ACKNOWLEDGMENTS

The second edition of *Northern California Coast* couldn't have been produced without the talented and dedicated staff at Sasquatch Books. (You wouldn't believe how much work it takes to publish this little book.) But if anyone deserves credit for creating this beast, it's my poor little Subaru. Together we literally drove to the Oregon border, flipped a U-turn, and made every right turn we could find that headed toward the sea. And through it all—the mud, the sand, the bone-jarring backroads—she never once let me down.

Next in line for recognition is Mona Behan, from whom I pilfered a sizable number of her flawless reviews, published in Sasquatch Books' *Northern California Best Places* (hey, if it works, don't fix it). Other contributors include reviewers Rebecca Poole Forée, Mary Anne Moore, and Maurice Read, as well as my ever-supportive editor, Kate Rogers.

Finally, I would like to thank everyone who housed, fed, informed, and befriended me during my journeys along the coast. Don't let anyone convince you that humankind is a selfish lot: the warmth, hospitality, and genuine selflessness I encountered from friends and strangers during my travels was constant and unwavering.

To all of you I dedicate this book.

—*Matthew Richard Poole*

HOW TO USE THIS BOOK

ACTIVITIES

The following symbols are used throughout this guide as a quick reference to activities and attractions along the coast.

 Arts and crafts, galleries

 Beaches, swimming, beachcombing, and water recreation

 Bicycling

 Entertainment: movies, theater, concerts, performing arts, and events

 Fishing (salt water and fresh)

 Food and drinks

 Golf

 Hikes and walks

 Kayaking and canoeing

 Kid friendly, family activities

 Lighthouses and historical sites

 Local produce, farmers markets, farm products, organic foods

 Parks, wilderness areas, outdoor recreation, and picnics

 Seals and sea lions

 Shops: clothing, books, antiques, souvenirs

 Views, scenic driving tours, attractions

 Whale watching, bird watching, and other wildlife viewing

RECOMMENDED
RESTAURANTS AND LODGINGS

At the end of each town section you'll find restaurants and lodgings recommended by our Best Places editors.

Rating System: Establishments with stars have been rated on a scale of zero to four. Ratings are based on uniqueness, value, loyalty of local clientele, excellence of cooking, performance measured against goals, and professionalism of service. In addition, we've included recommended bargain lodgings—the best place for the best price.

(*no stars*)	Worth knowing about, if nearby
☆	A good place
☆☆	Some wonderful qualities
☆☆☆	Distinguished, many outstanding features
☆☆☆☆	The very best in the region

|View| Watch for this symbol throughout the book, indicating those restaurants and lodgings that feature a coastal or water view.

Price Range: When prices range between two categories (for example, moderate to expensive), the lower one is given. Call ahead to verify.

$$$	Expensive. Indicates a tab of more than $80 for dinner for two, including wine (but not tip), and more than $100 for one night's lodging for two.
$$	Moderate. Falls between expensive and inexpensive.
$	Inexpensive. Indicates a tab of less than $35 for dinner, and less than $75 for lodgings for two.

Email and Web Site Addresses With the understanding that more people are using email and the World Wide Web to access information and to plan trips, BEST PLACES® has included email and Web site addresses of establishments, where available. Please note that the World Wide Web is a fluid and evolving medium, and that Web pages are often "under construction" or, as with all time-sensitive information in a guidebook such as this, may be no longer valid.

Checks and Credit Cards Most establishments that accept checks also require a major credit card for identification. Credit cards are abbreviated in this book as follows: American Express (AE); Diners Club (DC); Discover (DIS); MasterCard (MC); Visa (V).

Directions Throughout the book, basic directions are provided with each restaurant and lodging. Call ahead, however, to confirm hours and location.

Bed and Breakfasts Many B&Bs have a two-night minimum-stay requirement during the peak season, and several do not welcome children. Ask about a B&B's policies before you make your reservation.

Smoking Most establishments along the Northern California Coast do not permit smoking inside, although some lodgings have rooms reserved for smokers. Call ahead to verify an establishment's smoking policy.

Pets Most establishments do not allow pets; call ahead to verify, however, as some budget places do.

Index All restaurants, lodgings, town names, and major tourist attractions are listed alphabetically at the back of the book.

ABOUT BEST PLACES GUIDEBOOKS

Northern California Coast is part of the BEST PLACES® guidebook series, which means it's written by and for locals, who enjoy getting out and exploring the region. When making our recommendations, we seek out establishments of good quality and good value, places that are independently owned, run by lively individuals, touched with local history, or sparked by fun and interesting decor. Every place listed is recommended.

BEST PLACES® guidebooks, which have been published continuously since 1975, represent one of the most respected regional travel series in the country. Each guide is written completely independently: no advertisers, no sponsors, no favors. Our reviewers know their territory, work incognito, and seek out the very best a city or region has to offer. We provide tough, candid reports and describe the true strengths, foibles, and unique characteristics of each establishment listed.

Note: Readers are advised that the reviews in this edition are based on information available at press time and are subject to change. The editors welcome information conveyed by users of this book, as long as they have no financial connection with the establishment concerned. A report form is provided at the end of the book, and feedback is also welcome via email: books@SasquatchBooks.com.

NORTHERN CALIFORNIA COAST

THE MONTEREY COAST

A south-to-north sweep of the Monterey County coastline, beginning in Big Sur and ending north of Monterey at Moss Landing.

For the last 25 years, the Monterey coast has maintained a split personality. The handful of families who own most of the land south of Carmel—i.e., Big Sur—have endeavored to keep this rugged region as indigenous and unpopulated as possible. (In fact, Big Sur sustained a larger population a century ago than it does today.) The coastline north from Carmel, however, is just the opposite, a high-income haven blanketed with expensive homes, hotels, and boutiques. Try to find free parking or affordable lodging on a summer weekend, and the issue becomes readily apparent.

Problems aside, no one can dispute that the Monterey coast is a land of superlatives. It has one of California's most renowned scenic thoroughfares (17-Mile Drive), a slew of internationally renowned golf courses, the most popular aquarium in the nation, and even one of the most famous ex-mayors in America (Clint Eastwood). Combine all this with truly incredible coastal vistas—particularly around Big Sur—and it's not hard to see why the Monterey coast's 7 million annual visitors don't mind paying a little to park.

BIG SUR

When Spanish settlers first laid eyes on this 90-mile stretch of rugged, impassable coastline between Carmel and San Simeon, they deemed it *El País Grande del Sur,* or "the big country to the south" (that is, south of their colony at Monterey). Proving that there's nothing the English language can't butcher for the sake of brevity, El Sur Grande eventually mutated into Big Sur, an appellation that still does little to convey the unbelievable beauty bestowed on the land by Madre Nature. Mist-shrouded forests, plunging cliffs, cobalt seas, and nary a Starbucks or Taco Bell account for one of the most beautiful coastal drives in the country, if not the world. In fact, the region is so captivating that some folks favor giving it national park status; others, however, recoil in horror at the thought of involving the federal government in the preservation of this untamed land, and have coined the expression "Don't Yosemitecate Big Sur."

Despite Big Sur's popularity—summer weekends are unkind to the two-lane highway—the area has remained sparsely populated. Most visitors are day trippers vacationing in the Monterey area who come to see what all the fuss is about. The rest, aka those in the know, journey here for a few days of camping, backpacking, or luxuriating in the elegant (and exorbitantly priced) resorts. If you're only visiting for the day, start early, fill your tank, take a camera and binoculars, bring a jacket, wear comfortable shoes, drive slow, take a hike, then turn around at Julia Pfeiffer Burns State Park and do it all over again.

The only two naturally growing stands of Monterey cypress trees remaining on earth are at Point Lobos State Reserve and Pebble Beach on 17-Mile Drive.

ACTIVITIES

Point Lobos. Whether you're in Big Sur for a day or for a week, spend some time in the gorgeous 1,276-acre Point Lobos State Reserve (on Highway 1, 3 miles south of Carmel; (831)624-4909). More than a dozen trails lead to ocean coves, where you might spy sea otters, harbor seals, California sea lions, large colonies of seabirds, and, between December and May, migrating California gray whales. Wherever you trek through Big Sur, however, beware of poison oak (remember: Leaves of three, let it be).

Peruse the Point Lobos State Reserve's Web site at www.pt-lobos. parks.state.ca.us/.

Bixby Bridge. That magnificent arched span crossing over Bixby Creek Canyon is the Bixby Bridge, aka the Rainbow Bridge. At 268 feet high, 739 feet long, with a 320-foot arch, it's one of the world's highest single-span concrete bridges and a favorite stop for camera-wielding tourists. Photo tip: For the best shooting angle, drive a few hundred yards up the dirt road at the north end of the bridge (Old Coast Road).

Skip the $6 parking fee at Point Lobos State Reserve by parking alongside Highway 1 and walking (or biking) in. It's not only legal, the rangers recommend it.

Lighthouse. South of Bixby Bridge is the Point Sur Lighthouse, built in 1889 and towering 361 feet above the surf atop Point Sur, a giant volcanic-rock island easily visible from Highway 1. Inexpensive (though physically taxing) 2½-hour guided lighthouse tours are offered on weekends year-round and on Wednesdays in summer. Don't forget your jacket and $5 for admission. Call for schedule information. Off Highway 1, 19 miles south of Carmel in Big Sur; (831)625-4419.

State Park. A popular retreat for hikers and bicyclists is the 4,800-acre Andrew Molera State Park, the largest state park on the Big Sur coast. More than 15 miles of trails zigzag through grasslands, redwood forests, and along Big Sur River. A mile-long walk through a meadow laced with wildflowers leads to a 2-mile-long beach harboring the area's best tide pools. On Highway 1, 21 miles south of Carmel; (831)667-2315.

Old Coast Road. Across from the entrance to Andrew Molera State Park is the southern access point to Old Coast Road, a well-maintained (though bumpy) dirt road that passes through 10 miles of dense redwood groves and chaparral-covered ridges—with spectacular views of the coast—before exiting back onto Highway 1 at Bixby Bridge. A four-wheel-drive vehicle isn't necessary for the hour-long mini-adventure, but this isn't for the fainthearted, either.

Hiking. One thing Big Sur isn't short of is hiking trails. Pfeiffer–Big Sur State Park has dozens of trails—many with panoramic views of the sea—that crisscross the park's 810 acres of madrone and oak woodlands and misty redwood canyons. The Big Sur River meanders through the park, too, attracting anglers and swimmers hardy enough to brave the chilly waters. For overnighters, Pfeiffer–Big Sur offers 218 ultracivilized camping facilities that include showers, a laundry, a store, an amphitheater for ranger-led campfire talks, and (bless 'em) flush toilets. Park information: (800)444-7275 or (831)667-2315.

Beach. Though entrance to Pfeiffer–Big Sur State Park costs a hefty $5, the park's best attraction is free. Exactly $1^1/_{10}$ miles south of the park's entrance on Highway 1 is the unmarked turnoff to Sycamore Canyon Road, a narrow $2^1/_3$-mile paved road (motor homes can forget this one) that leads to beautiful but blustery Pfeiffer Beach, the only beach in Big Sur accessible by car. Even if the sun's a no-show, it's still worth a trip to marvel at the white-and-mauve sands, enormous sea caves, and pounding surf.

Miller Time. Three miles south of Nepenthe Restaurant is the Coast Gallery, a showplace for local artists and craftspeople featuring pottery, jewelry, and paintings, including watercolors by author Henry Miller, who lived nearby for more than 15 years. The gallery's casual Coast Cafe has a great view of the ocean and offers simple serve-yourself lunches of soup, sandwiches, baked goods, wine, and espresso drinks; Highway 1, Big Sur; (831)667-2301. The author's fans will also want to seek out the Henry Miller Library. In addition to a great collection of Miller's books and art, the library serves as one of Big Sur's cultural centers and features the art, poetry, prose, and music of locals; it's open Tuesday through Sunday, and is located just beyond Nepenthe restaurant on the east side of Highway 1; (831)667-2574.

The Big Sur-prize. If you only have the time or energy for one short hike while touring Big Sur, head for the secret cove at Partington Canyon. Don't bother looking for it on the map; it's not there. Instead, look for a long, horseshoe-shaped turn around a small canyon leading to the ocean, exactly 2 miles north of Julia Pfeiffer Burns State Park turnoff (you'll see several dirt pull-offs where you can park). Walk down the canyon toward the ocean, turn right at the "Underwater Forest" display, then left across the footbridge, and suddenly it's "Whoa! Where'd that come from?" A raging non sequitur in this remote valley is this 100-foot, hand-carved, timber-reinforced tunnel that leads to a dazzling hidden cove. Story goes John Partington built the tunnel for his tan-oak cutting and shipping operation, where sleds filled with tan-oak bark were pulled down the mountain and loaded onto ships anchored in the placid cove.

Julia's Park. At the southern end of the Big Sur area is Julia Pfeiffer Burns State Park. With 3,580 acres to roam— and a less-crowded feel to it than the region's other parks— you'll find some excellent day hikes here. If you just want to get out of the car and stretch your legs, take the ¼-mile Waterfall Trail to 80-foot-high McWay Waterfall, one of the few falls in California that plunges directly into the sea. Keep an eye open for the sea otters that play in McWay Cove; (831)667-2315.

"Most people don't know that the state parks in Big Sur are open year-round and never fill up— even in the summer. Also, your parking fee receipt is good for other state parks, too, so you only have to pay once to visit all the parks."
—Ted Guzowski, park ranger

The Molera Big Sur Trail Rides outfit offers guided horseback rides along the Big Sur coast. To reserve a pony, call (800)942-5486 or (831)625-5486.

RESTAURANTS

CAFE KEVAH ☆☆

 If your idea of communing with nature is a comfy chair in the shade, a leafy salad, and a view of the rugged coast, then grab a seat on the deck of the Cafe Kevah, located one flight of stairs below the fabled—and absurdly over-priced—Nepenthe Restaurant. Not only is Cafe Kevah's food wonderful (e.g., Australian lamb skewers with cous-cous, green mint pesto, and garlic toast; grilled salmon over tossed greens with a papaya vinaigrette; buttermilk waffles and fresh vegetable omelets), it's inexpensive, too—most menu items are under $10. The clincher, though, is the location: Perched 800 feet above the glim-mering Pacific, the cafe's deck has a phenomenal view of the Big Sur coastline. *On Hwy 1, 3 miles south of Pfeiffer–Big Sur State Park, Big Sur; (831)667-2344; Hwy 1, Big Sur; beer and wine; AE, MC, V; no checks; breakfast, lunch every day; $.*

BIG SUR RIVER INN ☆

The Big Sur River Inn is exactly the kind of restaurant you would expect to find in a mountain community—a large, rustic cabin (circa 1934), built and furnished entirely with rough-hewn woods, warmed by a large fireplace sur-rounded by comfy chairs, and occupied by jean-clad locals sharing the day's news over beers at the corner bar. In the summer most everyone requests a table on the shaded back deck, which overlooks a picturesque stretch of the Big Sur River. Since the restaurant caters to the inn's guests, it's open morning till nightfall. Breakfast is all-American (eggs, pancakes, bacon, omelets, and such), as is lunch and dinner. The menu offers a wide range of choices: pasta, burgers, chicken sandwiches, salads, fish 'n' chips, and a whole lot more. Recommended plates are the Black Angus Burger with a side of beer-battered onion rings, or a big platter of the Roadhouse Ribs served with cowboy beans. Wash either down with a cool glass of Carmel Brewing Co. Amber Ale, and you're ready to roll. *On Hwy 1, 2 miles N of Pfeiffer Big Sur State Park;*

(831)667-2700; Hwy 1, Big Sur; full bar; AE, DC, DIS, MC, V; no checks; breakfast, lunch, dinner every day.

LODGINGS

POST RANCH INN ☆☆☆☆

Travel & Leisure magazine hailed the 98-acre Post Ranch Inn "the most spectacular hotel on the Pacific Coast," and that might not be hyperbole. Discreetly hidden on a ridge in the Santa Lucia Mountains, architect Mickey Muennig's redwood complex was completed in April 1992. Muennig supposedly camped out on the property for five months before setting pencil to paper for his design, which had to conform to the strict Big Sur Coastal Land Use Plan. He propped up six of the inn's units (known as the Tree Houses) on stilts to avoid disturbing the surrounding redwoods' root systems, and sank others into the earth, roofing them with sod. The inn's deceptively simple exteriors are meant to harmonize with the forested slopes, while windows, windows everywhere celebrate the breathtaking vista of sky and sea that is Big Sur's birthright. Inside, the lodgepole construction and wealth of warm woods lend a rough-hewn luxury to the rooms. Earth tones, blues, and greens predominate, extending the link between the buildings and their environment.

"Environment," in fact, is a word you'll hear a lot around this place, which was named after William Post, one of the area's early settlers. The Post Ranch Inn is one of the new breed of eco-hotels, where the affluent can indulge in sumptuous luxury and still feel politically correct. The water is filtered; visitors are encouraged to sort their paper, glass, and plastic garbage; and the paper upon which guests' rather staggering bills are printed is recycled.

Despite this more-ecologically-correct-than-thou attitude, the folks behind the Post Ranch Inn haven't forgotten about the niceties of life. The 30 spacious rooms have spare—but by no means spartan—decor, including fireplaces, massage tables, king-size beds, and sideboards

When the El Niño storms of 1997–98 caused major landslides and road damage—closing Highway 1 for months—the ultra-luxurious Post Ranch Inn improvised by flying guests in by helicopter (for a wee fee, of course).

Post Ranch Inn architect Mickey Muennig supposedly camped out on the property for five months before setting pencil to paper for his design.

made of African hardwoods (nonendangered, naturally). Designer robes hang in the closets and whirlpool tubs for two adorn the well-equipped bathrooms. In the lobby and public areas, stereo systems fill the air with ethereal New Age music. A continental breakfast and guided nature hikes are included in the room rates; the massages, facials, herbal wraps, and yoga classes are not.

The Ranch also boasts a gorgeous, cliff-hugging restaurant that has been hailed as one of the best on the Central Coast. The **Sierra Mar Restaurant** serves a sophisticated brand of California cuisine in a serene expanse of wood and glass that lets you drink in the incredible views along with the costly wine. When you can wrest your eyes from the ocean and focus on the dinner menu, which changes daily, you might see such sumptuous starters as pine-smoked squab with ginger and cilantro; mussel soup with saffron and potatoes; and perhaps a salad of lettuces (organic, of course) mixed with shaved fennel, oranges, Parmesan, and a Campari vinaigrette. Main courses include such bounty as roast rack of venison with glazed chestnuts and huckleberries, truffled fettuccine with asparagus and English peas, and roasted guinea fowl with potato gnocchi and pearl onions. Finish off your feast with a plate of assorted house-made sweets—proof positive that politically correct need not mean diet deprived. *On Hwy 1, 30 miles S of Carmel; (831)667-2200, (800)527-2200, or (831)667-2800 (restaurant); On Hwy 1, PO Box 219, Big Sur, CA 93920; full bar; AE, MC, V; checks OK; lunch, dinner every day; $$$.* &

VENTANA COUNTRY INN RESORT ☆☆☆☆

 If one casts the Post Ranch as the brash newcomer, the Ventana must be seen as the revered granddaddy of the eco-hotel scene. Not that this stunning resort is showing its age—the Ventana is as fresh and up with the times as it was when it made its debut two decades ago. Set on the brow of a chaparral-covered hill in the Santa Lucia Mountains, this modern, weathered cedar inn is almost too serene and contemplative to be called decadent, yet too luxurious to be called anything else. Its spacious 59 rooms, decorated in an upscale country style and divided among 12 low-rise buildings, look out over the plunging forested hillsides, wildflower-laced meadows, and roiling waters of the Big Sur coast. Three houses are also available to rent; the rooms in the Sycamore and Madrone Houses have large private balconies and some of the best views of the ocean. Several rooms have fireplaces, hot tubs, and wet bars; rates climb in accordance with the amenities offered (peak-season prices range from approximately $200 to a whopping $900). A sumptuous breakfast is included.

The inn's other big draw is the **Ventana Restaurant,** which delivers panoramic patio views of 50 miles of coastline at prices that can be equally breathtaking. Although critics have been unanimous in praising its aesthetics, a revolving-door parade of chefs has kept them uncertain about the quality of the food since Jeremiah Tower's star turn here years ago. The current chef, Hamid Borna, serves ambitious dishes such as pan-seared, potato-wrapped salmon; oak-grilled Angus pavé with potato gratin; and chestnut-crusted ahi tuna. *On Hwy 1, 28 miles S of Carmel, 2½ miles S of Pfeiffer–Big Sur State Park; (831)667-2331 or (800)628-6500; Hwy 1, Big Sur, CA 93920; full bar; AE, DC, DIS, MC, V; checks OK; lunch, dinner every day; $$$.* &

DEETJEN'S BIG SUR INN ☆

During the '30s and '40s, travelers making the long journey up or down the coast used to drop in and stay the night with Grandpa Deetjen, a Norwegian immigrant. No doubt weary of houseguests, he constructed a cluster of redwood buildings with 20 rooms to accommodate them. Grandpa's idea of comfort was a bit austere, but then again, he never expected to charge $70 to $150 per night. Located in a damp redwood canyon, most cabins are divided into two units, each with dark wood interiors, hand-hewn doors without locks or keys (they can be secured with the hook and eye from within, though), and nonexistent insulation. Some have shared baths, and many are quite charming in a rustic sort of way, but they're definitely not for everyone. If you stay in one of the two-story units (some with fireplaces or wood-burning stoves), be sure to request the quieter upstairs rooms. The cabins near the river offer the most privacy.

Deetjen's Big Sur Inn Restaurant, which has garnered a loyal following, serves good Euro-California cuisine that takes advantage of local produce and seafood. The small menu varies seasonally and features half a dozen starters ranging from a warm poached pear stuffed with Stilton cheese and walnuts to the appetizer of roasted garlic, baked goat cheese, and grilled bell pepper served with tapenade and croutons. Several entrees are offered, including a fresh pasta selection that changes nightly and a roasted, sautéed, grilled, and steamed vegetable platter. Meat eaters will want to knife into such robust fare as the roasted rack of lamb with a honey-mustard and rosemary crust or an oak-grilled rib-eye steak. *On Hwy 1, 3 miles S of Pfeiffer–Big Sur State Park; (831)667-2377 or (831)667-2378 (restaurant); Hwy 1, Big Sur, CA 93920; beer and wine; MC, V; checks OK; breakfast, dinner every day; $$.*

RIPPLEWOOD RESORT ☆

With its 16 spartan cabins clustered along a rugged section of Highway 1, Ripplewood Resort is a wonderful place to go with a large group of friends. Try to book cabins 1 to 9, which are set far below the highway on the river, where the air is sweet with redwood. During the summer the popular units are typically booked four months in advance. The *Ripplewood Cafe* is comfortable and pretty and serves a good breakfast and lunch. The muffins, sticky buns, and pies are house-made, and the cinnamon French toast is a big favorite. For lunch try the marinated bean salad or the grilled Jack cheese sandwich slathered with green chile salsa. *On Hwy 1, about 1 mile N of Pfeiffer–Big Sur State Park (831)667-2242; Hwy 1, Big Sur, CA 93920; beer and wine; MC, V; no checks; breakfast, lunch every day; $$.*

BIG SUR CAMPGROUND AND CABINS

If $650 for a room at the Post Ranch Inn is a bit out of your price range, see if you can score one of the 13 adorable little A-frame cabins here, which start at about $80. Roughing it you're not: Each wood cabin comes with cozy country furnishings, wood-burning ovens, full kitchens, sleeping lofts, and even a patio. Several of the units sit along the Big Sur River, and each has a private bath and fireplace. In the summer, tent cabins are also available—with beds and bedding provided—or you can bring your sleeping bag and rough it at the 81 year-round campsites set in a large redwood grove. Guests often while away the day swimming or fishing in the river (steelhead season runs November 16 to February 28, on weekends, Wednesdays, and holidays only). Amenities include a store, laundry, playground, basketball courts, and inner-tube rentals. *On Hwy 1, about 3 miles south of Andrew Molera State Park; (831)667-2322; Hwy 1, Big Sur, CA 93920; MC, V; no checks; $–$$.*

CARMEL

In the not-so-distant past, Carmel was regarded as a reclusive little seaside town with the sort of relaxed Mediterranean atmosphere that was conducive to such pursuits as photography, painting, and writing. Robert Louis Stevenson, Upton Sinclair, and Ansel Adams all found Carmel so peaceful and intellectually inspiring as to settle down here.

Not anymore. The charmingly ragtag bohemian village of yesteryear has long since given way to a major tourist mecca brimming with chichi inns, art galleries, and house-and-garden marts offering $300 ceramic geese and other essentials. Traffic— both vehicular and pedestrian—can be maddeningly congested during the summer and on weekends, and prices in the shops, hotels, and restaurants tend to be gougingly high.

The funny thing is, no matter how crowded or expensive Carmel gets, nobody seems to mind. Enamored of the village's eclectic dwellings, outrageous boutiques, quaint cafes, and silky white beaches, tourists arrive in droves during the summer to lighten their wallets and darken their complexions. In fact, most

GETTING AROUND

Along with a ban on streetlights, franchises, and billboards, Carmel-by-the-Sea has also outlawed that scourge of modern society, the street address. That's right, no business or home within city limits has a numerical street address. Instead, people have homes with names like Periwinkle and Mouse House, and residents must go to the post office to pick up their mail. Fortunately, Carmel-by-the-Sea is small enough that this doesn't create much of a problem navigating your way around town, though a street map comes in real handy. The Carmel Business Association keeps a stack of free maps at the Carmel Visitors Center, located on San Carlos Street between 5th and 6th Avenues above the Hog's Breath Inn; (831)624-2522.

B&Bs are usually booked solid from May to October, so make your reservations far in advance and leave plenty of room on the credit cards—you'll need it.

ACTIVITIES

There are more than 90 art galleries in Carmel-by-the-Sea, a city measuring just 1 square mile.

Shopping Nirvana. Carmel is a wee bit o' heaven for shoppers. Even if you can't afford a lizard-skin gym bag or a Waterford crystal birdbath, it's still fun—and free—to window-shop among Carmel's oh-so-chic boutiques. Ocean Avenue has its share of tourist-schlock shops, it's true, but hit the side streets for some fine adventures in consumerland. Intriguing stores include Ladyfingers for jewelry (on Dolores Street between Ocean and Seventh Avenues); Handworks for beautifully made modern furniture and crafts (two locations, both on Dolores Street, one between Seventh and Eighth Avenues, and one between Fourth and Fifth Avenues); GJ's Wild West for Western clothes and accessories (on San Carlos Street between Fifth and Sixth Avenues); the Dansk II outlet for housewares (on Ocean Avenue and San Carlos Street); and the Secret Garden for pretty garden accessories (on Dolores Street between Fifth and Sixth Avenues). If you're looking for a gift for your teenager, head to On the Beach Surf Shop at Ocean and Mission

Streets, which has a huge selection of cool clothing. But wait, there's more! Just outside of town are two luxe suburban malls: the Barnyard (on Highway 1 at Carmel Valley Road) and the Crossroads (on Highway 1 at Rio Road).

Galleries. A thick cluster of quality art galleries can be found between Lincoln and San Carlos Streets and Fifth and Sixth Avenues. Particularly noteworthy is the Weston Gallery, which showcases 19th- and 20th-century photographers' works, including a permanent display featuring such famous Carmelites as Edward Weston, Ansel Adams, and Imogen Cunningham. Located on Sixth Avenue at Dolores Street; (831)624-4453.

Carmel's Beaches. If your sprees have left you shopped out, visit one of the town's fabled beaches. Carmel Beach City Park, at the foot of Ocean Avenue, tends to be overcrowded in summer (even though its chilly aquamarine water is unsafe for swimming), but the satiny white sand and towering cypresses are worth the price of sunbathing among the hordes. Better yet, head a mile south on Scenic Drive (the street running alongside the beach) to spectacular Carmel River State Beach, where the locals go to hide from the tourists. The Carmel River enters the Pacific here, and the nearby bird sanctuary is often frequented by pelicans, hawks, sandpipers, and the occasional goose. Middle Beach and Monastery Beach lie beyond.

Books & Bagels. The only thing better than a good bookstore is a good bookstore with a good cafe. Within the sea of Carmel's exorbitant boutiques and restaurants is the refreshingly unpretentious (and inexpensive) Thunderbird Bookshop and Cafe, located within the Barnyard shopping complex at Highway 1 and Carmel Valley Road. Peruse the largest book selection on the Central Coast, then sit your fanny at the adjacent cafe armed with a slice of quiche, a decaf latte, and your new read. Now that's vacationing. Open daily 10am to 8pm; (831)624-9414.

Carmel Mission. At the south end of Carmel on the corner of Rio Road and Lasuen Drive is the restored Mission San Carlos Borromeo del Río Carmelo, better known as the

If you don't feel like rambling through Carmel on your own, knowledgeable local Gale Wrausmann conducts leisurely, two-hour guided walking tours Tuesday through Saturday. Call (831)642-2700 for details or check out her Web site at www.carmelwalks.com.

Carmel Mission. Established in 1770, this was the headquarters of Father Junípero Serra's famous chain of California missions, as well as being his favorite (Serra is buried in front of the altar in the sanctuary). The vine-covered baroque church with its 11-bell Moorish tower is one of California's architectural treasures. The mission houses three extensive museums, and its surrounding 14 acres are planted with native flowers and trees. The cemetery has more than 3,000 graves of Native Americans who worked and lived in the mission; in place of a gravestone, many plots are marked by a solitary abalone shell. 3080 Rio Road at Lasuen Drive, several blocks west of Highway 1; (831)624-3600.

Trails of Solitude. If the Carmel crowds are starting to drive you buggy, head to the intersection of Mountain View Avenue and Forest Road (off Ocean Avenue) and bask in the glorious silence of Mission Trails Park. Even on the busiest weekends, the north end of the park is usually deserted, allowing those in the know a few hours' respite among the 35 shaded acres of tree-lined trails. Dogs are permitted, and plastic doo-doo bags are provided to keep things tidy.

Touring Tor House. Worth a gander is Tor House, the former home of poet Robinson Jeffers (it's still occupied by one of the Jeffers clan). Constructed over several years beginning in 1914, the rustic granite building looks as if it was transplanted from the British Isles. More intriguing, however, is the nearby four-story Hawk Tower, which Jeffers built for his wife, Una, with thousands of huge granite rocks he hauled up from the beach below his house. Guided tours of the house and tower are available for a fee on Friday and Saturday by reservation only. 26304 Ocean View Avenue at Stewart Way, Carmel-by-the-Sea; no children under 12; (831)624-1813.

Theater. Carmel has an active theater scene, perhaps best represented by the Pacific Repertory Theatre company, which puts on an outdoor musical and Shakespeare festival each summer and performs other classics such as *The Madness of George III* and *Death of a Salesman* in its indoor theater year-round. Tickets are reasonably priced; call (831)622-0700 or (831)622-0100 for details.

Johann's Bach in Town. The annual month-long Carmel Bach Festival offers numerous concerts, recitals, lectures, and discussion groups—some are even free. In addition to Bach masterpieces, you'll hear scores by Vivaldi, Scarlatti, Beethoven, and Chopin. The classical music celebration begins in mid-July; series tickets are sold starting in January, and single-event tickets (ranging from $10 to $50) go on sale in April. Call (831)624-2046 for tickets and (831)624-1521 for additional festival facts.

RESTAURANTS

PACIFIC'S EDGE ☆☆☆

Pacific's Edge, the Highlands Inn's flagship restaurant, is one of the best (and most expensive) dining establishments in the area, serving inspired California cuisine in a luxe setting blessed with panoramic views (reserve well in advance for a table at sunset). Starters might include farm-fresh artichokes with basil mayonnaise, potato-wrapped ahi tuna, or grilled quail with creamy rosemary polenta. Entrees range from grilled Monterey Bay salmon in an onion-rosemary sauce to roasted rack of lamb with white truffle potatoes. Chef Cal Stamenov also offers a nightly Sunset Dinner, a hand-picked selection of courses designed to create a truly memorable meal. *On Hwy 1, 4 miles S of Carmel; (831)624-3801 or (800)682-4811; gm@ highlands-inn.com; www.highlands-inn.com; full bar; AE, DC, DIS, MC, V; checks OK; brunch Sun, lunch, dinner every day; $$$.* &

ROBERT KINCAID'S BISTRO ☆☆☆

The master chef who created Monterey's ever-popular Fresh Cream restaurant returned to the peninsula in 1995 to open this temple to earthy haute cuisine. Wooden beams adorned with hanging dried flowers, golden-hued stucco walls, Provençal furnishings, and not one but two roaring stone hearths beckon visitors to relax. The older, moneyed clientele isn't here for the *charmant* French farmhouse atmosphere, though—they've come to sample Kincaid's culinary magic. His updated bistro fare includes such appetizers as an exceptionally

To find the perfect picnic-basket ingredients for a day on the beach, go to the Mediterranean Market on Ocean Avenue at Mission Street, which stocks a large selection of meats, cheeses, and wines; (831)624-2022.

creamy (and delicious) onion tart; delicate and delectable crab dumplings in two sauces (a honey-mustard and a dill sauce); and a baked Brie in white wine–butter sauce that may leave you feeling dangerously like Henry VIII after a state banquet. Main courses include sautéed red snapper Grenobloise (with bay shrimp, capers, and lemon) and a fillet of beef seared with green peppercorns, cream, and brandy. The *San Francisco Chronicle* deemed the roast duckling the best on the Monterey Peninsula, though it may be a mite dry and overcooked for some tastes. Desserts include mind-bendingly delicious treats such as Kincaid's signature chocolate bag with chocolate shake as well as pithiviers, a wonderfully light and tasty marriage of flaky puff pastry and almond cream. The service is both warm and impeccable, a rare combination, but the wine list disappoints: It's not as extensive as one would expect at a restaurant of this caliber and it's tipped toward pricier vintages. *217 Crossroads Blvd in the Crossroads Shopping Center at Hwy 1 and Rio Rd, Carmel; (831)624-9626; beer and wine; AE, DIS, MC, V; local checks only; lunch Mon–Fri, dinner Mon–Sun; $$$.* ⅙

SANS SOUCI ☆☆☆

True to its name, the folks at Sans Souci (French for "without worry") are determined that you'll never have to fret about the food or the service at their restaurant, which specializes in both classic and contemporary French cuisine. The candle-lit dining room has a beautiful bay window, a fireplace, fresh flowers, decorative wall sconces, and bright, cheery wallpaper bordered by white wainscoting. Despite the traditional white linens, silver, china, and crystal, Sans Souci isn't a bit stuffy. Owner John Williams' infectious sense of humor sets the tone of the place, and the young waitstaff is friendly yet highly professional. Chef Aaron Welsh's changing menu offers a large selection of appetizers, including escargots encased in filo pastry with garlic sauce, portobello mushrooms with spinach and a garlic-walnut vinaigrette, and sautéed foie gras with black currant sauce. Entrees on the seasonal menu might include duck with raspberry sauce;

a Roquefort-crusted filet mignon in cabernet sauce; or Dover sole with toasted almonds, hazelnut butter, and parsley. The desserts here put the "d" in decadent: luscious fruit soufflés, a classic tarte Tatin, and fresh fruit and ice cream–filled crêpes flambéed tableside. *On Lincoln St between 5th and 6th Aves; (831)624-6220; full bar; AE, MC, V; no checks; dinner Thurs–Tues; $$$.*

ANTON & MICHEL ★★

This longtime Carmel favorite overlooks the Court of the Fountains with its Louis XV lions and verdigris garden pavilions. Anton & Michel's elegant dining room has pink walls, white wainscoting, and tall, slender pillars adorned with curlicue cornices. Despite the interesting decor, the continental cuisine isn't very daring, but chef Max Muramatsu trained at Maxim's in Paris and Tokyo and his food is delicious and extremely well prepared. Standouts include the rack of lamb with an herb-Dijon mustard au jus, grilled veal with a spinach-Madeira sauce, and medallions of ahi tuna with a black-pepper-and-sesame-seed crust and a wasabe-cilantro sauce. Anton & Michel also offers traditional French desserts such as crêpes Suzette, cherries jubilee, and chocolate mousse cake with sauce Anglaise. Service is courtly, and the extensive wine list has garnered many *Wine Spectator* magazine awards. *On Mission St between Ocean and 7th Aves; (831)624-2406; www.critics-choice.com/restaurants/ anton; full bar; AE, DC, DIS, MC, V; no checks; lunch, dinner every day; $$$.* &

CASANOVA RESTAURANT ★★

The former home of Charlie Chaplin's cook, this sunny cottage with a Mediterranean feel attracts happy throngs of locals and tourists alike. Casanova specializes in Italian and French Country–style dishes; the pasta creations, such as linguine with seafood served in a big copper pot, are particularly fetching. Lunch on the big patio out back is informal and fun, with heaters keeping patrons warm on chilly afternoons. Inside, the cottage is a jumble of nooks and crannies decked out in rustic European decor.

Casanova prides itself on its extensive and reasonably priced wine list, including the well-received Georis merlot and cabernet, produced by one of the restaurant's owners. Cap off your meal with one of Casanova's superb desserts; the many choices include a Basque-style pear tart and a chocolate custard pie with whipped cream, nuts, and shaved dark and white Belgian chocolates. *On 5th Ave between San Carlos and Mission Sts; (831)625-0501; www.casanova-resto.com; full bar; MC, V; no checks; brunch Sun, lunch, dinner every day; $$.* &

FLYING FISH GRILL ☆☆

Hidden on the ground level of the Carmel Plaza shopping center, this ebullient newcomer is worth seeking out for its fun, stylish atmosphere and its delicious Pacific Rim seafood. The interior is a maze of booths and tables flanked by an expanse of warm, polished wood and crisp blue-and-white banners. Chef/owner Kenny Fukumoto offers such creative dishes as Yin-Yan Salmon (roast salmon on angel hair pasta sprinkled with sesame seeds and served with a soy-lime cream sauce); catfish fillets with fermented Chinese black beans, ginger, and scallions steamed in paper pouches; pan-fried Chilean sea bass with almonds, whipped potatoes, and a Chinese cabbage and rock shrimp stir-fry; and his specialty, rare peppered ahi tuna on angel hair pasta. A few meat dishes and a couple of flavorful clay pot dishes that you cook at your own table round out the menu. There's also a tempting lineup of desserts, including Chocolate Decadence, a warm banana sundae, and an assortment of delicate sorbets. *On Mission St between Ocean and 7th Aves in the Carmel Plaza; (831)625-1962; beer and wine; AE, DIS, MC, V; no checks; dinner every day; $$.*

LA BOHEME ☆☆

La Bohême is very small, very cute, and—depending on your luck—very good. The walls of this heart-flutteringly romantic restaurant are painted a pale blue and dotted with cream puff clouds. Two of the most sought-after tables are tucked inside a topsy-turvy little toy house—

part of the whimsical street scene mural. La Bohême serves only a prix-fixe menu, which changes nightly. Calendars list the entrees for an entire month, and patrons in the know make it a point to pick up this schedule as soon as they hit town. The three courses include a salad, a bowl of soup, and a main course—perhaps duck with a sherry sauce, filet mignon with a Roquefort-wine sauce, or prawns and scallops in a champagne sauce. The soups, such as salmon bisque, and the salads, with Carmel Valley organic greens, are universally wonderful. The entrees, alas, are less predictable, due to inconsistent meat preparation; cuts can range from splendidly pink and juicy to dull and overcooked. On the other hand, when everything works, La Bohême's cuisine ranks among the best in Carmel, at bargain prices to boot. At worst, you can console yourself with the rich but fluffy chocolate mousse or the velvety crème brûlée. *On Dolores St at 7th Ave; (831)624-7500; www.carmelnet.com/laboheme; beer and wine; AE, MC, V; no checks; dinner every day; $$.*

As a "dine" of the times, Carmel's La Bohême restaurant lists its monthly dinner schedule on the Internet at http://www.carmel net.com/laboheme.

LA DOLCE VITA ⭐⭐

Marcello Mastroianni and Anouk Aimee might have preferred sleeker surroundings, but those in the mood for authentic Italian food in a casual atmosphere will enjoy this restaurant, a local favorite. The terrace, which overlooks the street, is popular both for sunny lunches and moonlit dinners (heaters take the chill off when necessary). Decorated in an Italian-flag color scheme—green chairs, Astroturf, and plastic red-and-white tablecloths—it's a wonderfully unassuming place to sit back, sip a glass of wine, and revel in *la dolce di far niente*—the joy of doing nothing. The main dining room is a bit more gussied up; it resembles a cozy trattoria with slate floors, light wood furniture, and peach-toned walls bedecked with garlic braids. Specialties include the transporting ravioli alla Rachele (homemade spinach ravioli stuffed with crab and cheese in a champagne cream sauce, topped with scallops and sun-dried tomatoes) and gnocchi della nonna (fresh potato dumplings in either a tomato or Gorgonzola-sage-cream sauce—ask for a little of both). A range of individual-size pizzas is also available, along with *secondi piatti* ranging from traditional osso buco to calamari steak drizzled with sun-dried tomato pesto, lemon juice, and crisp Orvieto wine. The waitstaff can be a bit cheeky at times, but hey, with food this *bellissima*, you're not likely to get your feathers ruffled. *On San Carlos St between 7th and 8th Aves; (831)624-3667; beer and wine; MC, V; local checks only; lunch, dinner every day; $$.* &

RIO GRILL ☆☆

This noisy Southwestern-style grill is packed with a lively, young crowd from opening to closing. The salads, such as organic mixed greens with aged goat cheese, seasoned walnuts, and curry vinaigrette, are wonderfully fresh, and appetizers, like the ever-popular onion rings and fried Monterey Bay squid with orange-sesame dipping sauce, draw raves. The tasty barbecued baby back ribs and the herb-crusted chicken with crispy broccoli-corn risotto cakes are good bets for the main course, as is the pumpkin-seed-crusted salmon with chipotle-lime vinaigrette and roasted red pepper–potato cakes. Desserts include a killer olallieberry pie and caramel-apple bread pudding. While the atmosphere may be chaotic, the service isn't, and the grill boasts a large wine list, with many selections available by the glass. *101 Crossroads Blvd in the Crossroads Shopping Center at Hwy 1 and Rio Rd; (831)625-5436; 101 Crossroads Blvd, Carmel; www.critics-choice.com/restaurants/riogrill; full bar; AE, DIS, MC, V; no checks; brunch Sun, lunch, dinner every day; $$.* &

HOG'S BREATH INN

If rowdy crowds and music blasting so loud you can hardly think are your idea of a good time, then join the dinnertime melee at movie star and ex-Carmel mayor Clint Eastwood's place—just look for the fire-breathing hog out front. You'll always find a horde of tourists and locals cruising, carousing, and plowing their way through the better-than-average pub grub here. Many of the dishes are named after Eastwood's films, like the succulent Dirty Harry burger on a fresh-baked bun; the aptly named For a Few Dollars More 16-ounce New York steak; and the Sudden Impact sandwich, a broiled Polish sausage with Jack cheese and jalapeño peppers on a French roll. (A word to the wise: Prices vary wildly here—most dinner entrees will run you around $15 to $25, but the $7.25 burger or the $9.50 roast chicken might make your day.) Thanks to half a dozen heat lamps and fireplaces, you can eat outside on the brick patio, with its immense bucolic mural of Carmel Valley, in just about any weather. *On San Carlos St between 5th and 6th Aves; (831)625-1044; full bar; AE, DC, MC, V; no checks; brunch Sun, lunch Mon–Sat, dinner every day; $$.*

KATY'S PLACE ☆

When Katy's Place is closed for the day, there's no doubt about it—a big sign announces, "Kitchen's closed—this chick's had it!" When it's open, however, Katy's has a reputation for serving the best breakfasts in town. The country-kitchen-style restaurant specializes in comfort foods: big helpings and endless variations of pancakes, waffles, and eggs, including a dynamite eggs Benedict. Eat in the pretty dining room or on the patio under the redwood trees. *On Mission St between 5th and 6th Aves; (831)624-0199; beer and wine; no credit cards; local checks only; breakfast, lunch every day; $.* &

PATISSERIE BOISSIERE ☆

After you've shopped till you dropped in Carmel, this is the place to go to rest your bones while you refuel with some of the most divine desserts in town. For more than 30 years, this comfortable, European-style restaurant has turned out a tempting array of masterful cakes, tarts, mousses, and other delights, all displayed in big glass cases so you can visually caress each one before making your selection. Patisserie Boissiere is also a delightful spot for a light lunch or dinner in the pretty Louis XIV dining room. The predominantly French Country cuisine encompasses such offerings as a roasted chicken and spinach salad with jicama, apples, and caramelized walnuts; coquilles St. Jacques; lamb shanks; and salmon baked in parchment paper with fresh artichokes and lemon-basil butter. Take-out is available on weekdays, and there's an extensive espresso menu. *On Mission St between Ocean and 7th Aves; (831)624-5008; beer and wine; AE, MC, V; checks OK; breakfast Sat–Sun, lunch every day, dinner Wed–Sun; $$.* &

LODGINGS

HIGHLANDS INN   ☆☆☆

 This exquisite luxury hotel began as a clutch of cabins in 1916, but its rustic days are long gone. Set high above the rocky coastline south of Carmel with fine views of Yankee Point, the Highlands Inn is now a sprawling modern complex of glowing redwood and soaring glass. In the main lodge, a skylit promenade leads to a series of glass-walled salons built for watching sunsets. In the fireside lobby you'll find deep leather settees, a granite fireplace, a grand piano, and elaborate floral displays. Outside, flower-lined walkways connect the cottagelike collection of rooms and suites. Every suite and town-house unit comes with a full parlor, kitchen, and bath with a massive spa tub. The 142 guest rooms were completely refurbished in 1996, and jewel-tone accents in fabrics and carpeting substantially jazzed up the muted earth-tone color scheme. Most rooms have fireplaces, private decks, and fabulous views of the ocean, landscaped grounds, and evergreen-draped hills. Another perk is the inn's elegant three-star restaurant, Pacific's Edge (see Restaurants, above), and the less formal *California Market*, which boasts wonderful coastline views and serves casual, well-prepared California fare. *On Hwy 1, 4 miles S of Carmel; (831)624-3801 or (800)682-4811; PO Box 1700, Carmel-by-the-Sea, CA 93921; gm@highlands-inn.com; www.highlands-inn.com; AE, DC, DIS, MC, V; checks OK; California Market: breakfast, lunch, dinner every day; $$$.* &

MISSION RANCH ⭐⭐⭐

When Clint Eastwood—director, movie star, and former mayor of Carmel—was a young recruit stationed at Fort Ord 40 years ago, he happened to venture onto the Mission Ranch, and it was love at first sight. Once a working dairy farm, the ranch had become a humble roadhouse restaurant and motel—nothing special, perhaps, except for its magnificent natural setting. Nestled in back of the Carmel Mission, the Ranch overlooks a carpet of pastureland that gives way to a dramatic view of Carmel River Beach, with the craggy splendor of Point Lobos stretching just beyond. (Eastwood, by the way, wasn't the first to fall for that view. In 1879, Robert Louis Stevenson, hot in pursuit of his beloved—but inconveniently married—Fanny, was so taken with the vista that he made Point Lobos the setting for *Treasure Island*.)

Alas, over the years, termites, erosion, and lack of management interest had taken their toll on the ranch, and a developer was all set to raze the buildings in the late 1980s when Eastwood rode in to the rescue. He poured a ton of money and a lot of love into restoring the Victorian farmhouse, cottages, bunkhouse, and other buildings, determined to be true to the original spirit of the place. The result is simply wonderful. The peaceful, Western-style spread opened in 1992, offering everything a guest needs to feel comfortable and not a single silly frill. The 31 rooms, distributed among a clutch of pretty, immaculately maintained buildings, are sparsely but tastefully appointed, with props from Eastwood's films, such as the clock from *Unforgiven*, nonchalantly scattered among the furnishings. The 1857 Martin Family Farmhouse is a Victorian charmer, with six bedrooms and a handsome parlor complete with a grand piano and fireplace. Other structures include the old Bunkhouse (which has its own living room with a fireplace, dining room, and kitchen), the aptly named Meadow View Rooms (which are newer and more deluxe), the main barn, and the luxurious Hay Loft Bedroom. Handmade quilts grace the custom-made country-style wooden beds that are so large you literally have to climb into them, and

At no cost to you, the staff at Carmel's Tourist Information Service (aka RoomFinders) will help you find a place to stay in your price range—if one exists. They're located on Mission Street between Fifth and Sixth Avenues; (800)847-8066 or (831)624-1711.

each guest room has its own phone, TV, and bathroom. Rates include a continental breakfast served in the tennis clubhouse. The informal and Western-themed **Restaurant at Mission Ranch**, which operates under separate management, serves hearty American-style fare. The place's only flaw is that the piano bar can get a little rowdy, and guests in the structures closest to the restaurant may find themselves reaching for earplugs in the middle of the night. Otherwise, Stetsons off to Clint. *Dolores St at 15th Ave; (831)624-6436, (800)538-8221, restaurant: (831)625-9040; 26270 Dolores St, Carmel, CA 93923; MC, V; checks OK; brunch Sun, lunch Sat, dinner every day; $$-$$$.* &

CYPRESS INN ★★

This charming Mediterranean-style inn in the center of town recently has been treated to a much-needed renovation that brought it up to date while preserving its Old Carmel charm. The 33 guest rooms received new paint, furniture, carpets, and TVs, and the bathrooms have been outfitted in new ceramic or marble tile. Movie star and animal-rights activist Doris Day owns the inn, and pets, naturally, are more than welcome; the hotel even provides dog beds for its four-footed guests. Service is uniformly professional and courteous, and the rooms contain some thoughtful touches: fresh fruit, bottles of spring water, chocolates left on the pillow at night, and a decanter of sherry. Some have sitting rooms, wet bars, private verandas, and ocean views. There's a spacious Spanish-style living room with a comforting fire and a friendly bar that dishes out coffee and a continental breakfast in the morning, as well as libations of a more spirited kind at night. Posters of Doris Day movies add a touch of glamour and fun to the decor. *On Lincoln St at 7th Ave; (831)624-3871 or (800)443-7443; PO Box Y, Carmel-by-the-Sea, CA 93921; AE, DIS, MC, V; checks OK; $$$.*

THE HAPPY LANDING ★★

One could easily see Snow White puttering around contentedly in this B&B's garden courtyard, a storybook setting complete with gazebo, fountain, and a passel of stone gnomes. This aptly named pink-and-azure Comstock cottage, built in 1925 as a summer retreat for two lucky sisters from San Francisco, has been divided into seven cozy guest rooms. All rooms have private baths and televisions (but no phones), all but one are grouped around the courtyard, and three have fireplaces (havenots can console themselves with the large adobe-and-stone hearth in the reception room). The best rooms are the two spacious suites, which are equipped with wet bars, but all the rooms boast at least a few charming details befitting a Comstock creation: wood-beamed cathedral ceilings, stained-glass windows, hand-painted sinks, curved archways, and cunning little windows and doors in surprising places. Lovers of pristine modernity may not be comfortable here—some of the furniture is a bit down at the heels and the 1920s-era bathrooms in a few of the quarters might seem a little dowdy. A full breakfast is delivered to guests in the morning, and tea and sherry are served in the grand, antique-laden sitting room every afternoon. *On Monte Verde St between 5th and 6th Aves; (831)624-7917; PO Box 2619, Carmel-by-the-Sea, CA 93921; MC, V; checks OK; $$–$$$.*

LA PLAYA HOTEL ☆☆

 Almost regal in its splendor, this imposing 1904 luxury hotel spills down a terraced, bougainvillea-and-jasmine-strewn hillside toward the sea. Paths lit by gas street lamps wind among lush gardens with cast-iron gazebos and past a heated swimming pool festooned with mermaids, La Playa's mythical mascots. Unfortunately, such grandeur doesn't carry over to the hotel's 75 guest rooms, which, compared to the gorgeous courtyard and handsome lobby, are a disappointment, with thin walls, dull furnishings, and nary a green plant to offset the visual bombardment of terra-cotta pink and white. To do La Playa right, invest in one of the five cottages, some of which are nestled in the gardens. These have varying numbers of rooms, and four of them offer full kitchens, fireplaces, and private patios. The hotel's restaurant, the

Terrace Grill, has a fine view of the gardens and serves such tasty seasonal fare as artichoke ravioli, grilled shrimp risotto, and chicken breast stuffed with dried cherries, cranberries, and walnuts. *On Camino Real at 8th Ave; (831)624-6476 or (800)582-8900; PO Box 900, Carmel-by-the-Sea, CA 93921; full bar; AE, DC, MC, V; checks OK; breakfast, lunch Mon–Sat, brunch Sun, dinner every day; $$$.* &

SAN ANTONIO HOUSE ★★

Built in the late 1920s, this white-painted wood-shingle home with green trim has four cozy, wood-paneled rooms, each with antiques, a fireplace, a private bath, a refrigerator, and a telephone. In the morning, a breakfast of fruit, coffee cake, scones, and juice arrives at your door with the morning paper. Two rooms, the Doll House and the Patio Suite, have separate sitting areas. Stroll the gardens with their interesting little nooks and arbors, or walk down to Carmel Beach just one block away. *On San Antonio Ave between Ocean and 7th Aves; (831)624-4334; PO Box 3683, Carmel-by-the-Sea, CA 93921; MC, V; checks OK; $$$.*

THE STONEHOUSE INN ★★

This ivy-covered stone structure is one of those inns people return to again and again—and many have been coming back since it opened as a hostelry in 1948. Prior to that, the 1906 building was the home of Nana Foster, and the six prettily decorated guest rooms are named after local writers and artists who were her frequent guests. The Jack London Room has gabled ceilings, a queen-size brass bed, and a ruffled day bed with a sea view. The Sinclair Lewis Room has a king-size bed, a writing desk, and a fine view of the ocean (though who knows what Lewis—that loather of the bourgeois— would think of the giant teddy bears). Only the Ansel Adams and Robinson Jeffers rooms have private bathrooms—a definite detraction for some folks. Downstairs, you may lounge in the wing chairs before the fireplace and help yourself to wine and cheese in the early evening.

Huge bouquets of flowers enliven the house, and antique toy cars line the staircase. *On 8th Ave between Monte Verde and Casanova Sts; (831)624-4569 or (800)748-6618; PO Box 2517, Carmel-by-the-Sea, CA 93921; MC, V; checks OK; $$.*

THE GREEN LANTERN INN ☆

Built in 1925, the Green Lantern's rustic buildings are nestled among lush gardens just a few blocks above Ocean Beach. Renovated in 1993, the inn was treated to new wallpaper, carpets, and bathrooms, enhancing the place's Old Carmel charm. In 1996, it became a member of the Best Western hotel chain. Four of the 18 guest rooms have fireplaces, and a recently added mini-suite has a king-size bed, a dining alcove, a private deck, and a refrigerator. The staff is accommodating and a deluxe continental breakfast is served in the morning. *On Casanova St at 7th Ave; (831)624-4392; PO Box 1114, Carmel-by-the-Sea, CA 93921; www.travelweb.com; AE, DC, DIS, MC, V; no checks; $$.*

CARMEL RIVER INN

Families favor these 24 cottages and 19 motel units that offer utilitarian but homey accommodations at reasonable prices. Though the inn's close to the highway, noise isn't a problem because it is set back along the Carmel River and surrounded by a natural buffer of trees. The rustic Sierra-style units were refurbished after the floods of '95, but the cabins remain the best places to stay; a few have full kitchens or kitchenettes, and some have fireplaces and two bedrooms. Guests have use of a heated outdoor pool year-round. *On Hwy 1 at the bridge, S of Rio Rd; (831)624-1575 or (800)882-8142; PO Box 221609, Carmel, CA 93922; MC, V; no checks; $$.* &

PEBBLE BEACH

How much is a room and a round of golf at Pebble Beach these days? Put it this way: If you have to ask, you can't afford it. If the 6,000 or so residents of this exclusive gated community had their way, Pebble Beach would probably be off-limits to mere commoners. Perhaps more of an indignity, though, is the $7.25 levy required to trespass on their gilded avenues and wallow in envy at how the ruling class recreates. If you have no strong desire to tour corporate-owned hideaways and redundant—albeit gorgeous—seascapes along 17-Mile Drive, save your lunch money: you're not missing anything that can't be seen elsewhere along the Monterey coast.

ACTIVITIES

If paying $7.25 to tour 17-Mile Drive seems like highway robbery, drive the 5-mile coastline of Pacific Grove— along Sunset Drive and Ocean View Boulevard—3½ times for free instead. You'll hardly tell the difference.

17-Mile Drive. Five entrances, manned by spiffy security guards adept at making change, lead into this fabled enclave that serves as home and playground of the absurdly wealthy. Though it can be whizzed through in about 30 minutes, two to three hours is the average touring time. The $7.25 toll includes a map and guide, but all that's required to stay on course is to follow the dotted red line painted on the road. Aside from a few scenic overlooks, the third of the drive that passes through the Del Monte Forest is rather dull—a better bet is to double back along the coastal stretch. Among the 21 "points of interest" you'll see everything from a spectacular Byzantine castle with a private beach (the Crocker Mansion near the Carmel gate) to several tastefully bland California Nouvelle country-club establishments in perfectly maintained forest settings. Other highlights include the often-photographed gnarled Lone Cypress clinging to its rocky precipice above the sea; miles of hiking and equestrian trails winding through groves of native pines and wildflowers, with glorious views of Monterey Bay; and Bird Rock, a small offshore isle covered with hundreds of seals and sea lions (bring binoculars). Self-guided nature tours are outlined in a variety of brochures, available for free at the gate entrances and at the Inn at Spanish Bay and the Lodge at Pebble Beach (see Lodgings, below). On your way out, splurge on an $8 margarita at the Inn at Spanish Bay's oceanside cocktail lounge (hey, who's gonna know?). For more information, contact Pebble Beach Security at (831)624-6669.

GOLF COUNTRY

The Monterey coast is golf country, hosting some of the most famous (and lucrative) tournaments in the world. While all of the following courses are open to the public, green fees of up to $295 tend to keep the oceanside clubs rather exclusive. Not to worry, though—drive a little ways inland and the fees slice rather nicely.

Pebble Beach Golf Links: 6,799 yards, 18 holes, driving range, green fee $295 (nonguests); (800)654-9300.

The Links at Spanish Bay: 6,820 yards, 18 holes, green fee $210 (nonguests); (800)654-9300.

Spyglass Golf Course: 6,859 yards, 18 holes, driving range, green fee $225 (nonguests); (800)654-9300.

Laguna Seca Golf Course: 5,711 yards, 18 holes, green fee $55; (831)373-3701.

Bayonet/Blackhorse Golf Course: 6,982 and 6,396 yards, 18 holes each, driving range, green fees $50–$70; (831)899-7271.

Del Monte Golf Course: 6,007 yards, 18 holes, green fee $80 (includes cart); (831)373-2700.

Pacific Grove Municipal: 5,553 yards, 18 holes, driving range, green fee $35; (831)648-3175.

Poppy Hills Golf Course: 6,219 yards, 18 holes, green fee $130; (831)625-1513.

Rancho Cañada East & West: 6,113 yards, 18 holes, driving range, green fee $50–$70; (831)624-0111.

Though on week-days bicyclists can enter any gate into Pebble Beach for free, on weekends and holidays they may enter only through the Pacific Grove gate.

LODGINGS

THE INN AT SPANISH BAY

 Set on the privately owned 17-Mile Drive, this sprawling modern inn defines deluxe. Its 270 luxuriously appointed rooms and suites perched on a cypress-dotted bluff have gas fireplaces, quilted down comforters, and elegant sitting areas. Most have private patios or balconies affording gorgeous views of the rocky coast or the Del Monte cypress forest. Three of the most deluxe suites even come with grand pianos. The bathrooms, equipped with all the modern conveniences you could want, are appropriately regal. Hotel guests have access to the world-famous Pebble Beach, Spanish Bay, and Spyglass Hill golf courses, as well as eight championship tennis courts, a fitness club, an outdoor swimming pool, and miles of hiking and equestrian trails. Relax over a repast at the well-regarded **Bay Club**, serving fashionable northern Italian fare, or at **Roy's**, where Hawaiian master chef Roy Yamaguchi serves an artful blend of Asian-Pacific and European cuisine. *2700 17-Mile Dr, near the Pacific Grove entrance in Pebble Beach; (831)647-7500 or (800)654-9300; www.pebble-beach.com; full bar; AE, DC, MC, V; checks OK; Bay Club: dinner every day; Roy's: breakfast, lunch, dinner every day; $$$.* &

THE LODGE AT PEBBLE BEACH

 Despite greens fees that top $300, Pebble Beach remains the mecca of American golf courses, and avid golfers feel they have to play it at least once before retiring to that Big Clubhouse in the Sky. Until the rooms in the Lodge were renovated several years ago, this scattered cluster of accommodations surprised many guests with its rather run-down appearance—it was clear that golf and the spectacular natural setting, not the rooms, were Pebble Beach's principal allure. The guest rooms have been tastefully revamped, however, swathed in soothing earth tones and outfitted with a sophisticated, modern decor. There are 161 suites and rooms, most with private balconies or patios, brick fireplaces, sitting areas, and gorgeous views. All the usual upscale amenities are provided, from phones by the commode and honor-bar refrigerators to robes and cable TVs. The whole effect is very East Coast country club. Four restaurants cater to visitors, most notably **Club XIX**, which has been drawing raves since signing up Hubert Keller of San Francisco's Fleur de Lys as executive chef, and the **Cypress Room**, with a menu that offers several excellent methods of preparing fish— everything from poaching them in champagne to searing them in Cajun spices. *On 17-Mile Dr, near the Carmel gate in Pebble Beach; (831)624-3811 or (800)654-9300; www.pebble-beach.com; full bar; AE, DC, DIS, MC, V; checks OK; Club XIX: lunch, dinner every day; Cypress Room: breakfast, lunch, dinner every day; $$$.* ♿

PACIFIC GROVE

Established more than a century ago as a retreat for pious Methodists, this venerable Victorian seacoast village still retains much of its decorous old-town character, though it's loosened its collar a bit since the early days. Less tourist-oriented than Carmel and less commercial than Monterey, P.G. (as locals call it) is the place to settle down, buy a home, and raise 2.5 obedient children. The town has no graffiti, no raucous revelers, and not an unleashed dog in sight. P.G. exudes peace and tranquility—a city of gorgeous vistas, impressive architecture, and even reasonably priced accommodations just a jog from the sea.

ACTIVITIES

Coastal Trail. The best way to start your vacation in Pacific Grove is to stroll the 4 miles of trails that meander between Lover's Point Beach and Asilomar State Beach. Start at grassy Lover's Point (which, by the way, was named for lovers of Jesus Christ, not the more carnal kind), located off Ocean View Boulevard next to the Old Bath House Restaurant, and work your way west past the numerous white-sand beaches, tide pools, and rocky coves to Asilomar on the west side of Point Pinos. A second, shorter option is the mile-long Monterey Peninsula Recreation Trail, which parallels Ocean View Boulevard from Lover's Point to the Monterey Bay Aquarium. Be sure to keep an eye out for sea otters sleeping atop the kelp beds—there are tons of them here.

Butterflies. Pacific Grove bills itself as "Butterfly Town, U.S.A." in honor of the thousands of monarchs that migrate here from late October to mid-March. Two popular places to view the butterflies are the Monarch Grove Sanctuary (at Lighthouse Avenue and Ridge Road) and George Washington Park (at Sinex Avenue and Alder Street). To learn more about the

MONARCH BUTTERFLIES

Are the only insects known to migrate annually • Travel up to 2,000 miles between ancestral wintering sites • Can fly 100 miles a day at altitudes up to 10,000 feet • Live only 6 to 9 months, so are guided on their annual migration purely by instinct • Congregate in groups of up to 50,000 in a single grove • Feed on milkweed, a poisonous plant that makes them inedible to birds

monarchs, visit the informal and kid-friendly Pacific Grove Museum of Natural History, which has a video and display on the butterfly's life cycle, as well as exhibits of other insects, local birds, mammals, and reptiles. Admission is free. At the intersection of Forest and Central Avenues, Pacific Grove; (831)648-3116.

Lighthouse. At the tip of Point Piños (Spanish for "Point of the Pines") stands the Cape Cod–style Point Piños Lighthouse, the oldest continuously operating lighthouse on the West Coast: Its 50,000-candlepower beacon has shone since February 1, 1855. This National Historic Landmark is open to the public Thursday through Sunday from 1pm to 4pm, and admission is free. On Asilomar Boulevard at Lighthouse Avenue, Pacific Grove; (831)648-3116.

Victorian Beauties. P.G. is famous for its Victorian houses, inns, and churches, and hundreds of them have been declared historically significant by the Pacific Grove Heritage Society. Every October, some of the most beautiful and artfully restored are opened to the public on the Victorian Home Tour; call (831)373-3304 for details. If you can't make the tour, you can at least admire them from a distance along Lighthouse Avenue, Central Avenue, and Ocean View Boulevard.

Art Gallery. A perennial Best Art Gallery winner in the "Best of Monterey" survey by *Coast Weekly*, the nonprofit Pacific Grove Art Center has four galleries with rotating displays ranging from sculpture to photography to drawings and even children's artwork. Poetry readings, plays, workshops, and the occasional concert are also on the menu if you time it right. Open Wednesday to Saturday, noon to 5pm, Sunday 1pm to 4pm; 568 Lighthouse Avenue at Forest Avenue; (831)375-2208.

 Factory Outlets. Who would have guessed you could save money shopping in Pacific Grove? Within the American Tin Cannery factory outlet center are 40 high-quality clothing stores—Anne Klein, Bass, London Fog, Reebok, Big Dog—selling their wares for about half of what you'd normally pay. Particularly worth a look are the amazing deals at the Woolrich outlet, where most items are 50 percent off. It's open Sunday through Thursday 10am to 6pm, Friday and Saturday 10am to 8pm, and is located at 125 Ocean View Boulevard, around the corner from the Monterey Bay Aquarium; (831)372-1442.

For good books (particularly local guidebooks), coffee, and pastries, head over to Pacific Grove's most cerebral hangout, Bookworks. Open daily 8:30am to 10pm; 667 Lighthouse Avenue at Park Street; (831)372-2242.

RESTAURANTS

OLD BATH HOUSE RESTAURANT ★★★

 Although many locals are quick to dismiss the Old Bath House as a pricey tourist restaurant (and it is indeed guilty on both counts), the food is meticulously prepared and the setting is undeniably romantic. This former bath house at Lover's Point has a fine view of the rocky coast and a wonderful wood interior with a low, carved ceiling. Chef Jeffrey Jake, formerly at Domaine Chandon in Yountville and Montrio in Monterey, has breathed new life into the continental menu. Expect starters such as truffle-mousse pâté, grilled prawns and wild boar sausage, and artichoke ravioli with a lemon-nutmeg cream sauce. Entrees may feature braised petrale sole with fettuccine and chardonnay sauce, veal medallions crusted with pistachios and topped with lime butter, and soy-ginger-glazed filet mignon grilled with shiitakes. Tempting desserts include hot pecan ice-cream fritters and the aptly named Oceans of Chocolate (chocolate ice cream on chocolate pudding cake cloaked in chocolate fudge and white-chocolate chunks). The service is impeccable and the wine list extensive. *On Ocean View Blvd at Lover's Point Park; (831)375-5195; 620 Ocean View Blvd, Pacific*

Grove; www.critics-choice.com/restaurants/bath; full bar; AE, DC, DIS, MC, V; no checks; dinner every day; $$$.

TASTE CAFE & BISTRO ★★★

When it opened several years ago, Taste Cafe quickly developed a loyal and enthusiastic word-of-mouth following that remains the envy of several more established restaurants in town. You'll be hard-pressed to find higher-quality food for the same price anywhere else on the coast. Chef/owners Paolo Kautz and Sylvia Medina describe their preparations as a combination of rustic French, Italian, and California cuisines, and they work hard to glean the best and freshest produce, seafood, and meats from local suppliers. Start your meal with house-cured salmon carpaccio, butternut squash agnolotti, or an organic red oak leaf salad with crumbled blue cheese, balsamic dressing, sliced pears, and glazed pecans. Move on to entrees such as tortellini Florentine, marinated rabbit with braised red cabbage, and grilled pork medallions on mashed potatoes with shiitake sauce. Be sure to save room for one of Sylvia's wonderful desserts: warm brioche pudding with apricot coulis and crème fraîche, a hazelnut-chocolate torte, or a country-style apple galette with vanilla-bean ice cream and caramel sauce. Regulars elbow up to the wine and espresso bar. The word is out on this terrific restaurant, so be sure to call well ahead for reservations, especially for weekend dinners. *On Forest Ave at Prescott Ave; (831)655-0324; 1199 Forest Ave, Pacific Grove; beer and wine; no credit cards; checks OK; dinner Tues–Sun; $$.* &

CROCODILE GRILL ★★

Drawing on the sharp, exotic flavors of the Caribbean and Central and South America, Julio Ramirez's exciting, hybrid-Hispanic cuisine manages to cater to the tender sensibilities of *norteamericanos* without sacrificing authenticity. Lush tropical plants, photographs of Latin America, and dozens of crocodile chatchkas set an appropriate mood for fiery, flavorful, fish-focused meals. Starters include Bahamian seafood chowder, Salvadoran *pupusas* (fat tortillas stuffed with two cheeses and served with black beans and salsa), and—somewhat ironically considering this place's affection for large, toothy reptiles—alligator nuggets with passion-fruit dipping sauce. Specialties include Red Snapper Mardi Gras, smoked West Indian ribs, and spit-roasted Mayan chicken. Crocodile Grill's interesting selection of desserts includes mango cheesecake, chocolate–Brazil nut pie, and *paletas tropicales*, those delicious and refreshing frozen fruit treats so familiar to travelers in Mexico. A light bar menu is served from 4pm to 10pm, and you can chase down all that fiery food with a refreshing (if somewhat insincere) pitcher of Crocodile Tears (aka sangria). *On Lighthouse Ave at Congress Ave; (831)655-3311; 701 Lighthouse Ave, Pacific Grove; beer and wine; AE, DC, DIS, MC, V; no checks; dinner Wed–Mon; $$.* &

FANDANGO ☆☆

Fandango, the name of a lively Spanish dance, is the perfect moniker for this kick-up-your-heels restaurant specializing in Mediterranean country cuisine. It's a big, sprawling, colorful place with textured adobe walls and a spirited crowd filling five separate dining rooms; the glass-domed terrace in back, with its stone fireplace and open mesquite grill, is especially pleasant. Start with a few tapas—perhaps spicy sausage, roasted red peppers, or a potato-and-onion frittata. If you're feeling adventurous, order the Velouté Bongo Bongo, an exotic creamy soup with oysters, spinach, and Cognac, or the Couscous Algerois, a 130-year-old family recipe featuring lamb, vegetables, and North African spices. Other selections include the flavorful Paella Fandango (served at your table in a huge skillet), pasta puttanesca, bouillabaisse Marseillaise, osso buco, and a 26-ounce porterhouse steak. Fandango's wine list is one of the best in the area, with an impressive selection of French, California, Spanish, and Italian varietals. For dessert, try the profiteroles filled with chocolate ice cream and topped with hot fudge sauce. Olé! *On 17th St near Lighthouse Ave; (831)372-3456; 223 17th St, Pacific Grove; www.critics-choice.com/*

restaurants/fandango; full bar; AE, DC, DIS, MC, V; no checks; brunch Sun, lunch, dinner every day; $$$. &

PASTA MIA   ★★

A century-old Victorian house provides a homey backdrop for Pasta Mia's hearty Italian fare. The soup and appetizers tend to be tried-and-true standards, such as minestrone, mozzarella fresca, and carpaccio, but the house-made pastas include some intriguing choices. There's black-and-white linguine with scallops, caviar, cream, and chives, for instance, or half-moon pasta stuffed with pesto in a lemon-zest cream sauce dotted with chicken and sun-dried tomatoes. The corkscrew pasta with sausage and chicken in a pink sauce is satisfying and flavorful, as is the scampi in a light champagne cream sauce. *Secondi piatti* include a robust version of osso buco, pounded breast of chicken with a garlic, wine, and rosemary sauce, and a daily fresh fish preparation. Portions are generous in this friendly, informal restaurant, though service can be slow at times. *On Lighthouse Ave near 13th St; (831)375-7709; 481 Lighthouse Ave, Pacific Grove; beer and wine; AE, MC, V; local checks only; dinner every day; $$.* &

RED HOUSE CAFE   ★★

A trim, 103-year-old, brick red house in downtown Pacific Grove is the deceptively modest setting for some of the most adroit cooking on the Monterey Peninsula. Opened in 1996 by Laura and Chris D'Amelio (both formerly of Taste Cafe & Bistro), the Red House offers a handful of humble-sounding dishes at breakfast and lunch—items such as Irish oatmeal, Belgian waffles, pastries, a mixed green salad, roast beef on sourdough, a BLT, and eggs any way you like them as long as they're scrambled. Order at the counter, then take a seat on the porch with its smattering of wicker chairs and tables for two or in one of the snug, country-cottage dining rooms. After your food is served and you tuck into your warm pine-nut tart or chicken sandwich, you'll realize how even the simplest fare can be transporting if it's prepared by the right hands. Perfectly cooked, every dish demonstrates the kitchen's insistence on first-rate ingredients— heck, even the toast and jam tastes like a gourmet treat here. The Red House has been a locals' favorite ever since it opened, and its popularity is the only rub; traffic can back up at the counter as people wait to place their orders, creating some cramped conditions in the dining areas. *On Lighthouse Ave at 19th St; 662 Lighthouse Ave, Pacific Grove; (831)643-1060; beer and wine; no credit cards; checks OK; breakfast, lunch Tues–Sun; $.*

ALLEGRO GOURMET PIZZERIA ☆

With its merry festoons of garlic and red peppers, colorful Italian posters, and trilling Italian music, Allegro Pizzeria is the choice of locals in search of *la dolce vita* on the cheap. The handmade pizzas, which come either whole or in generous slices, have crisp, flavorful crusts, just the right amount of cheese, and well-seasoned sauces. You can choose your own favorite toppings or pick one of Allegro's creative combinations such as the quattro stagione (salami, artichoke hearts, mushrooms, anchovies, roasted garlic, and capers) or the del mare (shrimp, scallops, garlic, and mozzarella). The caesar salad is a local favorite, but try the Caprese for a change (tomato slices, fresh mozzarella, fresh basil, and olive oil, sprinkled with mint and served on a bed of organic romaine). Much to the delight of Allegro's many fans, another branch just opened in Carmel. Take-out is available at both locations. *In the Forest Hills Shopping Center, near Prescott Ave; (831)373-5656; 1184-E Forest Ave, Pacific Grove; beer and wine; AE, DIS, MC, V; checks OK; lunch Fri–Sun, dinner every day; $. ☆ ■ At the Barnyard at Hwy 1 and Carmel Valley Rd; (831)626-5454; 3770 the Barnyard, Carmel; beer and wine; AE, DIS, MC, V; checks OK; lunch Fri–Sun, dinner every day; $. ☆*

FISHWIFE ☆

Locals swear by this bustling and casual seaside restaurant. The decor is playful, with cloth parrots and toucans suspended from the ceiling and brightly colored fish-shaped pillows tossed about the waiting area. The long roster of seafood dishes includes fried calamari, grilled Cajun snapper, fillet of sole doré, and prawns Belize, as well as a number of daily specials featuring fresh seasonal fish. The Boston clam chowder is justly famous, as is the Key lime pie. For those who eschew eating our fine finned friends, the Fishwife also serves steaks and a couple of pasta dishes such as fettuccine with alfredo or pesto sauce. The reasonable prices and separate kids' menu make this a good choice for folks with children in tow. *On Sunset Dr in the Beachcomber Inn at Asilomar Beach; (831)375-7107; 1996½ Sunset Dr, Pacific Grove; www.critics-choice.com/restaurants/fishwife; beer and wine; AE, DIS, MC, V; no checks; brunch Sun, lunch, dinner Wed–Mon; $$.*

PEPPERS ☆

This Pacific Grove hot spot (pun intended) with strings of red chile peppers dangling from the ceiling is known for its house-made tamales and chiles rellenos. The delicately flavored seafood tacos, with mahi-mahi, swordfish, or salmon, and the spicy prawns Gonzalez, with tomatoes, chiles, cilantro, and lime juice, are also worth a try. The chips and salsa are dynamite, and a good selection of beers can cool your singed palate. Owner Scott Gonzalez is usually on hand to make sure everything runs smoothly; consequently, the service is always friendly even though the place is usually packed. *On Forest Ave by Lighthouse Ave; (831)373-6892; 170 Forest Ave, Pacific Grove; beer and wine; AE, DIS, MC, V; local checks only; lunch Mon, Wed–Sat, dinner Wed–Mon; $.*

LODGINGS
GRAND VIEW INN ☆☆☆

 Even in a town as rich in resplendent Victorians as Pacific Grove, this pristine and romantic inn stands out. Built in 1910 as the residence of Dr. Julia Platt, a marine biologist who became Pacific Grove's first female mayor, the Grand View was bought by the family who owns the Seven

Gables Inn next door (the two inns share the same garden). They lovingly restored this inn and opened it to the public in July 1995. A bit more casual and restrained in decor than its ornate sister, this charmer with the cheerful blue exterior has 10 guest rooms, all with bay views, high plaster ceilings with decorative detailing, eclectic antique furniture and light fixtures, queen-size beds, sitting areas, and beautifully appointed marble bathrooms. A full breakfast is served in the elegant first-floor dining room with its breathtaking view of Lover's Point; later in the day, the same room is the setting for a pleasant afternoon tea. Complimentary off-street parking is available, too. *On Ocean View Blvd at Grand Ave; (831)372-4341; 557 Ocean View Blvd, Pacific Grove, CA 93950; MC, V; checks OK; $$$.* &

THE MARTINE INN

 Perched like a vast pink wedding cake on a cliff above Monterey Bay, this villa with a Mediterranean exterior and a Victorian interior is one of Pacific Grove's most elegant bed and breakfasts. Built in 1899 for James and Laura Parke (of Parke-Davis Pharmaceuticals fame), the inn has 19 spacious guest rooms, all with private baths and gloriously unfussy, high-quality antiques, including lamps with interesting shades. Most rooms have fireplaces; all have views of the water or the garden courtyard with its delightful dragon fountain. If you feel like splurging, the Parke Room at the very top of the house is outstanding. Originally the master bedroom, it has a magnificent picture window, a four-poster canopy bed, and a massive, white brick fireplace. No matter which room you choose, you'll find a silver basket of fruit and a rose waiting for you upon arrival, and a newspaper at your door in the morning. Several intimate sitting rooms offset three large common areas: the library, the main dining room (with a dazzling view of the bay), and the breakfast parlor. There's also a pool table and an eight-person whirlpool bath in the old conservatory. The Martine serves an elaborate and well-prepared breakfast and offers wine and hors d'oeuvres in the late afternoon.

On Ocean View Blvd, 4 blocks from Cannery Row; (831)373-3388 or (800)852-5588; 255 Ocean View Blvd, Pacific Grove, CA 93950; www.virtualcities.com; AE, DIS, MC, V; checks OK; $$$. &

SEVEN GABLES INN ★★★

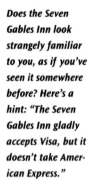

Does the Seven Gables Inn look strangely familiar to you, as if you've seen it somewhere before? Here's a hint: "The Seven Gables Inn gladly accepts Visa, but it doesn't take American Express."

An immaculate yellow mansion built in 1886 and surrounded by gardens, this family-run inn commands a magnificent view of Monterey Bay. Chock-full of formal European antiques, Seven Gables will seem like paradise to those who revel in things Victorian; those who prefer a more restrained, less fussy decor will do better elsewhere. Once you're ensconced in one of the 14 guest rooms, which are divided among the main house, a guest house, and a smattering of cottages, the warm and welcoming Flatley family will see to your every comfort. The beautifully appointed rooms feature ocean views, private baths, and queen-size beds. A pull-out-all-the-stops breakfast is served in the imposing dining room, and tea is set out every afternoon. *On Ocean View Blvd at Fountain Ave; (831)372-4341; 555 Ocean View Blvd, Pacific Grove, CA 93950; MC, V; checks OK; $$$.*

THE CENTRELLA

The aptly named Centrella (located smack in the center of town) combines the down-home glow of an Old West boardinghouse with the comfort and attentive service of a modern hotel. The front hallway of this spacious 1886 Victorian inn opens onto a large parlor overlooking a garden courtyard. The main building offers 21 rooms, and all but two have private baths. The upstairs rooms overlooking the garden are particularly attractive and comfortable, as are the two intimate attic suites with skylights and TVs. Outside, a brick path meanders through an old-fashioned garden of gardenias and camellias, leading to five well-equipped private cottages. For breakfast you'll find crisp waffles hot from the antique waffle iron, and in the evening look for dainty hors d'oeuvres served in the parlor. *On Central Ave at 17th St; (831)372-3372 or (800)233-3372; 612 Central Ave, Pacific Grove, CA*

93950; centrella@aol.com; www.centrellainn.com; AE, MC, V; checks OK; $$$. &

GATEHOUSE INN ☆☆

When State Senator Benjamin Langford built this ocean-view Victorian mansion in 1884, Pacific Grove was less a town than a pious Methodist meeting ground. Swathed in rules and regulations, it was separated from wicked, worldly Monterey by a white picket fence. Langford's domain is now an enticingly eccentric B&B. Decorated in an interesting mix of Victoriana and art deco, the inn's nine guest rooms have private baths and queen-size beds, with the exception of the Cannery Row Room, which has a king-size bed. The Langford Suite ranks as the inn's most luxurious, with an ocean-view sitting room, a fireplace, and a claw-footed bathtub that's just a step away from the bed and commands a stunning view of the coast (talk about soaking it all in!). You'll find delicious hors d'oeuvres, tea, and wine every evening and a full breakfast buffet in the morning. You can even help yourself to cookies and beverages from the kitchen any time of day or night. *On Central Ave at 2nd St; (831)649-8436 or (800)753-1881; 225 Central Ave, Pacific Grove, CA 93950; AE, DIS, MC, V; checks OK; $$$.* &

LIGHTHOUSE LODGE AND SUITES ☆☆

Less than a block from the ocean, the Lighthouse Lodge and Suites is really two entities with rather distinct personalities. The lodge, a Best Western property with an outdoor heated pool, consists of 68 motel-like rooms. Those seeking more luxurious accommodations should spring for one of the 31 newer suites down the road. The Cape Cod–style suites, all with beamed ceilings, plush carpeting, fireplaces, vast bathrooms with marble whirlpool tubs, large-screen TVs, mini-kitchens, and king-size beds, glow in peacock hues of purple, green, and fuchsia. The overall effect is a bit nouveau riche, but riche all the same. After a made-to-order breakfast in the fireside lounge, take a morning stroll around the grounds, cleverly landscaped with fountains and native plants.

On Lighthouse Ave at Asilomar Blvd; (831)655-2111 or (800)858-1249; 1150 and 1249 Lighthouse Ave, Pacific Grove, CA 93950; www.lhls.com; AE, DC, DIS, MC, V; no checks; $$ (lodge), $$$ (suites). &

ROSEDALE INN ★

While its name may conjure up images of pink petals and white lace, the Rosedale is more like an upscale motel, with woodsy flourishes such as a huge, carved redwood bear that welcomes guests. Despite a somewhat rustic appearance, each of the inn's 19 rooms is equipped with a wealth of electronic conveniences: multiple TV sets, a couple of phone lines, a whirlpool tub, a clock radio, a microwave, a VCR, and a hair dryer. The rooms are spacious, and some have kitchenettes. Located across the road from the Asilomar Conference Center, the Rosedale is well suited to conference-goers, business travelers, and families. *On Asilomar Blvd at Sinex Ave; (831)655-1000 or (800)822-5606; 775 Asilomar Blvd, Pacific Grove, CA 93950; AE, DC, MC, V; no checks; $$.* &

THE ASILOMAR CONFERENCE CENTER

Asilomar translates as "haven by the sea."

Many of the original buildings at Asilomar, located at the tip of the Monterey Peninsula on a wooded stretch of beach, were designed by famed Bay Area architect Julia Morgan. Donated to the YWCA by Phoebe Apperson Hearst and now owned by the State Division of Beaches and Parks, the Asilomar feels a bit like a grown-up Girl Scout camp, albeit a little more luxurious. Its 105 acres of parklike grounds include a large, heated swimming pool, wooded trails, and a fine beach where you can watch otters, seals, and, depending on the season, whales. There are 314 units in the complex; the older rooms, designed by Morgan, have hardwood floors and are much smaller and more rustic than the newer suites with their wall-to-wall carpeting, fireplaces, and kitchenettes. The apartment-style Guest Inn Cottage and Forest Lodge Suite can accommodate a large group or family. Breakfast is included in the price. There's also a cafeteria-style restaurant on the premises, but you're better off going into town to eat. *On Asilomar Blvd at Sinex Ave; (831)372-8016; 800 Asilomar Blvd, Pacific Grove, CA 93950; www.worldint.com/asilomar; MC, V; checks OK; $$.* &

MONTEREY

If you're looking for the romantically gritty, working-class fishing village of John Steinbeck's Cannery Row, you won't find it here. Even though Monterey was the sardine capital of the Western Hemisphere during World War II, overfishing (among other factors) forced most of the canneries to close in the early '50s. Resigned to trawling for tourist dollars instead, the city converted its low-slung sardine factories along Cannery Row into a rather tacky array of boutiques, knick-knack stores, yogurt shops, and—The Row's only saving grace—the world-famous Monterey Bay Aquarium.

As you distance yourself from Cannery Row, however, you'll soon see that Monterey also has its share of pluses that help even the score: dazzling seacoast vistas, stately Victorian houses, historic architecture, and a number of quality lodgings and restaurants. More important, Monterey is only minutes away from Pacific Grove, Carmel, Pebble Beach, and Big Sur, which makes it a great place to set up base while exploring the innumerable attractions lining the Monterey coast.

ACTIVITIES

Monterey Bay Aquarium. Monterey's top draw is the amazing Monterey Bay Aquarium, the largest and most popular aquarium in the nation. Formerly a boarded-up old cannery until David and Lucile Packard (of Hewlett-Packard electronics) got things rolling with a $55 million donation, the 221,000-square-foot building features over a hundred galleries—including one of the world's largest indoor, glass-walled aquarium tanks—with more than 350,000 specimens of animals, plants, and birds found in Monterey Bay. One of the aquarium's main exhibits is a 3-story, 335,000-gallon tank with clear acrylic walls that offers a stunning view of leopard sharks, sardines, anchovies, and other sea creatures swimming through a towering kelp forest. Even more impressive, however, is the Outer Bay, a million-gallon, record-breaking exhibit that show-

Stop by the Monterey Peninsula Visitors and Convention Bureau and pick up a free map and visitor's guide to Monterey, or visit their Web site at www.monterey. com. It's located at 380 Alvarado Street near the intersection of Pacific Street and Del Monte Avenue; (831)649-1770.

The 7-inch-thick walls of windows within the Monterey Bay Aquarium were built by a Japanese firm so protective of its technology that the aquarium staff was forbidden to observe the installation.

Surveys reveal that half of Monterey's tourists are drawn solely by the aquarium, spawning the unofficial town slogan, Where people once packed fish, today fish pack in people.

cases aquatic life living in the outer reaches of Monterey Bay. Schools of sharks, barracuda, yellowfin tuna, sea turtles, giant ocean sunfish, and bonito can be seen through the largest window on earth: an acrylic panel 15 feet high, 13 inches thick, and 54 feet long that weighs 78,000 pounds.

Three other popular exhibits are the Outer Bay's jellyfish exhibit, the bat-ray petting pool (not to worry, their stingers have been removed), and the two-story sea-otter tank, particularly at 10:30am, 1:30pm, and 3:30pm every day when the sea otters get to scarf down a mixture of clams, rock cod, and shrimp. In 1999, the Deep Sea exhibit opened with the largest collection of live deep-sea species in the world, many of which have never been part of an exhibit before.

Predictably, things get a little crowded on summer weekends, enough so that reservations are recommended in summer and on holidays. Open daily 10am–6pm (opens at 9:30am summer and holidays); 886 Cannery Row, Monterey; call (831)648-4888 for general information, (800)756-3737 for tickets.

Historical Walking Tour. To get the flavor of Monterey's heritage, follow the 2-mile Path of History, a walking tour of the town's most important historic sites and well-preserved old buildings—remember, this city was thriving under Spanish and Mexican flags when San Francisco was still a crude village. Free tour maps are available at various locations, including the Custom House, California's oldest public building (at the foot of Alvarado Street, near Fisherman's Wharf) and Colton Hall, where the California state constitution was written and signed in 1849 (on Pacific Street between Madison and Jefferson Streets). Call Monterey State Historic Park at (831)649-7118 for more information.

Maritime History. Nautical history buffs should visit the Maritime Museum of Monterey, which houses ship models, whaling relics, and the 2-story-high, 10,000-pound Fresnel lens, used for nearly 80 years at the Point Sur lighthouse to warn mariners away from the treacherous Big Sur coast; 5 Custom House Plaza, in Stanton Center near Fisherman's Wharf; (831)373-2469.

Shop & Go. The landmark Fisherman's Wharf, the center of Monterey's cargo and whaling industry until the early 1900s, is awash today in mediocre (or worse) restaurants and equally tasteless souvenir shops. Serious shoppers will be better off strolling Alvarado Street, a pleasantly low-key, attractive downtown area with a much less touristy mix of art galleries, bookstores, and restaurants. The best time to pick up a souvenir, however, is during the hugely popular Old Monterey Farmer's Market and Marketplace, held Tuesday afternoons year-round from 4pm to 8pm (4pm to 7pm in the winter) on Alvarado Street between Pearl and Del Monte Streets. It's a real hoot, with more than 100 vendors, musicians, and performers offering good grub and free entertainment.

A good day in Monterey: Renting bicycles or in-line skates at Adventures by the Sea (299 Cannery Row; (831)372-1807) and biking or skating the 3⅓-mile Monterey Bay Recreation Trail along the shore.

 Wynton Rome . . . For a toe-tappin' time in Monterey, visit on the third weekend in September, when top talents like Wynton Marsalis, Etta James, and Ornette Coleman strut their stuff at the Monterey Jazz Festival, one of the country's best jazz jubilees and the oldest continuous jazz celebration in the world. Tickets and hotel rooms sell out fast, so plan early (die-hard jazz fans make reservations at least six months before show time). Call (800)307-3378 for tickets and (831)373-3366 for more information. Monterey also hosts a Blues Festival in late June, which attracts a respectable but smaller crowd; (831)649-6544.

During the summer and fall, Monterey Whale Watch takes passengers on whale-watching excursions departing from Fisherman's Wharf. Call (831)375-4658 for reservations.

Kayaking Monterey Bay. One of the most enjoyable ways to spend a sunny day on the Monterey coast is paddling a sea kayak among the thousands of seals, sea lions, sea otters, and shorebirds that live within the Monterey Bay National Marine Sanctuary. No kayaking experience is necessary—just follow behind the instructor for an interpretive tour of the bay. For reservations call Monterey Bay Kayaks at (800)649-5357 or (831)373-5357, or visit the Web site at www.montereykayaks.com. Prices start at about $45 for the tours and $25 for rentals.

RESTAURANTS
FRESH CREAM   ✪✪✪

 One of the most highly rated restaurants on the California coast, Fresh Cream has a veritable mountain of rave reviews to its credit. It's easy to see why—from the delightful complimentary caviar-and-onion tartlet that starts each meal to the divine dessert at the end, the food here is exquisitely prepared and presented. Specializing in French cuisine with hints of California, Fresh Cream moved into handsome new quarters several years ago, and some of the tables afford pleasing views of Monterey Bay. Appetizers range from lobster ravioli with gold caviar to escargots in garlic butter with Pernod or a smooth-as-silk goose liver pâté with capers and onions. Executive chef Gregory Lizza's luscious entrees include roasted duck with black currant sauce, the definitive rack of lamb Dijonnaise, and a delicate poached salmon in saffron-thyme sauce. Vegetarians needn't feel left out; the tasty grilled seasonal vegetable plate is a cut above most veggie entrees. For dessert try the Grand Marnier soufflé or the amazing *sac au chocolat*, a dark chocolate pillow filled with a mocha milk shake. Service tends to be a bit on the formal side; the wine list is extensive and expensive. Dinner at Fresh Cream isn't cheap, to be sure, but it's worth the splurge. *At Suite 100C in the Heritage Harbor complex on Pacific St, across from Fisherman's Wharf; (831)375-9798; 99 Pacific St, Monterey; dining@ freshcream.com; www.freshcream.com; full bar; AE, DC, DIS, MC, V; checks OK; dinner every day; $$$.* ♿

MONTRIO ✩✩✩

It's rare indeed to find a haven where all the rough edges have been smoothed out, but that's the delightful state of affairs at this downtown Monterey hot spot. All's welcoming here, from the curved lines and soft-sculpture clouds that define the decor of this converted 1910 firehouse to the insightful, cordial waitstaff. The only even slightly edgy element is the food, which has the lusty, rough-yet-refined flavors characteristic of Rio Grill and Tarpy's, two other local favorites founded by Montrio co-owners Tony Tollner and Bill Cox. Indulge in such eloquent dishes as Dungeness crab cakes with spicy rémoulade and duckling with sun-dried cherry sauce. The Tuesday night special is another standout: a fork-tender fillet of beef on Roquefort ravioli that one must taste to comprehend—the distinct, exquisite flavors create a dish that's strong yet lilting. The wine list, which received *Wine Spectator* magazine's Award of Excellence, includes a passel of vintages by the glass. Or you can opt to sample a wee dram of single-malt Scotch or small-batch bourbon—and if it's thrills you seek, try a Black Death Martini, described on the menu as "soooo smooth it's scary." Surprisingly for such a stylish place, a kid's menu and crayons are available, which should keep junior diners as contented as their parents. *On Calle Principal near Franklin St; (831)648-8880; 414 Calle Principal, Monterey; www.critics-choice.com/restaurants/montrio; full bar; AE, DIS, MC, V; no checks; brunch Sun, lunch, dinner every day; $$$.* &

Locals' consensus: First Awakenings, a small cafe within the Tin Cannery Outlet Center at 125 Ocean View Boulevard, serves Monterey's best breakfast. Open daily 7am to 2:30pm; (831)372-1125.

STOKES ADOBE ✭✭✭

A historic peach-colored adobe built in 1833 for the eponymous town doctor is the setting for one of Monterey's most engaging restaurants. Co-proprietors Dorothea and Kirk Probasco (Kirk formerly managed Carmel's Rio Grill and Pacific's Edge at the Highlands Inn) didn't miss a trick when they opened Stokes in 1996, snagging Brandon Miller as head chef (think Campton Place and Tra Vigne), assembling a staff that is both well trained and friendly, and overseeing a redesign with a particularly skillful blend of old and new. The two-story adobe and board-and-batten house is surrounded by attractive gardens and reflects the Spanish character of Old Monterey. Inside, the large space has been divided into several airy dining rooms with terra-cotta floors, bleached-wood plank ceilings, Southwestern wooden chairs and tables, and white walls dotted with paintings. It's a soothing showcase for Miller's terrific food, which he describes as contemporary rustic Mediterranean: butternut squash soup with apple cider and maple crème fraîche, roasted spinach gratin with mussels and herbed bread crumbs, grilled lavender-infused pork chops with savory bread pudding and pear chutney, cassoulet of duck confit and homemade currant sausage with

If you think the Monterey coast looks beautiful at sea level, try seeing it from a hot-air balloon's perspective. Balloons-by-the-Sea offers sunrise flights daily by appointment and sunset flights in fall and winter. For more information, call (831)384-3483.

chestnut beans. Don't let the "rustic" label fool you; this is extremely refined cooking that respects the individual flavors of the high-quality ingredients. Desserts are wonderful here, including such winners as a warm apricot clafouti, chocolate espresso crème brûlée, and warm banana-rum bread pudding with vanilla crème Anglaise. A prix-fixe dinner is offered nightly—a real bargain at about $26 (and for another $20 you can get a carefully orchestrated selection of wines). *On Hartnell St at Madison St; (831)373-1110; 500 Hartnell St, Monterey; full bar; AE, MC, V; no checks; lunch, dinner every day; $$.* ♿

TARPY'S ROADHOUSE ☆☆☆

Worth a hop in the car for a spin on Highway 68, this exuberant restaurant features a broad, sunny patio shaded by market umbrellas out front and handsome Southwestern decor inside, with rustic, bleached-wood furniture, golden stone walls, and whimsical art. The menu indulges in a creative approach to traditional American food. Lunch emphasizes well-prepared sandwiches and salads, but dinner is when Tarpy's really shines. Appetizers might include grilled polenta with mushrooms and Madeira, fire-roasted artichokes with lemon-herb vinaigrette, and Pacific oysters with red wine–jalapeño mignonette. Entrees run the gamut from a bourbon-molasses pork chop or a Dijon-crusted lamb loin to sea scallops with saffron penne or a grilled vegetable plate with succotash. Desserts include lemon and fresh ginger crème brûlée, a triple-layer chocolate cake, and olallieberry pie. The wine list is modest and skewed toward the expensive side, but thoughtfully selected. *On Hwy 68 at Canyon Del Rey, near the Monterey Airport; (831)647-1444; 2999 Monterey-Salinas Hwy, Monterey; www.critics-choice.com/restaurants/tarpys; full bar; AE, DIS, MC, V; no checks; brunch Sun, lunch, dinner every day; $$$.* ♿

CAFE FINA ☆☆

 Many locals swear this is the only restaurant worth dining at on Fisherman's Wharf. And, indeed, Cafe Fina is a refreshing outpost of quality amid all the tourist-carnival trappings. Owner Dominic Mercurio offers fresh fish, mesquite-grilled chicken and beef, salads, house-made pasta with inventive herb sauces, and pizzas hot from the brick oven. Specialties are the seafood and pasta dishes, including the flavorful Pasta Fina (linguine with baby shrimp, white wine, olives, clam juice, olive oil, tomatoes, and green onions). The food is delicious and carefully prepared, the atmosphere is casual and fun, and the view is a maritime dream. *On Fisherman's Wharf; (831)372-5200; 47 Fisherman's Wharf, Monterey; full bar; AE, DC, DIS, MC, V; no checks; lunch, dinner every day; $$.*

Having trouble finding a vacancy? Call Resort-II-Me, the Monterey Bay area's most popular reservation service, at (800)757-5646 for a free recommendation in any price range.

LODGINGS

HOTEL PACIFIC ☆☆☆

 Like a Modigliani looming angular and bold in a gallery full of Fra Angelicos, this somewhat modern, neo-hacienda hotel stands out in the midst of Monterey's authentic old adobes. A sparkling fountain burbles beside the entrance; inside you'll find handwoven rugs, muted Southwestern colors, terra-cotta tiles, and beamed ceilings soaring above rounded walls. Connected by tiled courtyards, arches, and flowered pathways, a scattering of low-rise buildings holds 105 small suites. All rooms have private patios or terraces, fireplaces, goose-down feather beds, three telephones, and two TVs (one in the bathroom). Ask for a room on the fourth level with a panoramic view of the bay, or a room facing the inner courtyard with its large fountain. A deluxe continental breakfast is provided in the morning, and guests may indulge in afternoon tea. Complimentary underground parking is available, too. *On Pacific St between Scott St and Del Monte Blvd; (831)373-5700 or (800)554-5542; 300 Pacific St, Monterey, CA 93940; www.travelweb.com; AE, DC, DIS, MC, V; checks OK; $$$.* ♿

OLD MONTEREY INN ☆☆☆

Even those who feel they've seen it all on the bed-and-breakfast circuit are likely to be awed by the elegantly

To catch Monterey at its best, come in the spring or during the sunny Indian summer months; at other times, expect it to be foggy and slightly cool.

appointed Old Monterey Inn. Nestled among giant oak trees and gardens filled with rhododendrons, begonias, fuchsias, and ferns, this Tudor-style country inn built in 1929 positively gleams with natural wood, skylights, and stained-glass windows. The 10 beautifully decorated guest rooms, each with a private bath, are filled with charming antiques and comfortable beds with plump down comforters and huge, fluffy pillows. Most rooms have fireplaces, and although none have TVs or telephones, TVs may be brought into a few of the cable-equipped rooms upon request, and portable phones are available for guests. For the utmost privacy, request the lacy Garden Cottage, which has a private patio, skylights, and a fireplace sitting room. The deluxe Ashford Suite has a sitting area, a separate dressing room, a king-size bed, an antique day bed, and a panoramic garden view. Another standout: the handsome Library guest room, with its book-lined walls, stone fireplace, and private sun deck. Breakfast, taken in the dining room or *en suite*, might include baked apples, French toast, crêpes, cheese rolls, and curiosities such as coconut-lime muffins. You'll also find a delightful afternoon tea and evening hors d'oeuvres. There are plenty of low-key ways to pamper yourself around here, such as lounging at the picnic tables in the rose garden or strolling around the acre-plus grounds. *On Martin St near Pacific St; (831)375-8284 or (800)350-2344; 500 Martin St, Monterey, CA 93940; omi@ oldmontereyinn.com; www.oldmontereyinn.com; MC, V; checks OK; $$$.*

SPINDRIFT INN

 With its soaring four-story atrium and rooftop garden, the Spindrift is an unexpected and elegant refuge amid the hurly-burly tourist world of Cannery Row. Downstairs in this former bordello, plush Oriental carpets muffle your footsteps, and a tall pair of attractive—if politically questionable—Italian blackamoor statues keep you company in the fireside sitting room. Upstairs, all 42 rooms have feather beds (many with canopies)

with down comforters, fireplaces, hardwood floors, telephones, and tiled bathrooms with marble appointments. You'll also discover terrycloth robes, cable TVs, and nightly turn-down service. The corner rooms, with their cushioned window seats and breathtaking ocean views, are the best in the house. In the morning there will be a newspaper, a dewy rose, and a delicious breakfast of fruit, orange juice, croissants, and sweet rolls waiting outside your door on a silver tray. In the afternoon you are invited to partake of tea, pastries, wine, and cheese. *On Cannery Row at Hawthorne St; (831)646-8900 or (800)841-1879; 652 Cannery Row, Monterey, CA 93940; www.spindriftinn.com; AE, DC, DIS, MC, V; checks OK; $$$.* &

THE JABBERWOCK

 The Jabberwock, as you may recall, is a fearsome creature that sprang, gnashing its jaws and flashing its claws, from the fertile mind of Lewis Carroll. This inn has none of the menace but lots of the whimsy of his tale. The rooms bear names such as The Toves and Tulgey Woods and the delicious breakfast dishes (written on a board in backwards mirror-writing) are called "razzleberry flabjous" and "snarkleberry flumptious." Set well back from the hubbub of nearby Cannery Row, this 1911 former convent has seven guest rooms, five with private baths. The spacious and grand Borogrove Room boasts wraparound picture windows with views of the town and the inn's garden. The Mome Rath Room has a bed big enough for any beast. The large, beautifully landscaped garden has a pond, a waterfall, a nifty sundial, and, certainly no surprise, a rabbit—who's very late. *On Laine St at Hoffman Ave; (831)372-4777 or (888)428-7253; 598 Laine St, Monterey, CA 93940; MC, V; checks OK; $$.*

DEL MONTE BEACH INN

True to its name, this small, European-style hotel is right across the street from Del Monte Beach (and close to the majority of Monterey's other main attractions, including nearby Dennis the Menace Playground). Each of the 19 individually decorated rooms comes with period furniture, quilts, and fresh flower boxes hanging outside the window; three come with wharf and ocean views. There are no phones or TVs in the rooms, but there is a pay phone inside the inn and a TV in the library. Another plus is the sunny balcony out back that overlooks the garden. An added bonus is the free, buffet-style continental breakfast. Most rooms share a bath, and entertainment is limited to board games in the lounge, but quit your whining: with prices starting at $55 a night, you won't find a better deal in town. *At Park Ave; (831)649-4410; 1110 Del Monte Ave, Monterey, CA 93940; AE, DIS, MC, V; checks OK; $.*

CASTROVILLE

A young woman by the name of Norma Jean was crowned Castroville's first "Artichoke Queen" in 1947. Yes, Marilyn Monroe.

Gilroy made history with garlic; Castroville chose the artichoke. The undisputed Artichoke Capital of the World, Castroville celebrates its choke-hold on the artichoke market during the annual Artichoke Festival, held every third weekend in September. It's mostly small-town stuff: the crowning of the Artichoke Queen, a 10K run, artichoke cook-offs, and the Firefighters' Pancake Breakfast. If you have a few minutes to kill, you might want to check out the humongous cement version of the thistlelike plant, otherwise known as the Giant Artichoke Restaurant—it's good for a chuckle, a silly photo, and a bowl of artichoke soup; 11261 Merritt Street; (831)633-3204.

RESTAURANTS
LA SCUOLA   ★★

This *buonissimo* Italian restaurant on the main street of Castroville is a real find. Tucked away in a schoolhouse that's more than a century old, this elegant little place offers classic Italian staples such as veal Parmigiana, lasagne, and chicken Toscana. The most popular appetizer is a giant artichoke (naturally), prepared five different ways. The fettuccine with fresh Manila clams is very good (the house-made pasta comes perfectly al dente and the fresh clams explode with flavor), as is roasted garlic chicken in a mushroom and white wine sauce. The vegetable side dishes are cooked just enough to bring out their flavor and color, and the buttery, oven-roasted potatoes are delicately crisp on the outside and creamy-smooth within. The house wine, from the Moresco winery in Stockton, is also pretty good. *At Preston Rd, downtown; (831)633-3200; 10700 Merritt St, Castroville; beer and wine; AE, DIS, MC, V; no checks; lunch Tues–Fri, dinner Tues–Sat; $$.* &

MOSS LANDING

Nature lovers have long revered Moss Landing's Elkhorn Slough as a prime spot to study egrets, pelicans, cormorants, terns, great blue herons, and many other types of aquatic birds, not to mention packs of frolicking harbor seals and otters. Besides hiking or kayaking, one of the best ways to explore this scenic coastal wetland is to embark on an Elkhorn Slough Safari. Naturalist guides provide expert and enthusiastic commentary aboard a 26-foot-long pontoon boat; special activities (such as Bird Bingo) are provided for children; binoculars are available for rent; and coffee, soda, and cookies are served on the way back. The two-hour tours, which cost about $24 for adults, operate on a regular basis Friday through Sunday year-round; weekday tours can be arranged for groups of six or more; call (831)633-5555 for details and reservations or visit the Web site at www.elkhornslough.com.

RESTAURANTS
THE WHOLE ENCHILADA   ☆

Fresh seafood is the focus of this upbeat restaurant on Highway 1 with gaily painted walls, folk-art decorations, and leather basket chairs that lend an engaging south-of-the-border ambience. You'll find the usual lineup of burritos, tacos, chiles rellenos, and enchiladas on the comprehensive menu, but go for one of the more exotic regional specialties, such as Oaxacan chicken mole tamales or garlic prawns. Service is warm and efficient, and little touches like crayons and plastic mermaids clinging to the drink cups make this a place your kids will like, too. *On Hwy 1 at Moss Landing Rd; (831)633-3038; 7902 Hwy 1, Moss Landing; full bar; AE, DC, DIS, MC, V; no checks; lunch, dinner every day; $$.* ✦

THE SANTA CRUZ COAST

Long regarded as a seaside nirvana for dope-smoking hippies and anyone else eschewing the conventional lifestyle, the Santa Cruz coast simply ain't what it used to be—spend a day on the boardwalk and you'll see more bike locks than dreadlocks. What it all comes down to, of course, is money. Tourism is the big draw here: some 3 million annual visitors help fill the county's coffers; the county, in turn, does everything possible to make Santa Cruz a respectable, safe place to bring the family.

The result? A little of everything. Walk down gilded Pacific Avenue and you're bound to see the homeless mix it up with the alternative lifestylers within a sea of yuppie shops and shiny cafes. The cultural dichotomy is painfully manifest, but nobody seems to mind; rather, most locals are pleased with the turnout. As one resident put it, "Anything but Carmel."

A south-to-north sweep of the Santa Cruz County coastline, beginning at Aptos and ending north of Santa Cruz at Davenport.

The Santa Cruz County Conference & Visitors Council has an excellent Web site listing dozens of hotels, restaurants, sights, and activities in Santa Cruz County. Log on at www.scccvc.org.

APTOS

Other than a handful of B&Bs and a few state beaches and parks, Aptos has little in the way of tourist entertainment, leaving that messy business up to neighboring Capitola and Santa Cruz. The focus here is on quality lodgings in quiet surroundings. The only drawback is that the beaches are too far to walk to from town, but if you don't mind the short drive, Aptos is the ideal place for a peaceful vacation on the coast.

ACTIVITIES

Redwood Trails. The Forest of Nisene Marks State Park is one of the largest parks in central California and also one of the least known. The entire forest was clear-cut less than a century ago; today, however, a solid canopy of mostly second-growth redwoods shades the 2½-mile dirt road leading to the trailhead, where more than 30 miles of trails—ranging from cakewalks to lung-busters—disappear into the 10,000-acre forest. The most popular hiking trail is the Loma Prieta Grade, a 6-mile round-trip past the wooden remnants of a turn-of-the-century lumber camp (not far from the epicenter of the 1989 Loma Prieta earthquake). Mountain bikers and leashed dogs are also welcome. At the end of Aptos Creek Road off Soquel Drive; free; open year-round; (831)763-7062.

RESTAURANTS

CAFE SPARROW   ☆☆

Chef/owner Bob Montague opened this quaint French Country restaurant in June 1989. Then along came the Loma Prieta earthquake on October 17th (whose epicenter lay just a short distance away), and Montague had little more than a pile of rubble on his hands. Fortunately, he and his wife didn't throw in the towel, and their remodeled restaurant is indeed a gem of a dining spot, acting as a magnet for local gourmets. Two dining rooms, decorated with country furniture and a tentlike expanse of French printed fabric, provide a romantic backdrop for Montague's spirited culinary creations. Lunch may include a croissant layered with shrimp in lemon, fresh dill, and crème fraîche, or a bowl of creamed spinach with a vinaigrette salad and bread. Dinner, however, is when Montague puts on the ritz. Start with a pâté of fresh chicken livers seasoned with herbs and Cognac; prawns in an orange and pink peppercorn beurre blanc; or a fondue of white wine, herbs, and cheeses, served with vegetables and a baguette. Then progress to such entrees as a grilled chicken breast with pears topped with Brie; lamb chops in a rich red-wine and mint sauce; or pan-sautéed calamari steak with lemon, butter, and capers. Desserts are as decadent as you'd expect from a place that seems intent on spoiling its customers rotten. One unexpected touch: This sophisticated restaurant isn't afraid to be kid-friendly, and dishes tailored to tots are available. The wine list is far-ranging and agreeably priced, and the service is amiable. *On Soquel Dr near Trout Gulch Rd; (831)688-6238; 8042 Soquel Dr, Aptos; beer and wine; MC, V; checks OK; brunch Sun, lunch Mon–Sat, dinner every day; $$.*

LODGINGS

MANGELS HOUSE ★★

Set on an imposing green lawn in the middle of a red-wood forest, this Italianate mansion was built as a summer house for Spreckels sugar magnate Claus Mangels in 1886. British-born Jacqueline Fisher and her husband, Ron, who bought the estate in 1979, have decorated the six guest rooms in a daring, artful, whimsical way that enlivens the house's stately Victorian demeanor. One room sports a huge bed and chocolate-brown walls decorated with masks, shields, and other African souvenirs that sometimes shock guests expecting a more traditional approach to Victorian decor. Other rooms feature pastel stenciling that dances across the walls and dramatic modern vases atop antique marble sinks. Lavish breakfasts, served in the dining room, feature such delights as apple-puff pancakes, a spicy chile-cheese fluff, fresh fruit, and homemade scones. All in all, this is a comfortable, homey inn in a glorious natural setting. *On Aptos Creek Rd, on the road into the Forest of Nisene Marks State Park, ½ mile above town, (831)688-7982 or (800)320-7401; 570 Aptos Creek Rd, PO Box 302, Aptos, CA 95001; AE, MC, V; checks OK; $$–$$$.*

SEASCAPE RESORT ★★

This new condo-resort complex on 64 cliff-side acres offers spacious accommodations and plenty of creature comforts. The more than 200 guest suites (they're still building) are arranged in a cluster of three-story stucco buildings and are available in studio or one- or two-bedroom configurations. Each suite is outfitted with identical beach-house-style furnishings—not especially luxurious but pleasant enough—and comes with a fireplace, a private balcony or patio, a TV, a kitchenette, sitting and dining areas, a modem port, and an ocean view. Largely given over to corporate functions during the week, the complex segues into a haven for couples and families on the weekend. A paved path leads down to the beach, and guests enjoy member privileges at a nearby

Aptos had the unenviable honor of being the city nearest the epicenter of the 1989 Loma Prieta earthquake. A trail within the Forest of Nisene Marks leads to the exact point where the trouble began.

PGA-rated golf course and the Seascape Sports Club, which offers tennis, swimming, and a fully equipped gym. The resort also provides 24-hour room service, a children's program during the summer, and a spa offering massage and beautician services. Fresh seafood is the specialty at *Sanderlings*, the resort's airy, Florida-style restaurant with patio dining and gorgeous ocean vistas. *Seascape Resort Dr at Sumner Blvd; (831)688-6800 or (800)929-7727; 1 Seascape Resort Dr, Aptos, CA 95003; www.seascaperesort.com; full bar; AE, DC, MC, V; checks OK; breakfast, lunch, dinner every day; $$$.* &

BAYVIEW HOTEL BED AND BREAKFAST INN ☆

Built in 1878 on former Spanish land-grant property, the oldest hotel on Monterey Bay combines Old West ambience with up-to-date comfort. The steep staircase, book-lined parlor, and antiques recall Aptos' frontier past, but guests won't feel like they're roughing it. Each of the 11 rooms has its own phone, bath, and firm mattress resting in an antique frame; some have fireplaces and extra-large tubs. Occupying part of the first floor is the White Magnolia, a restaurant that opened in late 1997 featuring California cuisine with Pacific Rim accents. *On Soquel Dr at Trout Gulch Rd; (831)688-8654, (800)4-BAYVIEW, or (831)662-1890 (restaurant); 8041 Soquel Dr, Aptos, CA 95003; full bar; AE, MC, V; checks OK; brunch Sun, lunch Tues–Fri, dinner every day; $$–$$$.*

CAPITOLA

Founded in 1869 by lumber baron Frederick A. Hihn, Capitola is purport-edly California's oldest seaside resort.

Capitola's Mediterranean-style buildings, curved streets, white-sand beaches, outdoor cafes, and perpetually festive atmosphere seem more suitable for the French Riviera than Monterey Bay. The verdict? If you're staying on the coast for more than a day, a visit to this ultra-quaint hamlet is highly recommended. Park the car anywhere you can, feed the meter (bring quarters), spend an hour browsing the dozens of boutiques along the esplanade, then rest your bones at Zelda's sunny beachside patio with a pitcher of margaritas. That's the Capitola shuffle.

ACTIVITIES

Ocean Fishing. Even if you don't know an outboard from a Ouija board, the friendly staff at Capitola Boat & Bait have faith that you'll bring their fishing boats back in one piece. Around $60 buys you a four-person boat for the day, including an outboard motor, fuel, safety equipment, anchor, oars, seat cushions, and free maps of the hot fishing spots. Fishing gear can also be rented and one-day licenses purchased, so there's no excuse not to brave the open ocean just for the halibut. Open daily sunrise to 4pm; closed January to mid-Febuary. 1400 Wharf Road, at the end of Capitola Wharf; (831)462-2208.

RESTAURANTS

GAYLE'S BAKERY & ROSTICCERIA ☆☆

Take a number and stand in line. It's worth the wait at this wildly popular place, which is packed with local folk on weekend mornings. A self-service bakery and deli, Gayle's offers numerous imaginative sandwiches, pastas, casseroles, roasted meats, salads, cheeses, appetizers, breads, and treats. The variety is staggering and the quality topnotch. There's a good selection of wine, beer, bottled water, and espresso drinks, too. Once you've fought your way to the counter, you'll have the makings of a first-class picnic to take to one of the nearby parks or beaches. You can also eat your feast in the cafe's small dining area or on the heated patio. *On Bay Ave by Capitola Ave; (831)462-1200; 504 Bay Ave, Capitola; beer and wine; MC, V; checks OK; open 6:30am-8:30pm every day; $.* &

SHADOWBROOK RESTAURANT ☆☆

While locals are forever undecided about the quality of the food at Shadowbrook, they nevertheless insist that all Santa Cruz visitors dine here at least once in their lives. It's just such a fun place to eat—even its detractors delight in escorting their guests aboard the funicular that runs down through the ferny woods, past a waterfall, to the multistoried, woodsy restaurant bedecked in white lights.

That ship-shaped dock east of Capitola City Beach is the Palo Alto, built during World War I as part of the "concrete fleet." After the war, she was towed to nearby Seacliff, partially sunk, and used as a floating casino and dance hall. In 1965 the state purchased the $2 million ship for a buck and converted it into a fishing pier.

Lately, Shadowbrook has been paying more attention to the food, resulting in a well-crafted, seasonal California-Mediterranean menu. Starters might include artichoke hearts with lime-cilantro sauce; tender calamari strips served with a zesty pineapple-chile sauce; or a Tuscan salad with frisée, rock shrimp, pancetta, white beans, and goat-cheese croutons. Some of the better entrees are tender braised lamb shank, bacon-wrapped prawns with creamy polenta, and swordfish. Mud pie and cheesecake remain the most popular desserts. The best seat in the house is at the alfresco tables on the brickwork terraces, nestled romantically among rock gardens and rhododendrons. Management recently remodeled the entryway, allowing diners to eat in the informal bar area with a view of the waterfalls and gardens. *On Wharf Rd near the end of Capitola Rd; (831)475-1511; 1750 Wharf Rd, Capitola; michael@shadowbrook-capitola.com; full bar; AE, DC, DIS, MC, V; local checks only; brunch Sun, dinner every day; $$$.*

LODGINGS

THE INN AT DEPOT HILL ☆☆☆

Located in a turn-of-the-century train station, the Inn at Depot Hill is a dream of a place, with trompe l'oeil paintings on the walls and soft, sophisticated lighting that bathes everyone in an angelic glow. The 12 guest rooms, lavishly designed to evoke international ports of call, seem to have sprung directly from the pages of *Architectural Digest.* The terra-cotta–walled Portofino Room, patterned after a coastal Italian villa, sports a stone cherub, ivy, frescoes, and a brick patio. No less charming is the Stratford-upon-Avon, a faux English cottage with a cozy window seat. The Paris Room with its toile-covered walls dazzles in black and white, while the rather fussy Côte d'Azur boasts an ornate canopy bed with bronze vines climbing the four-posters. Every room has a TV and a VCR, a built-in stereo system, and a marble-appointed bathroom complete with a mini-TV and a coffee machine. In the morning, there's a buffet of pastries, cereal, and quiche, as well as a hot dish such as French toast or a spinach omelet. In the evening, you'll find sweets and wine in the downstairs parlor. You may also browse along the massive wall-length bookcase for a tome or videotape to borrow. *Monterey Ave near Park Ave, next to the railroad tracks; (831)462-3376 or (800)572-2632; 250 Monterey Ave, PO Box 1934, Capitola, CA 95010; lodging@innatdepothill.com; www.innatdepothill.com; AE, MC, V; checks OK; $$$.* &

SANTA CRUZ

For nearly a century, Santa Cruz has been synonymous with "beach and boardwalk," as if this seaside city of 50,000 exists solely to sustain what is now the only major beachside amusement park left on the Pacific Coast. Considering that the annual number of boardwalk visitors is 62 times greater than the city's population, it's no surprise that Santa Cruz's other highlights are all but ignored by the hordes of thrill-seekers who head straight for the waterfront each year.

Not that the boardwalk (now a cement walk) isn't worthy of the limelight. Ranked among the top amusement parks in the nation, with a higher attendance than either Marine World–Africa USA or Paramount's Great America, the privately owned amusement park has cleaned up its once-tarnished act by pouring a pile of money into improvements and security; the boardwalk is truly safe and clean these days. Then, of course, there's the legendary Giant Dipper, considered by those-who-would-know to be the greatest roller coaster ever built, and the

GETTING THERE

The most scenic route to Santa Cruz is along Highway 1 from San Francisco, which, aside from the "you fall, you die" stretch called Devil's Slide, lets you cruise at a steady 50mph along the coast. Faster but far less romantic is Route 17, which is accessed near San Jose from I-280, I-880, or Highway 101 and literally ends at the foot of the boardwalk. The exceptions to this are weekday rush hours and weekend mornings, when Route 17 tends to logjam while Highway 1 remains relatively uncrowded.

*Downtown Santa
Cruz is silly with
free parking: along
Cedar and Front
Streets there are 3
parking garages
and 16 surface lots
that offer 3 hours
of emancipated
parking.*

hand-carved horses of the Looff Carousel, the last bona fide
brass ring merry-go-round in North America. These two rides
alone are worth a walk down the boardwalk.

Yet even without its celebrated amusement park, Santa Cruz
would still be one of California's top coastal destinations. Where
else can you find a vibrant, cross-cultural (remember, this used
to be the LSD capital of the world) college town perched on the
edge of an immense bay teeming with marine life, ringed by
miles of golden beaches, and backed by dense redwood forests?
Remove those boardwalk blinders for a day, and you'll find out
that there's a whole lot more to Santa Cruz than cotton candy
and arcades.

ACTIVITIES

Power Shopping. When it comes to shopping, Santa
Cruz doesn't fool around. Walk down Pacific Avenue and
ay caramba! More than 250 shops and restaurants are crammed
into Santa Cruz's 29-block business district, which has recovered
rather nicely from the 1989 Loma Prieta earthquake (the epicenter was only 10 miles away). As you make your way down the
mall, look for the Octagon Building, an ornate, eight-sided Victorian brick edifice built in 1882 that has survived numerous
quakes. Previously serving as the city's Hall of Records, it's now
part of the McPherson Center for Art and History, which showcases 10,000 years of the area's past as well as contemporary art
of the Pacific Rim. Open Tuesday to Sunday, noon to 5pm (Fridays till 7pm); 705 Front Street at Cooper Street; (831)429-1964.

Sea Kayaking. The best ride on the boardwalk isn't the
Giant Dipper roller coaster, it's paddling a sea kayak along
the Santa Cruz coast. Vision Quest Kayaking, located on the
northeast end of the Santa Cruz Wharf, rents single-, double-,
and triple-seater kayaks for exploring the nearby cliffs and kelp
beds where a multitude of sea otters, seals, sea lions, and other
marine animals congregate. No experience is necessary, and all
ages are welcome. Guided tours are also available; (831)425-8445.

Redwoods State Park. The perfect antidote to an over-
dose of sun and sand is a walk through the redwoods at
Henry Cowell Redwoods State Park. Only a few miles from

On summer Friday nights, head to the Santa Cruz Beach Boardwalk and check out the free concerts at 6:30pm and 8:30pm, featuring the likes of the Shirelles, Chubby Checker, and Sha Na Na; (831)423-5590.

downtown Santa Cruz on Highway 9 (from Mission Street, turn north on River Street/Highway 9 and continue north), the 1,800-acre park has 20 miles of trails through thick, cool forests and golden meadows. Top pick for a leisurely walk is the ¾-mile Redwood Grove Trail, a wide and flat loop around an ancient stand of giant redwoods. On summer weekends at 2pm, docent-led tours of the Grove Trail start from the Nature Center, but call ahead first; (831)335-7077 or (831)335-4598. (Secret tip: About 1½ miles south of the main entrance on Highway 9 is the Ox Road Parking Lot. Park here—for free!—then take the short trail down to the locals' favorite swimming hole, the Garden of Eden.)

Marine Laboratory. Mildly entertaining for adults but a blast for kids are the aquarium and marine exhibits at the Joseph M. Long Marine Laboratory, a seaside research facility partly run by UC Santa Cruz. Top billing are the shallow touch tanks that allow visitors to handle—and learn about—sea stars, anemones, sea cucumbers, and other slimy sea creatures. You can also see scientists studying dolphins and sea lions in the lab's marine mammals pools. Behind the gift shop are the humbling skeletal remains of an 85-foot blue whale. There are plans underway to open a new Marine Discovery Center that will allow visitors to play marine scientist and learn firsthand about how researchers study the seas. Open Tuesday to Sunday, 1pm to 4pm; $2 for adults, kids 16 and under free. From Highway 1 in

Take the Beach Boys' advice—don't be afraid to try the greatest sport around. Learn to catch a wave at Club Ed Surf School, open year-round in front of the West Coast Santa Cruz Hotel just west of the Santa Cruz Wharf; (831)459-9283.

west Santa Cruz, turn south on Swift Street and right on Delaware Avenue to end; (831)459-4308.

Music & Dancing. One good thing about a college town—it knows how to party. The Cruz's coolest blues are at Moe's Alley, featuring live music (and dancing) nightly; 1535 Commercial Way; (831)479-1854. For traditional and modern jazz, there's the Kuumbwa Jazz Center, a nonprofit (and non-smoking) landmark that's been around for the past two decades; 320 Cedar Street; (831)427-2227. Local rock, reggae, blues, and world-beat bands mix it up at the Catalyst, which occasionally pulls in some big names, too; 1011 Pacific Avenue; (831)423-1336. Even bluegrass, Hawaiian, and folk music find a venue at cavernous Palookaville dance club, which also has its share of rock and reggae; 1133 Pacific Avenue; (831)454-0600.

Bike Rental. Santa Cruz is a bicycler's heaven. The pedal-friendly downtown area is flat and wide (ditto the wharf and boardwalk), and the shoreline bike path along West Cliff Drive is sensational. If you can't bring your own wheels, the Bicycle Rental & Tour Center rents touring, tandem, and mountain bikes at hourly, daily, and weekly rates, and even throws in free helmets, packs, maps and locks. 131 Center St, two blocks from the Municipal Wharf; (831)426-8687.

Surfing Museum. Within the small brick lighthouse building off West Cliff Drive is the Santa Cruz Surfing Museum. Photographs, videos, antique surfboards, and piles of other memorabilia depict the history and evolution of surfing around the world. After the tour, walk to the point's edge and watch the sea lions waddle around Seal Rock. (Open every day but Tuesday, noon–5pm; (831)429-3429.) Between the lighthouse and the boardwalk is that famous strip of the sea known as Steamers Lane, the summa cum laude California surfing spot (savvy surfers say this—not Southern California—is the place to catch the best breaks in the state).

Beach & Butterflies. At the north end of West Cliff Drive is Natural Bridges State Beach, named after archways carved into the rock formations here by the ocean waves (only one of the three original arches still stands). Popular with

A GOOD DAY IN SANTA CRUZ

9–10am:	Breakfast at Dale's Diner in Felton (see sidebar).
10am–noon:	A stroll through Henry Cowell Redwoods State Park.
Noon–1:30pm:	Lunch at Ristorante Avanti.
1:30–3:30pm:	Shop along Pacific Avenue.
3:30–5pm:	Sea kayaking from the wharf.
5–6:30pm:	A sunset walk along West Cliff Drive.
6:30–8pm:	Dinner at O'mei Restaurant.
8–10pm:	Browse the boardwalk.
10–11:30pm:	Decaf mocha and a good read at Bookshop Santa Cruz (see sidebar).

A consistent winner for Santa Cruz's "best breakfast" is Dale's Diner, a funky old restaurant in the mountain town of Felton that's renowned for its burly pancakes. Open 7am to 2:30pm every day; 6560 Highway 9, 6 miles north of Santa Cruz; (831)335-2000.

surfers, windsurfers, tide pool trekkers, and sunbathers, the beach does a brisk winter business as well: between October and March up to 200,000 monarch butterflies roost and mate in the nearby eucalyptus grove. Skip the $6 parking fee at the West Cliff Drive entrance and walk in from Delaware Avenue (just east of the entrance off Swanton Boulevard) for free; (831)423-4609.

 On the Wharf. If you had to pay just to drive down the famous Santa Cruz Wharf, you'd probably feel ripped off. Fortunately, you don't: The first 30 minutes of parking are free, which is plenty of time to rubberneck the touristy shops, fish markets, and seafood restaurants that line the side of this venerable octogenarian. Dining tip: Within the wharf's sea of pricey establishments is the Riva Fish House, a surprisingly inexpensive restaurant with good food and a superb view; Building 31, Municipal Wharf; (831)429-1223.

Santa Cruz's best hangout is Bookshop Santa Cruz, which has an enormous and diverse inventory (including a particularly good children's section) as well as the two other key elements to a good bookstore: plenty of places to sit and a good cafe. At 1520 Pacific Avenue; (831)423-0900.

 Coastal Walk. Santa Cruz's real premier attraction isn't the beach or boardwalk; it's the 2-mile walking-biking-jogging path along West Cliff Drive. Proof positive is that locals don't go anywhere near the boardwalk, but you can see them in droves exercising up and down the 2 miles of paved coastal trail from the wharf to Natural Bridges State Park. The best time to visit is at sunset, when the alternative-lifestylers gather near the lighthouse to bang their drums and flail around.

On the south end of West Cliff Drive is Lighthouse Field State Beach, the birthplace of American surfing and one of the few beaches in town where doggies are allowed.

"Every town needs at least one good dive bar—you know, the kind without any of that stupid shiny brass. The Avenue is ours; it's the last true dive bar in Santa Cruz."

—Frazer, bartender at the Avenue (711 Pacific Avenue at Laurel Street; (831)426-3434)

Localmotion. Locomotive buffs, kids, and closet tree-huggers should hop aboard the historic Roaring Camp train for a 6-mile, 1¼-hour round-trip excursion up the steepest narrow-gauge grades in North America. The steam-powered locomotive winds s-l-o-w-l-y through dense, cool redwood groves to the summit of Bear Mountain and back. A second train outfit, called Big Trees Railroad, offers an 8-mile ride through mountain tunnels and along ridges (with spectacular views of the San Lorenzo River) before stopping at the Santa Cruz Beach Boardwalk. Both trains are located on Graham Hill Road off Highway 17 in Felton (follow the signs), though the Big Trees Railroad can also be boarded at the east end of the boardwalk. Call for specific departure times. Roaring Camp: Trains run weekends December through March, daily rest of the year; (831)335-4484. Big Trees Railroad: Trains run weekends and holidays, September through November, with daily runs in summer; closed December through April; (831)335-4484.

Boardwalk Bargains. Save a bundle at the boardwalk by visiting on "1907 Nights." Every summer after 5pm on Monday and Tuesday, the Santa Cruz Beach Boardwalk celebrates the year it opened by reducing its prices to 50 cents a ride (it's normally $1.50 to $3), and two bits buys a hot dog, soft drink, cotton candy, or a red candy apple. At the end of summer the boardwalk also hosts "1907 Week," when you can get the same evening deals Monday through Friday before Labor Day; (831)423-5590.

RESTAURANTS

O'MEI RESTAURANT ☆☆☆

Named after a mountain in the Sichuan province of China, this acclaimed Chinese restaurant is a wondrous little paradox tucked into one of Santa Cruz's many strip malls. Owner/chef Roger Grigsby is not Chinese, nor are any of his cooks, but his food caters less to American sensibilities than do most Chinese restaurants. While you may order predictable northern Chinese offerings such as Mongolian beef and mu-shu pork, those with adventurous palates are better served if they forgo the old standbys. Pushing the envelope of Chinese cuisine, O'mei offers tasty provincial curiosities such as litchi chicken, leg of lamb sautéed with hot-and-sour cabbage, and an enchanting black sesame ice cream. Another plus: The limited but well-chosen wine list, with all wines available by the glass. *On Mission St near Fair Ave; (831)425-8458; 2316 Mission St, Santa Cruz; beer and wine; AE, MC, V; no checks; lunch Mon–Fri, dinner every day; $$.* &

OSWALD ☆☆☆

Thanks to chef Charlie Deal's adept cooking, reverence for fresh produce, and restrained spicing and saucing that let the flavors of the principal ingredients sing out loud and clear, this small California-French bistro will remind you of Berkeley's celebrated Chez Panisse. The dining room has a spare, arty look, with bold still-life paintings on the brick and pale-yellow-painted walls, high ceilings, wooden banquettes, and a petite wrought-iron-railed balcony set with a couple of tables. Chef Deal's small seasonal menu is supplemented nightly by a roster of specials that takes good advantage of the best meats and veggies in the markets that day (organic whenever possible). Expect starters such as plump pork and shrimp raviolis nestled in broth flecked with slivers of asparagus and mushrooms; steamed mussels with fried bread and aioli; and a butter lettuce salad with shaved fennel, delicate wedges of citrus, and green olives. Entrees might include savory Gruyère bread pudding with asparagus and leeks, buttermilk-fried chicken with an herbed potato and carrot chowder, and seared ahi tuna with scallion-potato cakes and a roasted beet and endive salad. There's always a very reasonably priced three-course vegetarian tasting menu, and desserts often feature seasonal fruit—two more indications of Deal's love affair with exceptional produce, no doubt fostered during his previous stint at San Francisco's famous Greens restaurant. The servers are knowledgeable and solicitous, and the wine list features a good lineup of both California and French offerings. *On Pacific Ave (use the parking lot on Cedar St and enter the restaurant through*

For organically grown produce, flowers, herbs, and other non-corporate-made goodies, shop at Santa Cruz's Farmers Market, held Wednesdays from 2:30pm to 6:30pm on Lincoln Street between Pacific Avenue and Cedar Street.

the courtyard), (831)423-7427; 1547 Pacific Ave, Santa Cruz; www.oswald.com; beer and wine; AE, DC, MC, V; local checks OK; dinner every day; $$. &

RISTORANTE AVANTI ★★★

Newcomers who take one look at this unpretentious restaurant set in a humble strip mall may be forgiven for thinking, "Three-star restaurant? I don't think so." Ah, but wait until they've tasted the food and sampled the considerate, professional service—they'll be sorry for doubting our stellar designation. In keeping with the Santa Cruz lifestyle, Avanti prides itself on serving "the healthiest meal possible" (think fresh, organic produce and free-range chicken, veal, and lamb). The modern, casual decor, with a long wooden counter dominating one of the small rooms and posters of Italy scattered throughout, provides a welcome setting for aromatic, seasonal dishes such as sweet squash ravioli with sage butter; lasagne primavera; spaghetti with wild mushroom and shallot duxelles; and orecchiette with salmon, Italian greens, mushrooms, and sun-dried tomatoes. The grilled lemon chicken, salmon with roasted garlic cream sauce, and balsamic-vinegar-marinated lamb chops also demonstrate the kitchen's skillful and delicate touch, and you simply can't go wrong with the daily specials. The ample and reasonably priced wine list contains selections from California, Spain, and Italy, and don't even think about skipping dessert—any of the ever-changing selections is worth an extra 20 minutes on the Stairmaster. *On Mission St near Bay St; (831)427-0135; 1711 Mission St, Santa Cruz; beer and wine; AE, MC, V; local checks only; breakfast, lunch, dinner every day, $$.* &

CASABLANCA RESTAURANT ★★

 There's nothing very Moroccan about this boardwalk bastion of California-continental cuisine, except, perhaps, the palpable air of romance. Soft music fills the candle-lit dining room, and stars wink on the water outside the window—you know, the sort of place where you get the urge to hold hands across the table. Chef Scott

Cater, who worked here in the '80s and recently returned to Casablanca, has crafted a regional American menu with European accents. Starters include fried calamari with a spicy lime dipping sauce, lobster chowder, and fried brie served with jalapeño jelly and toast rounds. Entrees range from grilled Hawaiian swordfish served on a bed of garlic-herb linguine to a cilantro-marinated chicken breast with garlic whipped potatoes and sun-dried-tomato pesto. Local wines share a book-length wine list with selections from Italy, Germany, France, and Australia. *On Main St at Beach St, on the waterfront; (831)426-9063; 101 Main St, Santa Cruz; full bar; AE, DC, DIS, MC, V; checks OK; brunch Sun, dinner every day; $$$.*

EL PALOMAR ★★

For a quick, inexpensive lunch, El Palomar, (831)425-7575, has a great taco bar across from its main restaurant at 1336 Pacific Avenue on the Pacific Garden Mall. Between 5pm and 8pm Monday through Thursday you can get $1.50 tacos, or $2 burritos, draft beers or margaritas.

Even on a rainy day, this vibrant restaurant hidden at the back of a former '30s hotel manages to create a sunny atmosphere. Maybe it's the tall vaulted-and-beamed ceiling painted in the Spanish manner, the huge mural depicting a Mexican waterfront village scene, or all the plants in big ceramic urns, but something about the place puts you in a good frame of mind even before the food shows up. When it does, your disposition is sure to be further enhanced. Peruse the imaginative, extensive menu while sipping an Ultimate Margarita and munching on delicate tortilla chips still warm from the oven. El Palomar is known for its seafood dishes, which are topped with exotic sauces, but traditional Mexican favorites such as burritos and tacos are also outstanding. A casual new sister restaurant, Cafe El Palomar, serves breakfast, lunch, and "taco cafe" fare beside the Santa Cruz harbor from 7am to 7pm. *On Pacific Ave in the Pacific Garden Mall, near Soquel Ave; (831)425-7575; 1336 Pacific Ave, Santa Cruz; full bar; AE, DIS, MC, V; local checks only; brunch Sun, lunch, dinner every day; $$. ₺ ■ Cafe El Palomar: On E Cliff Dr at the Santa Cruz Harbor; (831)462-4248; 2222 E Cliff Dr, Santa Cruz; beer and wine; MC, V; no checks; breakfast, lunch, early dinner every day; $. ₺*

CROW'S NEST ☆

 This large, multilevel seaside restaurant offers a heated, glassed-in deck that's an uncommonly pleasant place to watch boats cruise in and out of Santa Cruz Harbor. The food at the Crow's Nest isn't exactly gourmet, but the steaks, seafood, chicken, and salads are competently prepared and tasty. The staff is friendly and efficient, and there's a bar area for drinks and light eats. Young mateys can choose from a bargain-priced children's menu, then top off their meal with a little toy from the treasure chest. All in all, it's hard to think of a more relaxing and scenic place for a casual repast. *On E Cliff Dr at the Santa Cruz Harbor; (831)476-4560; 2218 E Cliff Dr, Santa Cruz; full bar; AE, DC, DIS, MC, V; no checks; lunch, dinner every day; $$.* &

PONTIAC GRILL ☆

Most everyone in town agrees that the Pontiac Grill is the best place to take the kids. The servers are decked out in pleated skirts and sweater vests, and each of the streamlined booths has a working mini-jukebox. The menu dishes up relentless automobile puns: appetizers are called "first gear," side orders are "spare parts," drinks are "heaters and coolants," drumettes with barbecue sauce are "chicken pistons." Of course, children love the french fries, onion rings, burgers, milk shakes, and the opportunity to color in the Pontiacs on the place mats. *Front St at Cathcart St; (831)427-2290; 429 Front St, Santa Cruz; beer and wine; MC, V; no checks; lunch, dinner every day; $.*

LODGINGS

THE BABBLING BROOK INN ☆☆

Ensconced in a fantastical garden with waterfalls, wishing wells, gazebos, and, of course, a babbling brook, Santa Cruz's oldest B&B offers 13 rooms, mostly named after famous artists. The mauve-and-blue Van Gogh Room has a private deck, a fireplace, a beamed ceiling, and a whirlpool tub for two. Peach and ivory predominate in the Cézanne Room, with its generous bath and canopy bed. The blue-and-white Monet Room has a corner fireplace, a canopy bed, a private deck, and a view of the waterfall and footbridge. In the morning, chatty and enthusiastic innkeeper Helen King lays out a delectable spread of fruit compote, banana muffins, croissants, French toast, fresh-squeezed orange juice, yogurt, fresh coffee, and more. She'll even whip up dishes for guests with special diets. You may eat in the luxurious dining room, on the flowery patio, or in your suite. *On Laurel St near California St; (831)427-2437 or (800)866-1131; 1025 Laurel St, Santa Cruz, CA 95060; www.virtual cities.com; AE, DC, DIS, MC, V; checks OK; $$-$$$.* &

Ninety percent of the brussels sprouts (yuck) grown in the United States are from Santa Cruz County.

THE DARLING HOUSE:
A BED AND BREAKFAST INN BY THE SEA ☆☆

 There are probably no better views (and no softer carpeting) in all of Santa Cruz than those you'll find at the Darling House, a Spanish Revival mansion built as a summer home for a Colorado cattle baron in 1910. From its postcard-perfect location in a posh residential neighborhood, you can see endless miles of gray-blue sea, boats, seagulls, and the lights of faraway towns. On chilly days you'll always find a fire crackling in the living room's glorious art deco fireplace. The Pacific Ocean Room, upstairs, is decorated like a sea captain's quarters, with a telescope and huge polished seashells. Across the hall, the Chinese Room features brightly colored lanterns and an exotic canopied Chinese wedding bed. The cottage out back has a kitchenette, a wood-burning stove, a living room, a claw-footed tub, and a queen-size canopy bed. Owners Darrell and Karen Darling have worked hard to preserve the house's intricate woodwork and have outfitted all eight guest rooms with museum-quality antiques. There's a hot tub in the backyard, and there are fluffy white robes in every closet. The incredibly attentive Darrell will even call a restaurant to make sure its evening menu is to your liking. Karen's breakfasts include fresh fruit, homemade granola made with walnuts from the Darlings' farm, and oven-fresh breads and pastries. *On W Cliff Dr between the pier and the lighthouse;*

(831)458-1958 or (800)458-1958; 314 W Cliff Dr, Santa Cruz, CA 95060; AE, DIS, MC, V; checks OK; $$$.

CLIFF CREST BED AND BREAKFAST INN ☆

History, the allure of an antique-laden Victorian house, and views of the Santa Cruz boardwalk and the bay beyond are all a part of this welcoming five-room B&B. With grounds designed by Golden Gate Park architect John McLaren, this 1887 Queen Anne inn is the former home of Lieutenant Governor William Jeter and his even more formidable wife, Jenny. Mrs. Jeter, who lived here until her death at age 99, reportedly used her cane to keep unruly nieces and nephews in line and insisted on driving her horse and buggy into town until the authorities prevailed upon the 89-year-old dowager to desist in 1949. These days, guests are greeted by the charming and, rest assured, far more easygoing hosts Bruce and Sharon Taylor. They'll invite you into their cozy sitting room/breakfast nook, complete with fireplace, antique furniture, old-time Jeter family photos—and a view of the boardwalk's roller coaster. Some painting and minor carpentry wouldn't be amiss, but the lack of these doesn't really detract from the feeling of old Santa Cruz charm fostered by the inn's intricate woodwork, stained glass, intriguing nooks, claw-footed tubs, and converted gaslight fixtures. The Rose Room boasts bay views, a sitting area, and an Eastlake bed, while the more modest Jenny's Room offers a window seat and a shower reputedly large enough for three (Aunt Jenny must be turning in her grave). Two other guest rooms have fireplaces. All the rooms are equipped with telephones, TVs are available upon request, and the complimentary full breakfast may be served in bed or on the garden terrace outside. *On Cliff St near 3rd St; (831)427-2609; 407 Cliff St, Santa Cruz, CA 95060; innkpr@cliffcrestinn.com; AE, MC, V; checks OK; $$–$$$.*

EDGEWATER BEACH MOTEL ☆

So old-fashioned it's retro-contemporary, the Edgewater hasn't changed many of its furnishings since the late

'60s—even the brochures (check out the beehive hairdos) are from 1966. The odd part is, everything is still miraculously new-looking, as if you've stumbled upon the set for *The Brady Bunch on Vacation*. The list of amenities runs long: all 17 rooms—including the family suites with kitchens, nonsmoking rooms, and rooms with fireplaces—have refrigerators, cable TV, phones, free coffee, and even access to a heated pool, sun deck, and a barbecue picnic area; most have microwaves. Parking is free, and the boardwalk is only a block away. Be sure to ask about the mini-vacation packages, which are a real deal. *Off the ocean end of Front St; (831)423-0440; 525 Second St, Santa Cruz, CA 95060; AE, DC, DIS, MC, V; checks OK in advance; $$.*

THE CARMELITA COTTAGES

From the street you'd never guess that this gaggle of whitewashed Victorian cottages is a hostel. Located a mere two blocks from the boardwalk in a quiet residential neighborhood, the Carmelita Cottages consist of simple dormitory-style cabins with three to five small beds per room (avoid the creaky bunk beds). All paths lead to the main house, which has a communal kitchen and comfy common rooms. Prices are about $13 per person (less than what you'd pay for parking at the boardwalk, which is free at the hostel), $40 for couples' rooms, and a bit more for family rooms. A morning chore is appreciated, lock-out is 10am to 5pm, and curfew is at 11pm (though no one seems to remember any of this). Reservations are a must during the summer, as are earplugs. *On Main St off Beach St, 2 blocks N of the wharf; (831)423-8304; 321 Main St, PO Box 1241, Santa Cruz, CA 95061; checks OK via mailed reservation; $.* &

DAVENPORT

About 10 miles north of Santa Cruz on Highway 1 is the former whaling and lumber-shipping town of Davenport, which now serves mainly as a snack stop for road-weary travelers. At the Whale City Bakery, Bar & Grill you can get an ample slice of hot apple or pecan pie for the road, but a better plan is to take your fixin's across the highway for an impromptu picnic underneath the cliff-side grove of cypress trees (open daily 6am to 8pm; 490 Highway 1, (831)423-9803).

ACTIVITIES

 What-a-Beach! Just a few years ago it used to be a secret, this pristine gold-sand beach near Davenport. Now there's not only a new parking lot, but a bus stop as well. No matter—it still remains the finest public beach between Santa Cruz and San Francisco, a postcard expanse of sand sheltered from wind and road noise by high bluffs. During high surf the waves put on quite a show smashing into the rocks. It's located exactly 1 mile south of Davenport on Highway 1. Park in the long, skinny lot across from Bonny Doon Road, climb over the railroad levee, and there she is: one of the most beautiful and secluded beaches in California.

LODGINGS

THE DAVENPORT BED & BREAKFAST INN ☆☆

 This pretty, rustic spot has a simple charm befitting this laid-back region of the coast. Artist-owners Bruce and Marcia McDougal have decorated the dozen rooms in a pleasing mélange of Native American, Victorian, and country motifs. If you're not likely to be bothered by traffic sounds from Highway 1 or music drifting up from the restaurant below, opt for one of the eight rooms in the main building. All have private baths and open onto a narrow wooden porch commanding inspiring views of the ocean and cliffs; the grandest, Captain Davenport's Retreat, features two walls of windows framing the splendid vista. If it's peace and quiet you're after, forgo the view and settle down in one of the four slightly smaller rooms in the annex next door. The room rate includes a full breakfast and a complimentary drink at the *New Davenport Cash Store Restaurant*, an attractive, Old West–style bar and dining establishment serving well-prepared American and Mexican fare. *On Davenport*

Ave right off Hwy 1; (831)425-1818 or (800)870-1817; 31 Davenport Ave, PO Box J, Davenport, CA 95017; inn@ swanton.com; www.swanton.com; full bar; inn: AE, MC, V, checks OK; restaurant: MC, V, no checks; breakfast, lunch, dinner every day; $$.

THE SAN FRANCISCO COAST

A south-to-north sweep of the San Mateo County coastline, beginning at the Año Nuevo State Reserve and ending at the Golden Gate Bridge in San Francisco.

It's sort of a mixed blessing, the almost ceaseless barrage of chilly winds and frigid, dangerous waters that predominates along the San Francisco coast. Too cold and cruel for profitable development—aside from a few sheltered coves such as Half Moon Bay—the stretch of shore between the Golden Gate and Santa Cruz has, for the most part, been left undisturbed and open to the public. While this is a boon for nature lovers, those in search of the perfect tan will probably be disappointed—sunshine tends to be an afternoon event. Be sure to dress warmly, pack your hiking boots, and dig around the closet for those binoculars, 'cause it's time to get next to nature.

PESCADERO

In the late 1800s, the clipper ship Carrier Pigeon crashed onto the rocks off Pigeon Point near Pescadero, spilling its load of white paint. Villagers, making the best of a bad situation, whitewashed their entire town.

Were it not for the near-mythical status of Duarte's Tavern, Pescadero would probably enjoy the sane, simple small-town life in relative obscurity. Instead, you can pretty much count on the town's population tripling on weekends as everyone piles into the bar and restaurant to see what all the hubbub is about. Whether it's worth the visit depends mostly on your interest in seeking out Duarte's holy recipe for artichoke soup.

ACTIVITIES

Farmers Market. A few miles east of Duarte's Tavern on Pescadero Road is Phipps Ranch, a sort of everlasting farmers market. Bring a little cash and load up on the huge assortment of fresh, organically grown fruits and vegetables (including an amazing selection of dried beans) or browse the nursery and gardens. June through late May you can pick your own olallieberries, strawberries, and raspberries in the adjacent fields. Open daily 10am to 6pm; 2700 Pescadero Road; (650)879-0787.

General Store. About 7 miles north of Pescadero on Highway 1 is the turnoff to Highway 84 and the legendary San Gregorio General Store. Since 1889, this funky old place has been providing the nearby ranching and farming community a bewildering assortment of "shoat rings, hardware, tack, bullshit, lanterns," and just about everything else a country boy needs to survive. It's truly worth a gander, particularly on Saturday and Sunday afternoons when the Irish R&B or Bulgarian bluegrass bands are in full swing. Open daily, 9am to 6pm; located 1 mile up Highway 84 from the Highway 1 intersection; (650)726-0565.

 Nature Reserve. At the turnoff to Pescadero is one of the few remaining natural marshes left on the central California coast, the Pescadero Marsh Natural Preserve. The 600 acres of wetlands—part of the Pacific flyway—are a refuge for more than 160 bird species, including great blue herons that nest in the northern row of eucalyptus trees. Passing through the marsh is the mile-long Sequoia Audubon Trail, accessible from the parking lot at Pescadero State Beach on Highway 1 (the trail starts below the Pescadero Creek Bridge). Docent-led tours take place every Saturday at 10:30am and every Sunday at 1pm, weather permitting. Call (650)879-2170 for recorded info about the walks.

Seaside Sex Show. You're not the only one having fun in the sun: For a seaside sex show, pull off Highway 1 between the coastal towns of Pescadero and Davenport (22 miles north of Santa Cruz) at Año Nuevo State Reserve, a unique and fascinating breeding ground for northern elephant seals. A close encounter with a 16-foot-long, 2½-ton male elephant seal waving his humongous schnoz is an unforgettable event. Even more memorable is the sight of two males fighting and snorting (they can be heard for miles) over a harem of a few dozen females. The reserve is open year-round, but you'll see hundreds of these marine mammals during their mating season, which starts in December and continues through March. To access the reserve during the mating season you must have a reservation on one of the 2½-hour naturalist-led tours (held rain or shine from December 15 through March 31). The tours are terrific and tickets are cheap, but they sell out fast, so plan about two months ahead (and don't forget to bring a jacket). Call Park Net for tickets at (800)444-4445; for more information call (650)879-2025.

The Pigeon Point Lighthouse, one of the most photographed lighthouses in the United States, offers self-guided tours from 8am till sunset, and 40-minute guided tours on Saturdays and Sundays from 11am to 4pm ($2). Call (650) 879-2120 for more information.

RESTAURANTS

DUARTE'S TAVERN   ★★

Duarte's (pronounced "DOO-arts") is a rustic gem, still
owned and operated by members of the family that built
it in 1894. Back then it was a place to buy a 10-cent shot
of whiskey on the stagecoach ride from San Francisco to
Santa Cruz. Now Duarte's is half bar, half restaurant,
though it's still set in an Old West–style wood-and-stucco
building near Pescadero's general store. The bar is dark
and loud, filled with locals drinking beer, smoking, and
spinning tales. The unassuming restaurant next door has
checkered tablecloths and terrific coastal fare. Most of
the fruits and vegetables come from the Duartes' own
farms. Start with the flavorful cream of artichoke or
green chile soup. The salads are a bit unimaginative, but
the greens are fresh. For your entree, there are about a
dozen kinds of fresh fish daily, as well as a selection of
sandwiches, chops, and steaks. Portions are generous,
but save room for dessert—the fruit pies are the stuff of
local legend. After your meal, walk down the road to visit
the oldest church on the Northern California coast and
the interesting old graveyard just beyond it. *On Stage Rd
at Pescadero Creek Rd; (650)879-0464; 202 Stage Rd,
Pescadero; full bar; AE, MC, V; local checks only; breakfast,
lunch, dinner every day; $$.* &

LODGINGS

PIGEON POINT HOSTEL

 Located halfway between San Francisco and Santa Cruz at
the base of one of the tallest lighthouses on the Pacific
Coast, Pigeon Point Hostel has a 270-degree view of the
ocean that can't be matched anywhere in the region. The
hostel's four buildings were originally home to the Coast
Guard lighthouse staff until high-tech lighthouse elec-
tronics gave them the boot. The 52 bunks are separated
into his and hers, but for few extra dollars per night you can
make your own foghorn noises in one of the couples-only
rooms. The facilities are clean and comfortable, and the

price—$15—can't be beat. The hot tub overlooking the ocean is well worth the $3-per-half-hour fee (guests only). Reservations are strongly recommended, although some bunk beds are held for walk-ins starting at 4:30pm. *On Hwy 1 south of the Pescadero turnoff; (650)879-0633; 210 Pigeon Point Rd, Pescadero, CA 94060; MC, V; checks OK; $.* &

HALF MOON BAY

Most Bay Area families know Half Moon Bay as the pumpkin capital of the West, where thousands of pilgrims make their annual journey in search of the ultimate Halloween jack-o'-lantern. Since 1970 the Half Moon Bay Art & Pumpkin Festival has featured all manner of squash cuisine and crafts, as well as the Giant Pumpkin weigh-in contest, won recently by a 974-pound monster. A Great Pumpkin Parade, pumpkin-carving competitions, pie-eating contests, and piles of great food pretty much assure a good time for all; for more information call the Pumpkin Hotline at (650)726-9652.

Pumpkins aside, Half Moon Bay is a jewel of a town, saved from mediocrity by diverting its historic Main Street well away from the fast-food chains and gas stations of Highway 1. The locals are disarmingly friendly, actually bestowing greetings as you walk along the rows of small shops and restaurants. Then, of course, there are the 4 miles of golden crescent-shaped beach,

"I love everything about Half Moon Bay: the fog, the rolling hills, the cows . . . even the coyotes, except for when they eat my cats."
—Half Moon Bay resident Marta Drury

GETTING THERE

The fastest way to Half Moon Bay is to take the Highway 92 exit off of Interstate 280, which leads straight into town. Far more scenic, however, is the drive along Highway 1, which, aside from Devil's Slide, moves right along at a 50mph clip. For some strange reason there are no obvious signs pointing the way to downtown Half Moon Bay (many travelers mistakenly assume Highway 1 is the downtown area). The entrance to Main Street is located about two blocks up Highway 92 from the Highway 1 intersection. Head toward the Shell station, then turn south onto Main Street until you cross a small bridge.

Serious green
thumbs know that
Half Moon Bay
Nursery, located on
Highway 92, 3
miles east of the
Highway 1 intersec-
tion, has one of the
finest selections of
indoor and outdoor
plants in Cali-
fornia. Open daily,
9am to 5pm; 11691
San Mateo Road;
(650)726-5392.

one of the prettiest in all of California; bustling Pillar Point
Harbor, launching point for whale-watching and deep-sea-
fishing trips; and myriad hiking and biking trails along the coast
and into the redwood forests. Combine this with an array of
commendable accommodations and restaurants and you have
the perfect ingredients for a peaceful weekend getaway.

ACTIVITIES

Fishing & Whale Watching. It's hard not to like a
big ol' fishing harbor. The pungent aroma of the
sea, the rows of rusty trawlers, and the salty men and women
tending to endless chores evoke a sort of Hemingwayish sense of
romance. Pillar Point Harbor, 4 miles north of Half Moon Bay
off Highway 1, is just that sort of big ol' fishing harbor. Visitors
are encouraged to walk along the pier and even participate in a
fishing trip. Captain John's Fishing Trips, (650)726-2913 or
(800)391-8787, and Huck Finn Sportfishing, (650)726-7133 or
(800)572-2934, each charge around $55, including rod and reel,
for a day's outing—a small price to pay for 60 pounds of fresh
salmon. Between January and March, whale-watching trips also
depart daily.

Biking. The best way to explore the small, flat town of
Half Moon Bay and its beaches is on a mountain bike.
Lucky for you, they're available for rent at the Bicyclery at 432
Main Street in Half Moon Bay. Prices range from $6 an hour to
$24 all day. Helmets—also for rent—are required; (650)726-
6000. Be sure to ask one of the staffers about the best biking
trails in the area, particularly the wonderful beach trail from
Kelly Avenue to Pillar Point Harbor.

Farmers Market. If you like vegetables, you'll love the
Andreotti Family Farm. Every Friday, Saturday, and
Sunday one of the family members slides open the old barn door
at 10am sharp to reveal a cornucopia of just-picked artichokes,
peas, brussels sprouts, beans, strawberries, and just about whatever else is growing in the adjacent fields. The Andreotti enter-
prise has been in operation since 1926, so it's a sure bet they
know their veggies. The barn is located at 227 Kelly Avenue,

halfway between Highway 1 and the beach in Half Moon Bay; (650)726-9461. Open till 6pm year-round.

Skip the $5 state beach parking fee at Half Moon Bay by parking along Medio Ave off Highway 1, or at Surfer's Beach, the first dirt parking lot south of Pillar Point Harbor.

Maverick Beach. If the name sounds familiar, that's because this local Half Moon Bay surf spot made national headlines as the site where famed Hawaiian surfer Mark Foo drowned in 1995 after being thrown from his board by a 20-foot wave. On calmer days, though, secluded Maverick Beach is still a good place to escape the weekend crowds because, although everyone's heard about the beach, few know where it is and you won't find it on any map. Here's the dope: From Capistrano Road at Pillar Point Harbor, turn left on Prospect Way, left on Broadway, right on Princeton, then right on Westpoint to the West Shoreline Access parking lot (on your left). Park here, then continue up Westpoint on foot toward the Pillar Point Satellite Tracking Station. Take about 77 steps, and on your right will be a trailhead leading to legendary Maverick Beach a short distance away.

Wine-Tasting. Wine-tasting in Half Moon Bay? Wine not? While the actual Obester Winery is located up north in the Anderson Valley, its satellite Wine-Tasting and Sales Room is only a few miles from Half Moon Bay up Highway 92. It's a pleasant drive—passing numerous fields of flowers, Christmas tree farms, and pumpkin patches—to this wood shack filled with award-winning grape juice. Behind the tasting room is a small picnic area that's perfect for an afternoon lunch break. Open daily, 10am to 5pm; 12341 San Mateo Road; (650)726-9463.

Kayaking. If you're one of those Type A people who can't just lie on the beach and relax, California Canoe & Kayak has the answer. For $89 they'll take you out on the bay for a 7-hour lesson in the fundamentals of the sea. Sure, it's expensive, but the rewards are priceless. Classes are usually held from 9am to 4pm Saturdays and Sundays, May through October (call to confirm); rentals are also available. CCK is located on Pillar Point Harbor at the Half Moon Bay Yacht Club; (650)728-1803.

Redwood Forest. The best place to hike and mountain-bike around Half Moon Bay is Purisima Creek Redwoods, a little-known sanctuary frequented mostly by locals. Located on the western slopes of the Santa

Cruz Mountains, the preserve is filled with fern-lined creek banks, lush redwood forests, and fields of wildflowers and berries that are accessible to hikers, mountain bikers, and equestrians along miles of trails. From the Highway 1/Highway 92 intersection in Half Moon Bay, drive 1 mile south on Highway 1 to Higgins Purisima Creek Road and turn left, then continue 4½ miles to a small gravel parking lot—that's the trailhead; (650)691-1200.

Golfing. The ocean-side 18-hole Half Moon Bay Golf Links, designed by Arnold Palmer, is rated among the top 100 courses in the country, as well as number one in the Bay Area. Green fees are a bit steep, however, ranging from $85 to $115. Reserve your tee time as far in advance as possible. The course is located at 2000 Fairway Drive at the south end of Half Moon Bay next to the Half Moon Bay Lodge; (650)726-6384.

RESTAURANTS

PASTA MOON   ★★

Recent renovations have left this popular establishment spruce and spacious but, alas, the Moon's kitchen may be on the wane. It was once widely regarded as the area's best coast-side restaurant, but the nouveau-Italian fare hasn't been up to past standards lately (perhaps executive chef Sean David Lynd needs to spend more time personally manning the stove). Fortunately, the baked-on-the-premises focaccia is still heavenly and the house-made pasta seldom disappoints; tempting possibilities include squash ravioli in sage butter sauce and tagliatelle with spicy Calabrese sausage and mushrooms. *Secondi piatti* might include roasted chicken and Tuscan potatoes or a braised lamb shank with garlic mashed potatoes. Pizza lovers can select from a wide range of thin-crust creations, including a daily special, cooked in the open kitchen's wood-burning oven. *At the N end of Main St in the Tin Palace, near Hwy 92; (650)726-5125; 315 Main St, Half Moon Bay; beer and wine; AE, DC, DIS, MC, V; local checks only; brunch Sun, lunch, dinner every day; $$.* &

SAN BENITO HOUSE ★★

A pastel blue Victorian on Half Moon Bay's Main Street, San Benito House has a candle-lit dining room that's one of the prettiest on the Central Coast, decorated with country antiques, vases of fresh flowers, and paintings by local turn-of-the-century artists. At lunch, the deli cafe turns out topnotch sandwiches on very fresh house-made bread—perfect to eat in the garden or on one of the nearby beaches. A trio of chefs—owner Greg Regan, Carol Mickelsen, and Lidia Machado—presides over the kitchen at dinnertime, turning out such interesting California-Mediterranean fare as homemade ravioli stuffed with fennel, fontina, and toasted almonds with creamy leek sauce; fillet of beef with Gorgonzola and herb butter; and salmon topped with a lemon-caper vinaigrette on a bed of lentil ragout. Desserts are terrific here, and may include such caloric wonders as a strawberry-rhubarb crêpe served with crème Anglaise and strawberry sauce, chocolate-espresso custard with Chantilly cream, and a pear poached with ginger and port wine. Too stuffed to move? Consider spending the night upstairs in one of the dozen modest but cheerful guest rooms (the one above the garden is the best). *Corner of Main and Mill Sts; (650)726-3425; 356 Main St, Half Moon Bay; full bar; AE, DC, MC, V; no checks in the restaurant, advance checks OK in the hotel; lunch (deli cafe only) every day, dinner (main restaurant only) Thurs–Sun; $$.*

A midday hot spot in Half Moon Bay is the tiny Garden Deli Cafe, a hole-in-the-wall lunch counter that cranks out huge, topnotch sandwiches on thick house-made bread. At 356 Main Street; open daily 11am to 3pm; (650)726-3425.

SUSHI MAIN STREET ★★

The food is Japanese, the decor is Balinese, and the background music might be anything from up-tempo Latin to bebop American. Hard to envision, yes, but these elements come together beautifully at Sushi Main Street, a funky yet tranquil oasis in the heart of town. The alluringly offbeat ambience blends Eastern elements such as the intricately carved wooden door and assorted Indonesian antiques with contemporary Western details like spot lighting, towering flower arrangements, and even a surfer-dude waiter complete with a Dobie Gillis goatee.

Grab a seat at the L-shaped sushi bar, pull up a chair at one of the rust-colored asymmetrical slate tables, or, if you're feeling limber, plunk yourself down at the large, low table designed for traditional cross-legged dining. Next, order the super-smooth sake (served room temperature in a traditional wooden box) and a kelp salad (a crisp, sesame-laden mixture of Japanese seaweeds) before diving into your main course.

You can choose from a wide range of sushi and sashimi, from arctic surf clams to marinated mackerel. (For 40 cents extra, they'll even toss some uncooked quail eggs into your sushi rice.) Frankly, you're better off sticking to sushi and sashimi here—other typical Japanese dishes such as beef teriyaki and shrimp tempura are on the menu, but the kitchen doesn't seem to have the same enthusiasm for their preparation. For a Zen sense of wholeness, top off your meal with green-tea ice cream or a dessert roll with papaya, plum paste, sesame seeds, and teriyaki sauce. *On Mill St just off Main St; (650)726-6336; 696 Mill St, Half Moon Bay; www.SushiMainSt.com; beer and wine; MC, V; checks OK; lunch Mon–Sat, dinner every day; $$.* ⅙

2 FOOLS CAFE AND MARKET ☆☆

Opened in 1993, this small, pleasantly modern restaurant has become a favorite with locals and visitors alike. Breakfast includes waffles and breakfast burritos, while the lunch menu concentrates on wonderfully fresh salads and sandwiches made with tasty, unusual breads. Dinner entrees run the gamut from a tangy buttermilk-roasted free-range chicken to an unusually subtle meat loaf (vegetarians can opt for the nut loaf alternative) to a simple but satisfying fried calamari with herb aioli. There's a special menu for tykes, and on warm days, diners of all ages might find the patio out back an inviting option. Everything on the menu may be ordered to go, and an ever-growing array of wines, teas, olives, jellies, and organically grown goodies is available for purchase. *On Main St near Mill St; (650)712-1222; 408 Main St, Half*

Moon Bay; beer and wine; MC, V; local checks only; breakfast, lunch every day, dinner Tues–Sun; $$. &

LODGINGS

CYPRESS INN ON MIRAMAR BEACH ★★★

 With Miramar Beach literally 10 steps away, this wonderful modern inn is *the* place to commune with the ocean. From each of its 12 rooms you not only see the ocean, you hear it, smell it, even feel it when a fine mist drifts in with the morning fog. The handsome wooden building, set at the end of a residential block, has beamed ceilings, skylights, terra-cotta tiles, colorful folk art, and warm, rustic furniture made of pine, heavy wicker, and leather—sort of a Santa-Fe-meets-California effect. Each room has a feather bed, a gas fireplace, its own bath, and an unobstructed ocean view. Most have private balconies, and the enormous penthouse also boasts a two-person soaking tub. Proprietors Dan Floyd and Suzie Lankes, who also own the stylish Inn at Depot Hill in Capitola, added a conference room, an outdoor hot tub, and four guest rooms that have such amenities as built-in stereo systems and hidden TVs. (The older rooms don't come with televisions, but the obliging innkeepers will put one in your room if you ask.)

The Cypress Inn's breakfast is far above the standard B&B fare—expect fresh juices, croissants, a fruit parfait, and made-to-order entrees such as eggs Benedict and the inn's signature peaches-and-cream French toast. In the afternoon you'll find an elaborate feast of wine and hors d'oeuvres (perhaps prosciutto and melon, freshly baked quiche, and fresh fruit pie) in the common room. And if the proximity to the sea, engaging decor, great food, and flawless service aren't enough to relax you, make a reservation with the in-house masseuse. *Head 3 miles N of the junction of Hwys 92 and 1, turn W on Medio Rd, and follow it to the end; (650)726-6002 or (800)83-BEACH; 407 Mirada Rd, Half Moon Bay, CA 94019; www.cypressinn.com; AE, MC, V; checks OK; $$$.* &

MILL ROSE INN ★★

One of the oldest bed and breakfasts on the Peninsula coast, the Mill Rose Inn fancies itself an old-fashioned English country house, with an extravagant garden and flower boxes as well as all the requisite lace curtains, antique beds, and nightstands. Romantics may love it here, but the inn's profusion of fabric flowers and slightly garish wallpapers (think William Morris on LSD) take it over the top for many folks; frankly, the overall effect is more Harlequin romance than authentic British country manor. But, heck, that can be fun, too—and the rooms are spacious and chock-full of creature comforts, the hosts are friendly, and the hot tub, tucked inside a frosted-glass gazebo, is quite enjoyable on a chilly coastal evening. The six guest rooms have private entrances and private baths, king- or queen-size feather beds, fireplaces (with the exception of the Baroque Rose Room), and views of the garden. They also have telephones, televisions with cable and VCRs, well-stocked refrigerators, fresh flowers, chocolates, and liqueurs. Two rooms, the Bordeaux and Renaissance Suites, have sitting rooms as well. In the morning, you'll find a newspaper outside your door and a full breakfast that you can enjoy in the dining area or in the privacy of your room. *On Mill St, 1 block W of Main St; 615 Mill St, Half Moon Bay, CA 94019; (650)726-9794; www.millroseinn.com; AE, DIS, MC, V; checks OK; $$$.*

THE ZABALLA HOUSE ★★

The oldest building in Half Moon Bay, this 1859 pastel blue Victorian offers a few amenities that go beyond the usual B&B offerings—including the ghost that reportedly walks through the wall in room 9 now and then. Homey, pretty, and unpretentious, the nine guest rooms in the main house are decorated with understated wallpaper and country furniture. Some have fireplaces, vaulted ceilings, or garden views. None have telephones, but three rooms have TVs. The gardens that once surrounded the building have been sacrificed for a recent addition (designed and painted to mimic this historic structure) housing stores, offices, and three attractive (and costlier) private-entrance suites. These new suites may lack spooks, but they offer some appealing extras: kitchenettes, double whirlpool tubs, VCRs, and private decks. Each is decorated differently: Casablanca-inspired number 10 is a charming, airy room with skylights, ceiling fans, and light wood-and-wicker furniture; number 11 has a French country look; and room 12—the most opulent—uses red velvet and plaster pillars, busts, and cornices to create an over-the-top classical look that will thrill some and be Greek to others. Whether you're staying in the annex or the original structure, in the evening you may partake of wine, hors d'oeuvres, and cookies by the fireplace in the main house's snug, antique-filled living room. Come morning, guests are treated to a lavish buffet breakfast. *On Main St at the N end of town; (650)726-9123; 324 Main St, Half Moon Bay, CA 94019; www.whistlere.com/zaballa; AE, DIS, MC, V; checks OK; $$–$$$.*

OLD THYME INN ☆

A comfortable and informal B&B, this 1899 Victorian house sits on the quiet southern end of Main Street. Floral wallpapers and bedspreads, rustic antiques, and lots of teddy bears grace the seven cozy guest rooms, each of which is named after one of the fragrant herbs in the inn's garden. The Thyme Room has a double whirlpool tub, a fireplace, and a queen-size canopy bed. Behind the main house is a spacious detached unit, the Garden Suite, with a queen-size four-poster bed, a fireplace, a double whirlpool tub under a skylight, a TV with a VCR, and a refrigerator stocked with complimentary beverages. Hosts George and Marcia Dempsey are eager to please and knowledgeable about the area's attractions and restaurants. A full breakfast, served in the parlor, includes such items as Swedish egg cake, quiche, cinnamon-raisin scones, and seasonal fruit; refreshments are also provided in the evening. *On Main St near Filbert St; (650)726-1616; 779 Main St, Half Moon Bay, CA 94019;*

oldthyme@coastside.net; www.inntraveler.com/oldthyme;
AE, MC, V; checks OK; $$–$$$.

PRINCETON-BY-THE-SEA

In the past dozen years, the 180 (give or take) boats of Pillar Point Harbor have pulled in nearly 10 million pounds of seafood, sold mostly in the Bay Area.

At the north end of Half Moon Bay is the small, quiet community of Princeton-by-the-Sea, anchored by the industrial-strength Pillar Point Harbor, a major supplier to San Francisco's seafood market. Until recently it was a one-hotel town, but within the last couple of years Princeton has beefed up its tourism market by adding two new hotels and the Mezza Luna restaurant, all of which are highly recommended.

RESTAURANTS

MEZZA LUNA ★★

Looking rather snazzy in its fashionable new digs at Pillar Point Harbor (a considerably better location than the cinder-block edifice it previously occupied), Mezza Luna is about as authentic as Italian food—and staff—gets. The gaggle of suave, sexy Italian waiters (you'd swear the accents are fake) make dining here a real event as they sing arias, make jokes, and serve *secondi Italiano* with unfeigned flourish. Be sure to start with the *antipasto della casa*, a platter of marinated grilled vegetables doused with the perfect blend of extra-virgin olive oil and red wine vinegar. For dinner the *penne alla calabrese*—perfectly cooked tube pasta quenched with a tangy tomato sauce, fresh mushrooms and house-made pork sausage, topped with aged ricotta cheese—is strongly recommended, as is the fresh salmon in a creamy brandy sauce (trust me, it's good). After dessert, dance off your dinner in the adjoining nightclub, which offers live music on the weekend. *4 miles N of Half Moon Bay on Hwy 1, and W on Capistrano Rd; (650)728-8108; 459 Prospect Way, Princeton-by-the-Sea; MC, V; checks OK; lunch, dinner every day; $$.* &

BARBARA'S FISH TRAP ★

 To get any closer to the ocean than Barbara's Fish Trap, you'd have to get your feet wet. Situated on stilts above the beach, the Fish Trap has indoor and outdoor dining with panoramic views of Half Moon Bay. The decor is classic fish 'n' chips style (complete with checkered plastic tablecloths, fishnets on the walls, and a wooden fisherman by the door), but the food is a cut above. Barbara's Fish Trap offers a selection of deep-fried seafood (calamari, rockfish, scallops, and prawns) as well as broiled fish such as Cajun-spiced snapper. The garlic prawns and steamed mussels are other good bets, and the french fries are fat and tasty. Kids can order from the children's menu, while adults may choose from more than 50 kinds of beer. *4 miles N of Half Moon Bay on Hwy 1, and W on Capistrano Rd; (650)728-7049; 281 Capistrano Rd, Princeton-by-the-Sea; beer and wine; no credit cards; checks OK; lunch, dinner every day; $$.*

LODGINGS

BEACH HOUSE INN

 Don't let the rather plain faux–Cape Cod facade fool you: The Beach House Inn is a first-class hotel, the kind you will want to return to year after year. It offers 54 ocean-view suites, each handsomely designed and decorated with stylish furnishings, modern prints, soothing yellow tones, and spectacular views of the bay and harbor (sunsets on the private deck with some bubbly are a must-do). Every guest room comes fully loaded with a king-size bed and down comforter (as well as a queen-size sleeper sofa), large bathrooms with separate showers and deep-soaking tub, wood-burning fireplace, component stereo system with CD player, private patios or deck access, two color TVs and VCR, *four* telephones with data ports and voice mail, and a kitchenette with microwave and refrigerators. Tip: Opt for one of the corner rooms, which offer more expansive views for the same price. Facilities include a heated pool, ocean-view whirlpool tub, fitness room, and sauna. Complimentary continental breakfast is served daily in the lobby. *On Hwy 1, 3 miles north of Half Moon Bay; (650)712-0693 or (800)315-9366; 4100 North*

Cabrillo Hwy, Half Moon Bay, CA 94109; www.beach-house.com; AE, DC, DISC, MC, V; checks OK; $$$.

PILLAR POINT INN ☆☆

 Located on a bustling harbor with a commercial fishing fleet, sportfishing and whale-watching charters, a few popular restaurants, and a busy pier, this modern inn is surprisingly quiet. Cheery and reminiscent of Cape Cod, the inn's 11 sunny, smallish rooms have harbor views, private baths, gas fireplaces, feather beds, and televisions with VCRs. Breakfast, served in the common room, includes coffee, juice, warm muffins, granola, and a hot dish such as waffles, scrambled eggs, or crêpes. Guests who request a spot of afternoon tea can enjoy it by the fire in the living room or outside on the sun deck. *4 miles N of Half Moon Bay on Hwy 1, then W on Capistrano Rd; (650)728-7377 or (800)400-8281; 380 Capistrano Rd, Princeton-by-the-Sea; PO Box 388, El Granada, CA 94018; AE, MC, V; checks OK; $$$.*

HARBOR HOUSE ☆

 If all you're looking for is a cozy, quiet, moderately priced inn with a clear view of the ocean, you'll be very satisfied with Chris Mickelsen's Harbor House. Each room is simply yet pleasantly decorated with natural wood and wicker furnishings, queen-size beds with down comforters, kitchenettes, tile floors, TVs, telephones, and a fireplace. A major plus is that rooms also come with private decks or patios overlooking the cool blue Pacific. The "penthouse" is a barn-sized studio overlooking the ocean that could easily house and feed a Girl Scout contingent—a real bargain for families or groups. There's even access to a gym across the street. *On Princeton Ave, 3½ miles N of Half Moon Bay, W of Pillar Point Harbor; (650)728-1572; 346 Princeton Ave, Princeton-by-the-Sea, CA 94019; AE, MC, V; checks OK; $$.*

MONTARA AND MOSS BEACH

Don't take it personally if you've never heard of Montara or Moss Beach; these two neighboring towns between Pacifica and Half Moon Bay have had a long history of being discreet. During the Prohibition years, bootleggers stored their illegal wares along the hollowed-out sea cliffs below and depleted them at the Moss Beach Distillery above. Today, despite the excellent selection of beaches and tide pools in the area, Montara and Moss Beach are anything but tourist towns—for shopping, dining, and such, you'll need to take a short drive down to Half Moon Bay.

One of the most serene, pleasant walks in the Moss Beach area is along the bluffs above the Fitzgerald Marine Preserve, which loops through a grove of century-old, wind-sculpted Monterey cypress. From the preserve's main entrance off California Avenue, walk toward the beach and you'll see the trailhead on your left.

ACTIVITIES

Marine Reserve. At high tide, one wonders what all the excitement is about, but come back to the James V. Fitzgerald Marine Reserve at minus low tides and wow! Thirty-five acres of tidal reef house more than 200 species of marine animals—sea anemones, urchins, snails, hermit and rock crabs, starfish, sponges—making it one of the most diverse tidal basins on the West Coast (and one of the safest, thanks to a wave-buffering rock terrace 50 yards from the beach). It's okay to touch the marine life as long as you don't pick it up, but nothing—not even a rock—is available as a souvenir. Call the reserve before coming to find out about the tide and the docent-led tour schedules (tours are usually on Saturdays). No dogs are allowed, and rubber-soled shoes are recommended. Located at the west end of California Avenue off Highway 1 in Moss Beach; (650)728-3584.

Nude Beach. Here's something you don't see often—a clothing-optional beach run by the government. Gray Whale Cove State Beach, a glorious little gold-sand beach hidden between two enormous bluffs, is located on the southern slope of Devil's Slide, 1½ miles north of the Chart House (heading south, look for the first dirt parking lot on your left). It's open 9am to sunset, costs $7.50 weekends and holidays, $6.50 weekdays (kids 12 and under are fee), and no cameras or binoculars are permitted; (650)728-5336. Warning: Be very careful when crossing the highway on foot, as cars come screaming around the corner.

Hiking/Biking Trail. Across from Whale Cove State Beach is McNee Ranch State Park, virtually unknown and recognizable only by the rusty yellow gate blocking the trailhead. The first part of the 3¾-mile hiking/biking trail to the top of Montara Mountain is a real lung-buster, but the reward—unsurpassed views of the entire Bay Area and beyond—makes it worth the effort.

State Beach. About a mile south of Gray Whale Cove is Montara State Beach, a ½-mile-long cove with silky-soft sand that's superior even to Half Moon Bay's. Since this is the first free public beach south of San Francisco that's worth a hoot, it's often packed on summer weekends. Dogs are allowed on a leash. If the parking lot is full at the north end of the beach, try parking next to the Chart House Restaurant at the opposite end.

RESTAURANTS

MOSS BEACH DISTILLERY ☆☆

 Used by bootleggers during Prohibition to store their illicit wares, this coastal grande dame was treated to a $2 million facelift in 1997, and the old gal's never looked better. With its blue-painted walls, cozy dining alcoves, and massive patio and windows affording magnificent ocean views, the cliff-side landmark still has its beguiling 1920s beach-house atmosphere, but new state-of-the-art kitchens have been installed, the old dirt parking lot paved, a downstairs dining area added, and the decor enhanced with mahogany ceilings, discreet spot lighting, and some rather racy stained-glass tableaux featuring celebratory bare-breasted women. The food has gotten considerably better, too, with new chef Scott Monfils (formerly of San Francisco's Fog City Diner) in charge of the kitchen. Gone is the pedestrian surf-and-turf fare that used to be the Distillery's lot; in its place are tasty, creative California-Mediterranean dishes such as grilled portobello mushrooms with cabernet sauce, shrimp tempura with a ginger vinaigrette, and a fork-tender pork chop enlivened by a mustard-shallot sauce and leek-buttermilk mashed potatoes. As if the views, historical setting, and good food weren't enough, the Distillery also lays claim to a couple of resident ghosts, including the famous Blue Lady, a flapper-era beauty who's said to haunt the place searching for her faithless lover. If you're not in the mood for a complete meal, grab a seat on the patio at sunset, curl up in one of the blankets the management thoughtfully provides, and enjoy a drink and some treats from the bar menu as the sun slowly sinks into the Pacific. *On Beach Way at Ocean Blvd (from Hwy 1, take the Cypress Ave turnoff and turn right on Marine Blvd, which turns into Beach Way), Moss Beach; (650)728-5595; full bar; DC, DIS, MC, V; no checks; brunch Sun, lunch Mon–Sat, dinner every day; patio menu available all day, every day; $$.* &

LODGINGS

SEAL COVE INN   ★★★

Karen Brown Herbert (of *Country Inns* guidebook fame) knows what makes a superior bed and breakfast, and she didn't miss a trick when she and her husband, Rick, set up their own several years ago. The result is a gracious, sophisticated B&B that somehow manages to harmoniously blend California, New England, and European influences in a spectacular seacoast setting. The large, vaguely English-style country manor has 10 bedrooms that overlook a colorful half-acre wildflower garden dotted with birdhouses. All of the rooms have woodburning fireplaces, fresh flowers, antique furnishings, original watercolors, grandfather clocks, hidden televisions with VCRs, and refrigerators stocked with free beverages. One thing's for sure: You won't starve here. Early in the morning, you'll find coffee and a newspaper outside your door, and later Herbert serves a full breakfast, wherever you prefer to eat. In the afternoon, wine and hors d'oeuvres are offered in the dining room, and at night, chocolates appear on the pillows of your turned-down bed.

The inn's extravagant backyard garden fronts open parkland with seaside meadows and a miniforest of cypress trees. On the other side of the park, about a quarter of a mile away, is the Fitzgerald Marine Reserve, one of the area's best spots for exploring tide pools. Nearby are some interesting local restaurants, horseback riding on the beach, and a seaside bike trail. *6 miles N of Half Moon Bay on Hwy 1, then W on Cypress Ave; (650)728-7325; 221 Cypress Ave, Moss Beach, CA 94038; sealcove@ coastside.net; AE, DIS, MC, V; checks OK; $$$.* &

POINT MONTARA LIGHTHOUSE HOSTEL

 Sorta funny that the only two secluded oceanfront accommodations on the entire San Francisco Peninsula are hostels, but why should the rich get all the perks? Ten to fifteen dollars buys anyone a bunk for the night at the Point Montara Lighthouse Hostel, perched right on the edge of a cliff next to a functioning lighthouse. Family and couples' rooms are available by reservation, and guests even have access to an outdoor redwood hot tub ($5 per half hour). Hot showers, modern kitchens, a cozy common room, and laundry facilities make this a real deal. *Off Hwy 1 between Montara and Moss Beach; (650)728-7177; 16th St, Hwy 1, Montara, CA 94037; MC, V; no checks; $.* &

OCEAN BEACH

On summer nights it's not uncommon to see bonfires burning along Ocean Beach at the edge of Golden Gate Park.

When San Francisco citizens and surfers say they're going to "the beach," they're talking about Ocean Beach, which stretches for 3 straight miles from Cliff House to Fort Funston. Alas, because of the consistently chilly west winds and deadly riptides, most beachgoers are forced to bundle up and walk along the shoreline or ride bicycles atop the esplanade—a remnant of the early days when the beach, the Cliff House, and Playland-on-the-Beach (now a condominium complex) were all part of the city's fabled seaside resort. If the weatherman mentions a heat wave, though, you can be sure parking will be scarce along the Great Highway as the locals take advantage of a rare thing (and so should you).

ACTIVITIES

Fort Funston. It's a sure bet most San Franciscans have never heard of Fort Funston and even fewer have been there, which, considering all the park has to offer, is their loss. Located at the south end of Ocean Beach (off Skyline Boulevard), Fort Funston has a little something to entertain everyone. Kids and equestrians? How about horse and pony rides? Dog owners? On the weekend it looks like a leash-free kennel show. Fort Funston is even one of the nation's premier hang-gliding spots: a wheelchair-accessible viewing deck has been built on the bluff so that spectators can watch the pilots run off the edge (always a nerve-rattling thrill). Combine all this with miles of easy walking trails along the dunes and down to the nearly-deserted beach and it becomes a mystery why Fort Funston is still so little known.

Those strange-looking steel plates and cement ridges in the parking lot at Fort Funston are the remnants of a NIKE missile launching pad.

THE PRESIDIO

For more than 200 years the Presidio served as San Francisco's principal military outpost, originally commandeered for its strategic importance and later retained for its private golf course. Though the Army still occupies a few officers' homes and barracks, the majority of the 1,480-acre installation has been turned over to the Golden Gate National Recreation Area (GGNRA) and is open to visitors as part of the largest urban park in the world. Think of it as a playground for all ages, a verdant oasis-by-the-bay filled with forts, beaches, and trails that are tempting enough to lure San Francisco's joggers, bicyclists, and windsurfers out of their apartments and into the fog.

GETTING THERE

Navigating your way into, through, and out of the Presidio is almost comical. Even locals get temporarily turned around as they attempt to negotiate the maze of winding roads, dead ends, and maddening loops, so don't even attempt the journey without a map. The smartest approach is to head due west on Geary Boulevard to the end, stop by the GGNRA visitors center behind the Cliff House Restaurant, and plunk down $2.50 for "The Official Map & Guide to the Presidio." Open daily 10am to 5pm; (415)556-8642.

Story has it a lone World War II gunner spotted a tall, thin, black shape off the waters of the bay and was convinced it was a submarine periscope. After he fired the only "shot in anger" of San Francisco's entire military arsenal, the cormorant flew away.

Museum. If there was ever a museum that was truly "fun for all ages," it's the Musée Mécanique, a glorious old trove of antique mechanical amusement machines that actually work (providing you have a pocket full of quarters). Watch the children cower in fear as Laughing "Fat Lady" Sal—of San Francisco's Playland-at-the-Beach fame—gives her infamous cackle of a greeting, or see what Grandmother the Fortune Teller has to say about your future. Most older kids congregate around the far-less-imaginative video games in back. Behind the arcade museum is Camera Obscura, a replica of Leonardo da Vinci's invention that reflects and magnifies an image of nearby Seal Rocks and Ocean Beach on a giant parabolic mirror. Both are located directly below the Cliff House Restaurant at 1090 Point Lobos Avenue. Open daily 11am to 7pm (open earlier on weekends); (415)386-1170.

War Memorial. Of all the war memorials within the Presidio, the most poignant is the tribute to the men of the USS *San Francisco*. Sections of the actual bridge of the warship—riddled with enormous holes from enemy gunfire—flank a series of bronze plaques depicting the sad, heroic story of the 107 men lost in one of the fiercest close-quarter battles in naval history. At the end of El Camino del Mar, one block up from the Cliff House.

Historical Site. The Cliff House's glory days may be gone for good, but business is still booming thanks to the busloads of tourists who pass through daily to see the adjacent Sutro Bath ruins, San Francisco's version of the Acropolis. All that remains of the illustrious 3-acre spa is its ugly concrete foundation, but that's apparently good enough for the tour companies. Time better spent is at the Sutro Bath photo exhibit at the visitors center below the Cliff House Restaurant, followed by a short walk to the charming—and practically deserted—Sutro Park across the street: the 200-degree view of the coast from atop the castle-like garden wall is outstanding.

Secret Overlook. Here's a little-known spot to escape the crowds, explore the rusty gun batteries, and revel in an amazing bay view: From Lincoln Road at the northwest end of the Presidio, turn west on Langdon Court, swing left around the cinder-block building, and there it is—the Fort Scott overlook, home of one of the best views on the California coast and the perfect launching point for the magnificent 1½-mile Coastal Trail, which curves along the Presidio's bluffs.

Presidio Tours. To inquire about a wide array of free guided tours of Presidio highlights—everything from bike rides to pier crabbing and cemetery walks—call the Presidio visitors center at (415)561-4323. The top tour pick is Fort Point, where park rangers clad in authentic Civil War garb play soldier, loading and firing a smoothbore cannon from within the pre-Civil War brick fortress (open Wednesday–Sunday, 10am–5pm). After the tour, take a bayside walk along the Golden Gate Promenade, the most popular and scenic jogging route in the city. The 4-mile path, which starts (or ends) at Fort Point, leads past the windsurfers off Crissy Field, around the Yacht Harbor, and along the Marina Green toward Fort Mason and Aquatic Park.

"Aaahhh! There's a rat, there's a rat!"
—Presidio tourist, when approached by a squirrel for a handout

GOLDEN GATE BRIDGE BY THE NUMBERS

Total length:	8,981 feet
Span:	6,450 feet
Cost:	$35 million
Completion date:	May 28, 1937
Date paid in full:	July 1971
Engineer:	Joseph B. Strauss
Road height:	260 feet
Tower height:	746 feet
Swing span:	27 feet
Deepest foundation:	110 feet under water
Cable thickness:	36½ inches
Cable length:	7,650 feet
Steel used:	83,000 pounds
Concrete used:	389,000 cubic yards
Miles of wire cable:	80,000
Gallons of paint annually:	10,000
Color:	international orange
Rise, in cold weather:	5 feet
Drop, in hot weather:	10 feet
Traffic:	3 million vehicles per month
Toll:	$3 (southbound only)

Why blow a fortune on a mediocre lunch or dinner at the Cliff House Restaurant when you can enjoy the same magnificent ocean view from the fireside cocktail lounge at Phineas T. Barnacle (or PTB as they call it) next door? A small, inexpensive, buffet-style deli takes care of the appetite, while the full bar helps recharge your batteries.

China Beach, at the end of Seacliff Avenue off El Camino del Mar in the well-to-do neighborhood of Seacliff, is the only safe swimming beach in San Francisco (that is, when the water's warm enough) aside from Aquatic Park on the bay. Great for kids.

A Walk on the Windy Side. There are certain things everyone should do at least once in life, and one of those is to walk across the world-famous Golden Gate Bridge. Simply driving across won't work; to feel the bridge swaying under your feet as you peer 260 feet down to certain death—now that's living. It's a 1¼-mile stroll across and takes about an hour round-trip. Pedestrians and bicyclists must use the path on the east side of the bridge, which is open daily from 5am to 9pm (bicyclists have to use the west side on weekends). Free parking is available at both ends of the bridge, but the lots are usually full on summer weekends. Dress warmly or you'll be sorry.

THE MARIN COAST

When you consider that the San Francisco Bay Area has more people than the entire state of Oregon, and that Marin County has the highest per capita income in the nation, you would expect its coastline to be lined with gated communities and fancy resorts. Truth is, you won't find even a Motel 6 along the entire Marin coast, due partly to public pressure against development, but mostly because of the inaccessibly rugged, heavily forested terrain (it may *look* like a 15-minute drive from San Francisco on the map, but 90 minutes later you'll probably still be negotiating hairpin curves down the side of Mount Tamalpais). The only downside to the Marin coast's limited development is the scarcity of affordable lodgings; expensive B&Bs reign supreme, which is fine if you don't mind blowing $150 a night for a bed and bagel. Otherwise, the Marin coast is just short of Eden, a veritable seaside playground for city-weary nine-to-fivers in search of a patch of green or square of sand to call their own for a day.

A south-to-north sweep of the Marin County coastline, beginning at the Marin Headlands and ending at Dillon Beach just north of Point Reyes.

THE MARIN HEADLANDS

On a sunny San Francisco day, there's no better place to spend time outdoors than in the Marin Headlands. For more than a century following the Civil War, this vast expanse of grass-covered hills and rocky shore was off-limits to the public, appropriated by the U.S. Army as a strategic base for defending the bay against invaders. Remnants of obsolete and untested defenses—dozens of thick concrete bunkers and batteries recessed into the bluffs—now serve as playground and picnic sites for the millions of tourists who visit each year.

There's a wealth of scheduled activities offered daily within the 15-square-mile Golden Gate National Recreation Area—birding clinics, bunker tours, wildflower hunts, geology hikes—but most visitors are satisfied with poking their heads into a bunker or two, snapping a photo of the San Francisco skyline, and driving home. For a more thorough approach, buy the handy $1.50 "Marin Headlands Map and Guide to Sites, Trails, and Wildlife", at the Information Center at Fort Barry (follow the signs in the Headlands), and plan your day from there. Free hiking, mountain biking, and pet-friendly trail maps are available, too. The center is open daily from 9:30am to 4:30pm; (415)331-1540.

Call (415)331-1540 for a current schedule of the free ranger-led walks through the Marin Headlands; topics range from bird-watching to wildflowers and war relics. Then again, why walk? Tennessee Valley Miwok Stables offers interpretive guided horseback rides to nearby Muir Beach and various headland highlights; (415)383-8048.

*Only in California:
"Whale Hotline—
(415)474-0488."*

*Battery Townsley,
built in 1940, had
two mounted 16-
inch-caliber rifles
that could fire a
2,100-pound shell
more than 25 miles
with pinpoint accu-
racy. Many of the
guns that never
fired a shot in
defense were sold
to the Gillette Com-
pany for conversion
to razor blades.
Seems it was a close
shave after all.*

ACTIVITIES

Mammal Center. A popular Marin Headlands attraction is the Marine Mammal Center, a volunteer-run hospital for injured and abandoned mammals-of-the-sea. It's virtually impossible not to melt at the sight of the cute sea lions and elephant and harbor seals as they lie in their pens (the center's staff, being no dummies, take donations right on the spot). Signs list each animal's adopted name, species, stranding site, and injury—the latter of which is usually human-caused. Located at the east end of Fort Cronkhite near Rodeo Lagoon, the Marine Mammal Center is open daily from 10am to 4pm and admission is free; (415)289-SEAL.

Lighthouse. Closed to the public for several years due to storm damage, the precariously perched 1877 Point Bonita Lighthouse is once again thrilling those tourists brave enough to traverse the long, dark tunnel and seven small footbridges leading to the beacon. (Because the cliffs along the passageway are so steep, one 19th-century lighthouse keeper rigged ropes around his children to prevent them from slipping into the raging sea below.) The reward for such bravery is, among other things, a rare and sensational view of the entrance to the bay.

GETTING THERE

To reach the Marin Headlands, head north across the Golden Gate Bridge, take the Alexander Avenue exit, and make your first left onto cliff-hugging Conzelman Road, which climbs high above the bay—with magnificent views of the bridge and city—before ending at Point Bonita 5 miles west. Easy, huh? Getting back to the city, though, is a little trickier because of the one-way roads. Heading east on Bunker Road, either turn right on McCullough Road to get back to Conzelman Road, or continue on Bunker Road through the tunnel and back onto Highway 101. For a spectacular scenic route out of the headlands, turn left immediately after exiting the tunnel. The road will take you through East Fort Baker, past the pier, underneath the Golden Gate Bridge, and back on Highway 101 toward San Francisco.

Call for tour times, and be sure to inquire about the full-moon tours, which take place twice a month by reservation only; (415)331-1540.

As the World Terns. To witness the teeming sea and bird life—puffins, albatrosses, terns, whales, dolphins, seals, sea lions, and more—that congregates on and around the distant Farallon Islands, call the nonprofit Oceanic Society Expeditions at (415)474-3385 and reserve a space on its 63-foot boat. The exceptional tour, which lasts eight or nine hours and costs about $65 per person, departs from the Fort Mason area in San Francisco's Marina district at 8:30am on Saturdays, Sundays, and occasional Fridays. Shorter, less expensive excursions to see gray whales are available, too.

Bird-watching. Within the Marin Headlands is Hawk Hill, one of the most remarkable avian sites in the western United States and the biggest hawk lookout in western North America. More than 20,000 birds reside here or pass through annually, including 21 species of hawks. The best time to visit is during September and October, when thousands of birds of prey soar over the hill each day. (Located above Battery 129, where Conzelman Road becomes one-way.)

LODGINGS
MARIN HEADLANDS HOSTEL ☆

Formerly known as the Golden Gate Hostel, the Marin Headlands Hostel is the only public lodging on the Headlands. The converted army hospital—shaded under a canopy of eucalyptus trees—holds 66 bunks, a few "couples" rooms, a huge clean-up-your-own-mess kitchen, a game room with ping pong and pool tables, and a large common room with TV, VCR, sofas, fireplace, piano, and other distractions. In 1995 the hostel acquired the adjacent commander's home, a plush 37-bed spread with Oriental carpets, two kitchens, and four carved-oak fireplaces (obviously, this is the place you want to request first). Bunks are a mere $12 a night ($35 for two for a double room), and hostel-association membership is not required (though a current photo ID is). BYO food because there are no restaurants or stores within the Headlands. *At Fort Barry in Bldg 941, 200 yards southeast of the Headlands Information Center; (415)331-2777; Fort Barry, Bldg 941, Sausalito, CA 94965; DIS, MC, V; no checks; $.* ♿

MUIR WOODS

When you stand in the middle of Muir Woods surrounded by a canopy of ancient redwoods towering hundreds of feet skyward, it's hard to fathom that San Francisco is less than 6 miles away. In this den of wooden giants tourists speak in hushed tones as they crane their necks in disbelief, snapping photographs that don't begin to capture the immensity of these living titans.

Although Muir Woods can get absurdly crowded on summer weekends, you can usually circumvent the masses by hiking up the Ocean View Trail and returning via Fern Creek Trail. Admission is free, but a donation box is prominently displayed to stoke your conscience. Picnicking is not allowed, although there is a snack bar (and gift shop) at the entrance. It's typically cool and damp here, so dress appropriately. Muir Woods is located at the end of Muir Woods Road off the Panoramic Highway (from Highway 101 in Sausalito, take the Stinson Beach/Highway 1 exit and head west); open 8am to sunset, (415)388-2595.

ACTIVITIES

Muir Beach. Three miles west of Muir Woods, along Highway 1, is a small crescent-shaped cove called Muir Beach. Strewn with bits of driftwood and numerous tide pools, Muir Beach is a more sedate alternative to the beer-'n'-bikini crowds at the ever-popular Stinson Beach up north. If all you're looking for is a sandy, quiet place for some R&R, you may want to park the car right here and skip the trip to Stinson altogether (swimming, however, isn't allowed at Muir Beach because of the strong rip currents).

RESTAURANTS
THE PELICAN INN ☆☆

One of the better ways to spend a Sunday afternoon in the Bay Area is to take a leisurely drive to this homey little English pub, grab a table at the glassed-in patio or by the fireplace, and gorge yourself proper on a steaming shepherd's pie. Rack of lamb, prime rib, and a few fish dishes are also on the menu, and in the bar you'll find a goodly number of British, Irish, and Scottish beers on tap. After lunch, burn a few calories with a stroll down Muir Beach. *On Pacific Way off Hwy 1 at the entrance to Muir Beach; (415)383-6000; 10 Pacific Way, Muir Beach; beer and wine; MC, V; no checks; lunch, dinner every day May 1 to Oct 31 and holidays year-round (lunch, dinner Tues–Sun Nov 1 to Apr 30); $$.*

LODGINGS
THE PELICAN INN ☆☆

Romantic intentions of a homesick expatriate led to the creation of this 16th-century English Tudor country inn, and by God if it isn't filled with convivial dart-playing chaps chugging pints of bitter as lovebirds snuggle in front of the hearth's glowing fire in the inn's pub (see Restaurants, above). The inn, named after Sir Francis Drake's ship the *Pelican*, has seven small yet cozy rooms with canopy beds, leaded-glass windows, heavy brocade curtains, and English antiques (the top pick is room 3 with its authentic Half-Tester bed). There's also a "snug" (i.e., common room) for lounging by the fire or playing the piano. In the morning, guests are treated to an authentic English breakfast of bangers and eggs, toast and marmalade, and—but of course—a cuppa. *On Pacific Way off Hwy 1 at the entrance to Muir Beach; (415)383-6000; 10 Pacific Way, Muir Beach, CA 94965; beer and wine; MC, V; no checks; breakfast (guests only) every day year-round; lunch, dinner every day May 1 to Oct 31 and holidays year-round; lunch, dinner Tues–Sun Nov 1 to Apr 30; $$.*

GREEN GULCH FARM ZEN CENTER ☆

When was the last time your bodhisattva spirit—the spirit of kindness—had a vacation? Green Gulch Farm, a Soto Zen practice center hidden in a lush, verdant valley near Muir Beach, offers fantastically priced "guest practice retreats" for those interested in learning the art of Zen meditation. If you participate in the retreat, there's a minimum three-night stay (Sunday through Thursday only), and you are expected to attend *early*-morning meditations (read: 5am), then work until noon with the community. After that, you're on your own to wander down to Muir Beach, hike through Muir Woods or on the trails surrounding Green Gulch, participate in classes on Buddhism, or do whatever else your karma desires. Rates are an enlightening $30 per person per day ($50 for double occupancy), *including* three squares a day. You may also stay here on a nightly basis Sunday through Thursday without participating in any of the center's programs, but it will cost about twice as much. *Off Hwy 1, a few miles west of the Muir Woods turnoff; (415)383-3134; 1601 Hwy 1, Sausalito, CA 94965; no credit cards; checks OK; $.* ⟨♿⟩

STINSON BEACH

For recorded weather and surf conditions at Stinson Beach call (415)868-1922.

On those treasured weekend days when the fog has lifted and the sun is scorching the Northern California coast, blurry-eyed Bay Area residents grab their morning papers and beach chairs, pile into their cars, and scramble to the sandy shores of Stinson Beach—the North Coast's nice-try answer to the fabled beaches of Southern California.

Stinson is one of Northern California's most popular beaches, a 3½-mile stretch of beige sand that offers enough elbow room for everyone to spread out beach blankets, picnic baskets, and toys. Although swimming is allowed and lifeguards are on hand from May to mid-September, notices about riptides (not to mention the sea's toe-numbing temperatures and the threat of sharks) tend to discourage folks from venturing too far into the water. Joined at the hip with *la playa* is the town of Stinson Beach, which does a brisk summer business serving lunch alfresco at the numerous cafes.

GETTING THERE

Stinson Beach is located right off Highway 1 at the base of Mount Tamalpais in Marin County, 10 miles from San Francisco as the crow flies but a winding 20 miles as the wheel turns. To reach the beach from the Bay Area, take the Stinson Beach/Highway 1 exit off Highway 101 just north of Sausalito and follow Highway 1 all the way to the shore. A few miles before you reach the ocean, there's a fork in the road (the Muir Woods turnoff) that allows wimpy drivers to avoid the thrilling cliff-side drive along Highway 1 by taking an inland detour along Panoramic Highway, which isn't as scenic as its name suggests but dumps you right into town.

About a mile south of Stinson Beach off Highway 1 is Red Rock Beach, one of the few nude beaches on the Marin coast. It's easy to miss, since you can't see it from the road: Park at the first dirt pull-off on your right after leaving Stinson Beach and look for a steep trail leading down to the beach.

ACTIVITIES

The Merchant of Venice Beach. Ol' Billy would have been proud to see the turnout at Stinson Beach's Shakespeare at the Beach, which is packed to the partitions every weekend with sold-out crowds. The 125-seat outdoor theater is a real charmer, encircled on all sides by 20-foot walls with grass for flooring and plastic lawn chairs for seats. The elevated performance space, though, is the real thing, complete with faux balconies, arched entrances, and a raked stage. The theater is located next to the Stinson Beach Post Office at Highway 1 and Calle del Mar. Show times are Friday at 7pm and Saturday and Sunday at 6pm, May through October, and you can get tickets ($15 for adults, $12 for kids under 18) in advance by calling (415)868-9500. Dress warmly, bring a blanket, and hiss only when appropriate.

Kayaking. There are plenty of adventurous things to do around Stinson. For example, Scott Tye, a kayak instructor for Off the Beach Boats in downtown Stinson Beach, offers two-hour lessons on the basics of sea and surf kayaking. Rentals are surprisingly cheap (about $25 for four hours for surf kayaks), and they even include a kayak that can hold an entire nuclear family. Body boards and surfboards are available for rent as well. Call (415)868-9445 or drop by the shop at 15 Calle del Mar next to the Stinson Beach Post Office.

Wildlife Sanctuary. A short drive north of Stinson Beach on Highway 1 leads to Bolinas Lagoon, a placid saltwater expanse that serves as refuge for numerous shorebirds and harbor seals hauled-out on the sandbars. Across from the lagoon is the Audubon Canyon Ranch's Bolinas Lagoon Preserve, a 1,014-acre wildlife sanctuary that supports a major heronry of great blue herons. This is the premier spot along the Pacific Coast to watch the immense, graceful seabirds as they court, mate, and rear their young, all accomplished on the tops of towering redwoods. Admission is free, though donations are requested. Open mid-March to mid-July on Saturday, Sunday, and holidays, 10am to 4pm, and by appointment for groups. 4900 Highway 1, Stinson Beach; (415)868-9244.

RESTAURANTS

THE PARKSIDE CAFE ☆

During the day this popular neighborhood cafe bustles with locals and Bay Area beachgoers who stop for an inexpensive breakfast or lunch before shoving off to Stinson Beach around the corner. Morning favorites are omelets, blueberry pancakes, and the not-to-be-missed raisin-walnut bread. For lunch there are basics like burgers, grilled sandwiches, and soups, as well as a few daily specials. Once the beach crowd departs, chef Jim White starts preparing the evening menu, which includes a wide variety of dishes ranging from lamb chops and roast chicken to mussel linguine, seafood pizza, and baked eggplant. On sunny days dine alfresco on the brick patio; otherwise, cozy up to the fire. For a quick bite to go, the cafe's snack bar sells great burgers, fries, and shakes daily from March through September, and on weekends from October through February. *On Arenal Ave off Calle del Mar in downtown Stinson Beach; (415)868-1272; 43 Arenal Ave, Stinson Beach; beer and wine; AE, MC, V; local checks only; breakfast, lunch every day; dinner Thurs–Mon; $.*

LODGINGS

CASA DEL MAR ★★★

 After stints as a lawyer and a fisherman, proprietor Rick Klein jumped headfirst into the B&B business by designing, building, and running the Casa del Mar, a beautiful Mediterranean-style haven that overlooks Stinson Beach. Each of the six sun-drenched rooms has large windows (with views of Mount Tamalpais, the ocean, or the spectacular terraced garden), French doors that open onto a private balcony, and a private bath. The spartan but comfortable furnishings include a few cushy chairs and a platform bed topped with a down comforter and piles of pillows. Fresh flowers and whimsical artwork by local artists brighten the rooms while the sound of the ocean provides the ambience. Breakfast features an ever-changing array of wonders such as fresh fruit compote, spinach and mushroom quiche, Spanish frittata, and fresh baked breads. *Heading N into Stinson Beach, turn right at the fire station onto Belvedere Ave; (415)868-2124 or (800)552-2124; 37 Belvedere Ave, PO Box 238, Stinson Beach, CA 94970; Inn@StinsonBeach.com; www.Stinson-Beach.com; AE, MC, V; checks OK if mailed 2 weeks in advance; $$$.*

STEEP RAVINE ENVIRONMENTAL CABINS ★

 How much would you expect to pay for a night in a romantic oceanside cabin with its own small, secluded beach? $200? $300? Try 30 bucks. Once the private get-away of powerful Bay Area politicians (who lost their long-term leases in a battle with the state, poor dears), this cluster of small cabins is now available to those lucky enough to snag a reservation and who don't mind bringing their own sleeping bag and pad. Platform beds, wood-burning stoves, and nearby running water and out-houses are provided, but there is no electricity, and fire-wood costs an extra $4. Each cabin sleeps up to five, and whether you plan to go solo or bring four friends, the low per-night rate stays the same (though only one car per cabin is allowed). *Off Hwy 1, a mile S of Stinson Beach (look*

"*Responsible woman seeks peace and tranquillity at Stinson. Looking for a small cottage or special place to call home. Will pay up to $900 a month.*"
—*From the message board at Stinson Beach Books*

"*Nine hundred dollars sounds about right, though I remember when you could rent a place around here for 50 bucks a month.*"
—*Stinson Beach Fire Chief and long-time resident Kendrick Rand, when asked about escalating property values*

for a paved turnout and a brown metal sign); reservations required 10 days to 7 months in advance; call Park Net at (800)444-4445; MC, V; checks OK if received within 6 days of making reservation; $.

STINSON BEACH MOTEL ☆

If you can't afford the Casa del Mar, try this place. The Stinson Beach Motel has five small rooms and one apartment nestled in a cute little garden setting, each individually decorated with aging yet homey furnishings and private baths. Rates are quite reasonable, and the small apartment, which sleeps up to four, is a steal, given the prime location in downtown Stinson Beach. Try to reserve room 7, which is separated from the rest and offers the most privacy. *On Hwy 1 at the S end of Stinson Beach near the fire station; (415)868-1712; 3416 Hwy 1, PO Box 64, Stinson Beach, CA 94970; MC, V; checks OK if received 10 days in advance; $$.*

BOLINAS

Smiley's Schooner Saloon in Bolinas has live music—anything from jazz to country, blues, or rock—every Friday and Saturday night, but be prepared to shell out $7 for the cover charge.

A sort of retirement community for aging rock stars, spent novelists, and former hippies, Bolinas is one of the most reclusive towns in Northern California. Residents regularly take down highway signs pointing the way to their rural enclave, an act that, ironically, has created more publicity for Bolinas than any road sign ever did. As a tourist, you don't have to worry about being chased out of town by a band of machete-wielding Bolinistas, but don't expect anyone to roll out the welcome mat, either. The trick is to not look like a tourist, but more like a Bay Arean who's only here to buy some peaches at the People's Store.

ACTIVITIES

Organic Market. There couldn't be a better antithesis to the corporate supermarket mentality than the Bolinas People's Store, a town landmark that's famous for its locally grown organic produce (don't confuse it with the much larger general store down the street). It's a little hard to find, hidden at the end of a gravel driveway next to the Bolinas Bakery, but it's worth searching out just to see (and taste) the difference between Safeway and the Bolinas way. Open 8:30am to 6:30pm daily; (415)868-1433.

The Bolinas Bay Bakery & Cafe in downtown Bolinas is renowned for its cinnamon buns made with organic flour.

 Tidepooling, Bird-watching, & Hiking. Three side trips near Bolinas offer some adventurous exercise. Just before entering downtown Bolinas, turn right (or west) on Mesa Road, left on Overlook Road, and right on Elm Road and you'll dead-end at the Duxbury Reef Nature Reserve, a rocky outcropping with numerous tide pools harboring a healthy population of starfish, sea anemones, snails, sea urchins, and other creatures that kids go gaga over.

The Point Reyes Bird Observatory is one of the few full-time ornithological research stations in the United States.

If you continue west on Mesa Road, you'll reach the Point Reyes Bird Observatory, where ornithologists keep an eye on more than 400 feathered species. Admission to the visitors center and nature trail is free, and visitors are welcome to observe the tricky process of catching and banding the birds. It's open daily 15 minutes after sunrise until sunset. Banding hours vary, so call (415)868-0655 for exact times and (415)868-1221, ext 40, for recorded general information.

At the very end of Mesa Road is the Palomarin Trailhead, a popular hiking trail that leads into the south entrance of Point Reyes National Seashore. The 6-mile round-trip trek—one of Point Reyes' prettiest hikes—passes several small lakes and meadows before it reaches Alamere Falls, a freshwater stream that cascades down a 40-foot bluff onto Wildcat Beach.

LODGINGS

THOMAS'S WHITE HOUSE INN ★★

 Thomas's White House Inn is Bolinas personified—charming, offbeat (e.g., the bathroom doubles as an aviary), and surrounded by incredible vistas. Lounging on the immense and beautifully landscaped front lawn—it alone is worth the room rate—you get a sweeping view of the Bay Area coastline from Marin to Half Moon Bay. The two guest rooms are located upstairs and boast cathedral ceilings and window seats ideal for gazing out at the sea. The larger room has a more rustic feel, with old pine furnishings and an antique steamer trunk, while the smaller room is decorated in softer tones with white wicker and lace. Owner Jackie Thomas serves a simple continental breakfast. *Kale Rd (call for directions), Bolinas; (415)868-0279; PO Box 132, Bolinas, CA 94924; www.coastallodging.com/thomas/thomas.html/; no credit cards; checks OK; $$.*

POINT REYES

Think of Point Reyes as Mother Nature's version of Disneyland, a sort of outdoor-lover's playground with one doozy of a sandbox. Hiking, biking, swimming, sailing, windsurfing, sunbathing, camping, fishing, horseback riding, bird-watching, kayaking: all are fair game at this 71,000-acre sanctuary of forested hills, deep-green pastures, and undisturbed beaches. Point Reyes is hardly a secret anymore—millions of visitors arrive each year—but the land is so vast and varied that finding your own space is never a problem (like the old saying goes, if you want to be alone, walk up).

There are four towns in and around the Point Reyes National Seashore boundary—Olema, Point Reyes Station, Inverness Park, and Inverness—but they are all so close together that it really doesn't matter where you stay, because you'll always be within a stone's throw of the park. While the selections of lodging in Point Reyes is excellent, it's also expensive, with most rooms well over $150 per night. Be sure to make your reservation far in advance during the summer and holidays, and dress warmly: Point Reyes gets darn chilly at night.

ACTIVITIES

Lighthouse. On the westernmost tip of Point Reyes at the end of Sir Francis Drake Highway is the Point Reyes Lighthouse, the park's most popular attraction. Even if you loathe lighthouse tours, go anyway: the drive alone—a 45-minute scenic excursion through windswept meadows and working dairy ranches (watch out for cows on the road)—is worth the trip. When the fog burns off, the lighthouse and the headlands provide a fantastic lookout point for spying gray whales and thousands of common mures that inundate the rocks below. Visitors have free access to the lighthouse via a thigh-burning 308-step staircase. Open 10am to 4:30pm, Thursday to Monday, weather permitting; (415)669-1534.

GETTING THERE

Point Reyes is only 30 miles northwest of San Francisco, but it takes at least 90 minutes to reach by car (it's all the small towns, not the topography, that slows you down). The easiest route is via Sir Francis Drake Boulevard from Highway 101 south of San Rafael; it takes its bloody time getting to Point Reyes, but does so without any detours. A much longer but more scenic route: Take the Stinson Beach/Highway 1 exit off Highway 101 just south of Sausalito and follow Highway 1 north. As soon as you arrive at Point Reyes, stop at the Bear Valley Visitors Center on Bear Valley Road (look for the small sign posted just north of Olema on Highway 1) and pick up a free Point Reyes trail map. (Open weekdays 9am–5pm and weekends 8am–5pm; (415)663-1092.)

Drakes Estero, the large saltwater lagoon within the Point Reyes peninsula, produces nearly 20 percent of California's commercial oyster yield.

Oyster Farm. That mighty pungent aroma you smell on the way to the Point Reyes Lighthouse is probably emanating from Johnson's Oyster Farm. It may not look like much—a cluster of trailer homes, shacks, and oyster tanks surrounded by huge piles of oyster shells—but that certainly doesn't detract from the taste of fresh-out-of-the-water oysters dipped in Johnson's special sauce. Eat 'em on the spot, or buy a bag for the road; either way, you're not likely to find California oysters as fresh or as cheap anywhere else. Open 8am to 4pm Tuesday through Sunday; located off Sir Francis Drake Boulevard about 6 miles west of Inverness; (415)669-1149.

Kayaking Tomales Bay. A popular Point Reyes pastime is ocean kayaking. Don't worry, the kayaks are very stable and there are no waves to contend with because you'll be paddling through placid Tomales Bay, a haven for migrating birds and marine mammals. Rental prices at Tomales Bay Sea Kayaking start at about $35 for half a day ($65 for a double-hulled kayak), and you can sign up for a guided day trip, a sunset cruise, or a romantic full-moon outing. Instruction, clinics, and boat delivery are available, and all ages and levels are welcome. The launching point is located on Highway 1 at the Marshall Boatworks in Marshall, 8 miles north of Point Reyes Station. It's

POINT REYES TOP PICKS

Limantour Beach for bird-watching, swimming, and dog-walking

Kehoe Beach during spring wildflower blooms

Bear Valley Trail for an easy, beautiful walk through the woods to the beach

Hearts Desire Beach at Tomales Bay for kids, warmer water, and the safest swimming ($3 fee)

Palomarin Trailhead for prettiest hike

McClures Beach for tidepooling and solitude

Stewart Trail for serious mountain biking

Estero Trail for casual mountain biking

Drakes Beach for swimming, beach fires, and lunch at the small cafe

open in the summer Friday through Sunday from 9am to 6pm and by appointment; (415)663-1743.

Mountain Biking. As most ardent Bay Area mountain bikers know, Point Reyes National Seashore has some of the finest mountain-bike trails in the region—narrow dirt paths winding through densely forested knolls and ending with spectacular ocean views. A trail map is a must (available for free at the Bear Valley Visitors Center), since many of the park trails are off-limits to bikes. If you didn't bring your own rig, you can rent a mountain bike at Bear Valley Inn and Rental Shop, located at the intersection of Bear Valley Road and Highway 1 in Olema; (415)663-1958.

RESTAURANTS

MANKA'S INVERNESS LODGE ☆☆☆

Half the fun of dining at Manka's is waiting for your table. Sit in the lobby's plush high-backed chairs, warm your toes by the small wood-burning fireplace, and watch in fascination as one of the cooks kneels beside you to grill the house-made wild boar sausages over the fire: it's like being in a freaking Jack London novel. To complement the hunting lodge illusion, Manka's serves "unusual game, local line-caught fish, oysters pulled from the bay, and bounteous greens from down the road and over the hill." Appetizers range from grilled California quail with wild-mushroom sauce to fire-roasted figs with black-pepper syrup. And the entrees? How about pan-seared elk tenderloin, black buck antelope chops with sweet corn salsa, and wild Canadian pheasant with mashed potatoes? The divine desserts—such as the cinnamon-croissant pudding with warm caramel sauce— are made from scratch, and the wine list is longer than the drive to get here. *On Argyle St off Sir Francis Drake Blvd, 3 blocks N of Inverness; (415)669-1034 or (800)58-LODGE; beer and wine; MC, V; checks OK; brunch on special occasions only, dinner Thurs–Mon; $$$.*

Point Reyes Station is also known as "Mootown," due to its noontime cow siren.

THE STATION HOUSE CAFE ☆☆

For more than two decades the Station House has been a favorite stop for West Marin residents and San Francisco day trippers. The menu changes weekly, but you can count on chef Denis Bold to work daily wonders with local produce, seafood, and organic beef from Niman-Schell Farms. Breakfast items range from French toast made with Il Fornaio bakery's sweet challah to buckwheat pancakes and roasted vegetable frittatas. For dinner, start with a platter of local oysters and mussels, followed by a braised lamb shank (made with Guinness Stout), salmon with roasted yellow pepper sauce, or one of the Station House old standbys such as fish and chips with country fries and cole slaw. There's a good selection of wines, too. When the weather's warm, sit outside in the shaded garden area—particularly if you're eating breakfast here on a sunny day. In the summer barbecued oysters are often served on the patio. *On Main St in the center of Point Reyes Station; (415)663-1515; 11180 Shoreline Hwy, Point Reyes Station; full bar; DIS, MC, V; local checks only; breakfast, lunch, dinner every day; $$.* &

A great way to spend an afternoon in Point Reyes is browsing through the boutiques, galleries, bookstores, bakeries, antique stores, and saloons along the main strip in Point Reyes Station.

Short on lunch money? The Gray Whale Cafe in downtown Inverness serves all kind of salads, sandwiches, pastas, and pizzas for only $6. It's open daily 11am to 9pm (till 8pm winter); (415)669-1244.

TAQUERIA LA QUINTA ☆

Mexican folk music fills the air and bright colors abound at this exuberant restaurant, where most of the fare costs less than *seis dólares*. La Quinta (Spanish for "the country house") offers a large selection of Mexican-American standards, as well as vegetarian dishes and weekend seafood specials. The service is fast, the food is fresh, and the salsa is *muy caliente*. *At 3rd and Main Sts in Point Reyes Station; (415)663-8868; 11285 Hwy 1, Point Reyes Station; beer only; no credit cards; local checks only; lunch, dinner Wed–Mon; $.*

VLADIMIR'S CZECH RESTAURANT ☆

The first thing you're likely to notice when you walk into this dark, wood-paneled dining room is an old guy neatly dressed in traditional Czech attire. This is Vladimir Nevl, who since 1960 has been entertaining guests with his war stories as they boldly sample the chicken paprikash, Moravian cabbage roll, beef tongue, klobasa, and Hungarian goulash—all served with dumplings. On weekends the place tends to feel like a tourist trap and the service can be lackadaisical, but hey, when you gotta have beef tongue, you gotta have it. *On Sir Francis Drake Blvd in Inverness; (415)669-1021; 12785 Sir Francis Drake Blvd, Inverness; full bar; no credit cards; checks OK; lunch Wed–Sun, dinner Tues–Sun; $$.* &

Inverness' Czech-heavy population stems from a 1930s shipwreck in San Francisco Bay—several of the Czech deckhands jumped ship and settled here.

LODGINGS

MANKA'S INVERNESS LODGE ☆☆☆☆

What a difference a Grade makes. For years Manka's was a mediocre Czech restaurant, but when Margaret Grade and family took over in 1989, things changed. This former hunting and fishing lodge soon became one of the most romantic places to stay in California, as well as a wonderful place to eat (see Restaurants, above). Manka's offers a dozen accommodations, including four upstairs guest rooms that look as though they came out of a Hans Christian Andersen fairy tale—small and cozy, with tree-limb bedsteads, down comforters, high ceilings, and old-fashioned bathrooms. Rooms 1 and 2 extend out to large private decks overlooking Tomales Bay and have fireplaces and double tubs with showers open to the sky. Manka's also offers four handsome rooms in its Redwood Annex, and two spacious one-bedroom cabins with living rooms, fireplaces, and hot tubs. For the ultimate romantic—or family—retreat, reserve either the fantastic two-level/ two-bedroom/two-bath boathouse built out over the bay (equipped with a fireplace, deck, and kitchenette) or the Chicken Ranch, a private 19th-century hunting cabin. Friendly, refreshingly unpretentious, and surprisingly affordable, Manka's Inverness Lodge is *the* idyllic weekend getaway. *On Argyle St off Sir Francis Drake Blvd, 3 blocks N of Inverness; (415)669-1034 or (800)58-LODGE; PO Box 1110, Inverness, CA 94937; MC, V; checks OK; $$$.*

If you're having trouble finding a vacancy in Point Reyes, call the West Marin Network at (415)663-9543 for information on available lodgings.

BLACKTHORNE INN

With its four levels, five rooms, multiple decks, spiral staircase, skybridge, and fire pole, the Blackthorne Inn is more like a tree house for grown-ups than a B&B. The octagonal Eagle's Nest, perched on the top level, has its own sun deck and a 360-degree view of the forest (the bath, however, is located across the skybridge—something of a nuisance on blustery nights); the spacious Forest View and Hideaway Rooms, which share a bath, have sitting areas facing the woods; the outdoor treetop-level hot tub offers a great view of the stars. A country buffet breakfast, included in the room rate, is served on the upper deck when the sun is shining. *Take Sir Francis Drake Blvd to Inverness Park, then go ¼ mile up Vallejo Ave; (415)663-8621; 266 Vallejo Ave, Inverness Park; PO Box 712, Inverness, CA 94937; susan@blackthorneinn.com; www.blackthorneinn.com; MC, V; checks OK; $$$.*

DANCING COYOTE BEACH

The local Miwok Indians called falling stars "dancing coyotes"—something to ponder as you stare at the heavens through the skylit sleeping lofts of this bayside bed and breakfast. Hidden in a pine-covered cove and within easy walking distance of downtown Inverness, the four adjoining natural-wood cottages are painted in Southwestern pastels and equipped with simple furniture, private decks, fireplaces, and full kitchens. The Beach Cottage, with its small upper deck overlooking Tomales Bay, should be your first choice; Acacia Cottage, which gets a fair amount of traffic noise, should be your last, although you're allowed to bring your pooch into this one. The private lawn, beach, and sun deck are perfect spots for settling down with a good book. *On Sir Francis Drake Blvd, just N of Inverness; (415)669-7200; 12794 Sir Francis Drake Blvd, PO Box 98, Inverness, CA 94937; no credit cards; checks OK; $$.*

HOLLY TREE INN ★★★

Hidden within a 19-acre valley with a meandering creek and wooded hillsides is the blissfully quiet Holly Tree Inn. This family-owned B&B has four cozy guest rooms, each with a private bath (one with a fireplace) and decorated with Laura Ashley prints and country antiques. The large, airy living room has a fireplace and comfortable chairs where guests converse over afternoon tea. If privacy is what you're after, tucked in a far corner of the estate is the Cottage-in-the-Woods, a two-room hideaway with a small fireplace, a king-size bed, and an old-fashioned bathtub from which you can gaze at the garden. Families or honeymooners should inquire about the separate Sea Star Cottage—built on stilts over Tomales Bay—and the two-bedroom Vision Cottage; both have hot tubs. In the morning enjoy a bountiful country breakfast. *On Silverhills Rd off Bear Valley Rd, 1 mile from Point Reyes Station; (415)663-1554; 3 Silverhills Rd, Inverness Park; PO Box 642, Point Reyes Station, CA 94956; AE, MC, V; checks OK; $$$.*

TEN INVERNESS WAY ★★★

Follow the curving flagstone pathway through the garden and under the wisteria-laced entryway to this three-story Inverness bed and breakfast. Inside you'll find a fir-paneled living room with inviting couches facing a huge stone fireplace, and five comfortable guest rooms equipped with plush chairs, patchwork quilts, and private baths.

The best room is the Garden Suite: separated from the others by an entire floor, it has its own sitting room, kitchen, and private patio. The terrific breakfast—banana-buttermilk buckwheat pancakes, chicken-apple sausages, and fresh fruit prepared by innkeepers Barbara Searles and Mary Davies—will fortify you for a long day of hiking in the hills. When you return, soak your sore muscles in the garden hot tub. *On Inverness Way off Sir Francis Drake Blvd, at the N end of Inverness; (415)669-1648; 10 Inverness Way, PO Box 63, Inverness, CA 94937; MC, V; checks OK; $$$.*

POINT REYES SEASHORE LODGE ☆☆

For folks who want the beauty of the countryside combined with the creature comforts of the city, this is the place. Built in 1988, the three-story cedar inn has 21 guest rooms, most of which offer a fireplace, telephone, down comforter, whirlpool bath, and view of the exquisite garden. If price is no object, opt for one of the two-story suites with a sleeping loft, refrigerator, and the perk of having breakfast delivered to your room. One note of caution: The lodge is located on Highway 1, next to a restaurant that does a brisk (read noisy) business. For peace and quiet, ask for a room in the north wing, or reserve the Casa Olema Retreat, a detached cottage that sleeps up to eight and has a hot tub with room for eight

POINT REYES ABLAZE

In the early afternoon of October 3, 1995, an unattended and illegal campfire sparked a blaze that destroyed 12,000 acres within the Point Reyes National Seashore. The numbers are staggering: $40 million in damage, including 45 homes destroyed; 2,164 firefighters recruited (some from as far as Oregon) at a cost of $4 million; and 75 percent of hiking trails ruined. The good news is that about 80 percent of the park was left untouched, and rangers made the best of the situation by turning the burned portion of the park into a classroom on forest regeneration. Today the entire National Seashore is back in business and as beautiful as ever.

The block-long town of Olema marks the epicenter of the 1906 earthquake that devastated San Francisco.

as well. A continental breakfast, included in the nightly rate, is served in the lodge's common room. *On Hwy 1 at Sir Francis Drake Blvd in Olema; (415)663-9000 or (800)404-LODG; 10021 Hwy 1, PO Box 39, Olema, CA 94950; prsl@worldnet.att.net; www.placestostay.com; AE, DIS, MC, V; checks OK; $$$.* ♿

BEAR VALLEY INN ☆

Ron and JoAnne Nowell's pleasant and reasonably priced bed-and-breakfast inn is an ideal base for exploring Point Reyes. The two-story Victorian home, built in 1899, has three guest rooms and a shared bath (though a detached private bath is available with the Rose Room or King Room during the week). If you want the quietest space, ask for the Rose Room. After breakfast, Ron will be happy to give tips on where to bicycle in the area (he also runs the mountain bike rental shop next door). When you return from your day of exploring, plop yourself onto one of the overstuffed chairs and relax in front of the old wood-burning stove. *On Bear Valley Rd at the intersection of Hwy 1; (415)663-1777; 88 Bear Valley Rd, Olema, CA 94950; AE, MC, V; checks OK; $$.*

KNOB HILL ☆

Horse trainer Janet Schlitt rents out a cottage that stands atop a small bluff overlooking Point Reyes Mesa. Perfect for couples and horse owners, it comes with a stereo, wood-burning stove, private deck, a TV on request, and, if you brought along your horse, stable service. Schlitt also rents a very small (and very reasonably priced) room that's attached to her house and has a private bath, entrance, and garden area. Be sure to indulge in the optional breakfast of fresh baked goods and fruit, then hit the nearby trailhead to Tomales Bay or sign up for some horseback riding lessons with Schlitt. *From Highway 1 N of Point Reyes Station, turn W on Viento Way to Knob Hill Rd; (415)663-1784; 40 Knob Hill Rd, PO Box 1108, Point Reyes Station, CA 94956; no credit cards; checks OK; $$.*

POINT REYES HOSTEL

Isolated deep inside Point Reyes National Seashore is the Point Reyes Hostel. It's in prime location, just steps from numerous trails that lead deep into the National Seashore area. It offers 45 dormitory-style accommodations, including one room that's reserved for families. There are also two common rooms, each warmed by wood-burning stoves on chilly nights, and containing a fully equipped kitchen, barbecue, and patio. If you don't mind sharing your sleeping quarters with strangers, this is a $15-per-person deal that can't be beat. Reservations are strongly recommended. Reception hours are 7:30–9:30am and 4:30–9:30pm daily. *Off Limantour Rd; (415)663-8811; PO Box 247, Point Reyes Station, CA 94956; no credit cards; no checks; $.* &

TOMALES

Most people don't even know the town of Tomales exists, which is just fine with the handful of people who live here. Comprising not much more than a general store, two churches, and a superb little bakery, the tiny ranching community looks pretty much as it did a hundred years ago, which gives you an idea of the pace around here. It's in a prime location, though—only 30 minutes' drive from Point Reyes National Seashore, yet far enough away to avoid the traffic and commotion.

In 1927, 20-by-100-foot lots along Tomales Bay were offered for $69.50 to each new subscriber of the San Francisco Bulletin.

ACTIVITIES

Coastal Drive. One of the most scenic drives on the Marin coast is along Dillon Beach Road from Tomales. The 4-mile drive passes through windswept meadows with wonderful vistas of Tomales Bay, Point Reyes, and the Pacific before ending at the privately owned Dillon Beach campground. For a proper grand finale to the drive, turn right on Oceana Drive in Dillon Beach and continue to a vacant cul-de-sac. On a clear day you can see all the way to Bodega Bay.

Oyster Farm. Tomales is a popular stop for fresh raw and barbecued oysters. Since 1909, the Tomales Bay Oyster Company has been selling its wares right off the shore at 15479

If you're cruising along Highway 1 toward Tomales and happen to see a guy sweating over a huge metal grill in front of Tony's Seafood Restaurant, pull over— barbecued oysters don't get any better.

Highway 1 just south of Marshall. Choose from bite-size cocktails to big ol' hunkin' cowboys, all of which are sold by the dozen or in sacks of 100, should you be feeling randy enough. Those in the know bring their own knife, lemons, cocktail sauce, and even bags of charcoal for the nearby barbecue pits. Open daily 9am to 5pm; (415)663-1242.

LODGINGS

U.S. HOTEL ☆

With nothing more to go by than a photograph of the original inn—which burned down in 1920—the owners of the U.S. Hotel built it from the ground up in 1989. The result? This place is so evocative of a bygone era that you could film a Western here and never need a set decorator. The pleasingly plain interiors are a welcome alternative to the typical lace-and-patchwork B&B decor: each of the eight immaculate rooms has high ceilings, a private bath, and simple yet attractive faux-antique furnishings. While the staff could be a bit more accommodating, the reasonable room rates—which include a self-serve continental breakfast—more than compensate. *On Hwy 1 in the center of Tomales; (707)878-2742; 26985 Hwy 1, Tomales, CA 94971; MC, V; no checks; $$.*

THE SONOMA COAST

Mention Sonoma and everyone's immediate association is "wine country." What few Californians seem to know, however, is that Sonoma County gerrymanders a hefty chunk of the coast as well, more than 50 miles of mostly undeveloped shoreline from Bodega Bay to Jenner. And judging from the mostly vacant state parks and beaches, even fewer Californians seem to know what a good thing they're missing as they migrate lemming-like to Mendocino or Carmel. The Sonoma coast isn't for everyone, though; there's little in the way of shopping, sightseeing, and such. It's more of a place where inlanders return annually to bury themselves in a book, wiggle their toes in the sand, and forget about work for a while.

A south-to-north sweep of the Sonoma County coastline, beginning at Bodega Bay and ending at Jenner.

BODEGA BAY

When it comes to a selection of fancy restaurants, accommodations, and boutiques, Bodega Bay has a long way to go. As it stands, there is only one three-star lodge and restaurant, and the town's most venerable store sells taffy and kites. Which is odd, considering Bodega Bay is only a few hours' drive from the Bay Area, a good two to three hours closer than Mendocino, and has all the beautiful scenery and golden beaches you could possibly hope for. Even 15 minutes of international fame as the setting for Alfred Hitchcock's *The Birds* hasn't changed things much. Spend a few hours meandering through town and it becomes apparent that Bodega Bay is, for the most part, still just a working-class fishing town, the sort of place where most people start their day before dawn, mending nets, rigging fishing poles, and talking shop. But if all you want to do this weekend is breathe in some salty air and could care less about Gucci boutiques and dancing till dawn, come to Bodega Bay—ain't much here, which is precisely the point.

As you roll into Bodega Bay, keep an eye out for the Bodega Bay Area Visitors Center, located in the center of the town at 850 Highway 1. Load up on free maps, guides, and brochures, including the "Bodega Bay Area Map & Guide," which gives the exact locations of all the town's attractions; (707)875-3422.

ACTIVITIES

Walking Trails. Bodega Head, the small peninsula that shelters Bodega Bay, has two superb walking trails that follow the ocean. The first, a 4-mile round-trip trail, starts from the Head's west parking lot, leads past the Bodega

On Friday after-
noons between 2pm
and 4pm, docents
from the University
of California
Marine Biology Lab
on Bodega Head
conduct hour-long
guided tours of its
lab projects,
including numerous
tanks filled with a
variety of inter-
esting sea crea-
tures. Suggested
donation is $2;
(707)875-2211.

The Pacific Gas and
Electric Company
(PG&E) had started
to build a nuclear
power plant at
Bodega Head, but
after vehement
protests, the project
was scrapped. The
road to Bodega
Head and a giant
hole in the ground
(appropriately
dubbed Hole in the
Head) are all that
remain.

GETTING THERE

No matter which direction you're coming from, getting to Bodega Bay is a rather long haul; there are no fast, direct routes leading to this oceanside town. If you're approaching from the San Francisco area, the fastest (and most scenic) route is via Petaluma. From Highway 101, take the East Washington Street/Central Petaluma exit and turn west toward the town. After a straight shot though the center of Petaluma, you'll spend about 45 minutes on a pleasant drive through rolling green hills before reaching the bay. Note: Don't make the common mistake of taking the Bodega turnoff onto Bodega Highway. Bodega and Bodega Bay are two different towns.

Bay Marine Laboratory, and ends at the sand dunes of Salmon Creek Beach. An easier, 1½-mile round-trip walk begins in the east parking lot and encircles the edge of Bodega Head, branching off for an optional side trip to the tip of the point for a spectacular 360-degree view. From December through April, Bodega Head also doubles as one of the premier whale-watching points along the California coast. (From downtown Bodega Bay, turn west on Eastshore Road, then turn right at the stop sign onto Bay Flat Road and follow it to the end.)

Gone Fishing. A great way to spend a lazy afternoon in Bodega Bay is at the docks, watching the rusty fishing boats unload their catches. Tides Wharf, located at 835 Highway 1 in Bodega Bay, has the most active dock scene, including a viewing room near the processing plant that allows you to witness the fish's ultimate fate—a swift and merciless gutting by deft hands, followed by a quick burial in ice. Just outside, sea lions linger by the dock hoping for a handout; (707)875-3652.

Golfing. The only golf game in town—open to the public every day of the year—is the Bodega Harbour Golf Links, a championship 18-hole Scottish-style course designed by Robert Trent Jones, Jr. and situated near the Bodega Bay Lodge. A new warm-up center and practice facility has been added, which can be used free of charge by registered golfers. Rates range from $50 with cart on the weekdays to $80 with cart on weekends. Call (707)875-3538 for starting times.

Fun of a Beach. Linking Bodega Bay and the nearby town of Jenner are the Sonoma Coast State Beaches, 16 miles of pristine sand and gravel beaches, tide pools, rocky bluffs, hiking trails, and one heck of a gorgeous drive along Highway 1. While all the beaches are pretty much the same—divine—the safest for kids is Doran Park Beach, located just south of Bodega Bay. When the water's rough everywhere else, Doran is still calm enough for swimming, clamming, and crabbing (an added bonus: the adjacent Doran mud flats, a favorite haunt of egrets, big-billed pelicans, and other seabirds). Tide pool trekkers will want to head to the north end of Salmon Creek Beach (off Bean Avenue, 2 miles north of town) or Shell Beach, a small low-tide treasure trove 10 miles north of Bodega Bay near Jenner. If all you want to do is get horizontal in the sand, deciding which of the 14 beaches along Highway 1 looks the best will drive you nuts; just pick one and park.

Hitchcock's Bodega. Worth half an hour of any Hitchcock fan's day is a quick trip to the town of Bodega, located a few miles southeast of Bodega Bay off Highway 1. The attraction is a bird's-eye view of the hauntingly familiar Potter School House and St. Teresa's Church, both immortalized in Hitchcock's *The Birds*, which was filmed here in 1961. The two or three boutiques in downtown Bodega manage to entice a few visitors to park and browse, but most people seem content with a little rubbernecking and finger-pointing as they flip U-turns through the tiny town.

Fishy-Suave. If you've never been ocean fishing, be forewarned that it is an extremely complicated four-step process: (1) get on the fishing boat; (2) grab a pre-rigged fishing pole; (3) lower your line in the water when everyone else does; and (4) reel in the fish. Everything else, from taking the fish off the hook to cleaning it, is taken care of by the friendly deckhands, which makes deep-sea fishing pretty much idiotproof. On the fish-and-crab combination trips (even more fun than the regular fishing trips), you get to keep your catch as well as a few of the enormous Dungeness crabs caught in the traps set out on

Have you always dreamed of riding naked on the back of a wild white stallion, crashing through waves burned orange by the glimmering sunset? Well, keep dreaming, because the guides at Chanslor Horse Stables in Bodega Bay won't let you. You can, however, amble your little horsey across the dunes for $40. The 700-acre ranch, in operation since the 1850s, also has a petting zoo and pony rides for the kids. Open daily 8am to 8pm; 2660 Highway 1, north of Bodega Bay; (707)875-2721 (ranch), (707)875-3520 (stables). Reservations recommended.

the way to the fishing grounds. Both the fishing and fish-crab combo trips cost approximately $55 per person (rod-and-reel rental is an additional $7.50), and almost everyone takes home a gunnysack full of seafood. For information and reservations, call the Bodega Bay Sportfishing Center at (707)875-3344.

Clamming. How often do you have a legitimate, legal excuse to get down and dirty on a public beach? Well, as long as you're on the hunt for a sack of fresh clams, you can do it year-round at Bodega Bay. The only skill required is digging; the only equipment needed is a shovel and a sturdy bag. The rest is childishly straightforward: Find a good spot (hint: try the western side of Bodega Bay); wait for low tide; search the sand closest to the water for a small, bubbling siphon hole; then dig like heck with whatever's handy (a narrow clammer's shovel works best). What you'll discover is a long "neck" leading to a horseneck clam, the most abundant type of clam in Bodega Bay. A fishing license is required for anyone over 16 (one-day licenses are available at most sporting-goods stores and bait shops).

Whale Watching. Sure, spotting gray whales from shore is exciting, but nothing compares to getting within listening distance of the 40-ton cetaceans, so close you can actually hear the blast of the blowholes. From late December through April several of Bodega Bay's fishing charters offer whale-watching trips. One reputable outfit is Will's Fishing, (707)875-2323, which offers trips every weekend between November and April. The typical charge is about $20 per person, $15 for kids under 16; trips last about three hours (or seemingly forever if you get seasick, so bring Dramamine).

Fisherman's Festival. For a festive time in Bodega Bay, visit in April, when as many as 25,000 partyers tip their shucks and bottles at the annual Fisherman's Festival, a two-day orgy of lamb and oyster barbecues, Sonoma County wine tastings, craft fairs, pony rides, bathtub races, parades, kite-flying contests, live music, and dancing. The festival highlight is the Blessing of the Fleet, a colorful, jubilant boat parade in which clergymen stand on a vessel and bless the fishing fleet as it floats by. For more information, call the Bodega Bay Chamber of Commerce at (707)875-3422.

RESTAURANTS

THE DUCK CLUB

 Bodega Bay sure took its sweet time coaxing a premier chef to the coast, but now that Jeff Reilly (formerly the executive chef at Lafayette Park in Walnut Creek) is in town, gastronomes up and down the coast are coming to the Bodega Bay Lodge to sample his wares. "Sonoma County cuisine" best describes Reilly's penchant for local yields, with creations such as roasted Petaluma duck with Valencia orange sauce or a Sonoma-farm-fresh asparagus strudel bathed in a mild curry sauce. *Le poisson du jour* comes straight from the docks down the street. Large windows overlook the bay, so be sure to beg for a table with a view when making the required reservations. The Duck Club offers a lengthy wine list with an extensive selection of Sonoma County labels. *At the Bodega Bay Lodge, at the S end of Bodega Bay; (707)875-3525; 103 Hwy 1, Bodega Bay; beer and wine; AE, DC, DIS, MC, V; no checks; breakfast, dinner every day; $$$.* &

BREAKERS CAFE

If the Duck Club and Lucas Wharf Restaruant are both beyond your budget, Bodega Bay's Breakers Cafe is the answer. For breakfast, park your fanny among the numerous plants in the sun-filled dining room and feast on yummy Belgian waffles topped with hot spiced peaches and whipped cream. Lunch is mostly sand-wiches, burgers, and house-made soups, and dinner items range from fresh seafood to chicken, pasta, and low-fat vegetarian dishes. *In the Pelican Plaza at the N end of Bodega Bay; (707)875-2513; 1400 Hwy 1, Bodega Bay; beer and wine; MC, V; local checks only; breakfast every day, May 1 to Sept 30, lunch, dinner every day year-round; $.* &

LUCAS WHARF RESTAURANT AND BAR ■
LUCAS WHARF DELI

 Few tourists come to Bodega Bay just for the seafood, as you'll soon discover if you spend more than a day here. There are only two "seafood" restaurants in town, Tides Wharf and Lucas Wharf, and both do little to excite the palate. Yes, the fish is fresh off the boats, but the preparations are basic and uninspired (though the hundreds of people who dine here daily in the summer don't seem to mind). Also, don't expect the weather-beaten luncheonette you may remember from Hitchcock's *The Birds*—a recent $6 million renovation has transmogrified the place beyond recognition. The best tables offer views overlooking the ocean, and the bill of fare is seafood standard: oysters on the half shell, clam chowder, and fish caught from the restaurant's own boat. Prime rib, pasta, and poultry dishes are available as well. Your best bet, however, is to skip both Tides and Lucas Wharf restaurants and go next door to Lucas Wharf Deli, pick up a $6 pint of crab cioppino or a big ol' basket of fresh fish 'n' chips, and make a picnic of it on the dock. *On Hwy 1 at the S end of town; Restaurant: (707)875-3522; 595 Hwy 1, Bodega Bay; full bar; AE, DIS, MC, V; checks OK; lunch, dinner every day; $$.* & ■ *Deli: (707)875-3562; beer and wine; AE, DIS, MC, V; checks OK; take-out picnic items every day; $.* &

LODGINGS

BODEGA BAY LODGE ★★★

 Granted, the competition isn't very fierce, but it's safe to say that the Bodega Bay Lodge provides the Sonoma Coast's finest accommodations. It's the view that clinches it: All 78 rooms—recently remodeled in handsome hues of cardinal red and forest green, with wood-burning fireplaces and stocked minibars—have private balconies with a wonderful panorama of Bodega Bay and its bird-filled wetlands. Should you ever leave your balcony, a short walk through elaborate flower gardens leads to an outdoor fieldstone spa and heated swimming pool overlooking the bay. A fitness center, sauna, and complimentary morning newspaper are also part of the package. More proof of Bodega Bay Lodge's top standing is its Duck Club restaurant (see the review above), easily the Sonoma coast's best. *On Hwy 1 at the S end of town; (707)875-3525 or (800)368-2468; 103 Hwy 1, Bodega*

Bay, CA 94923; bbl@woodsidehotels.com; www.woodside-hotels.com; AE, DC, DIS, MC, V; checks OK; $$$. ♿

INN AT THE TIDES ☆☆

In Bodega Bay the architectural style of most structures is nouveau Californian—wood-shingled boxes with lots of glass—and the Inn at the Tides is no exception. Perched on a hillside overlooking Bodega Bay, it offers 86 units with bay views, spacious interiors, and contemporary (albeit dated contemporary) decor, and all with the usual amenities of an expensive resort: terrycloth robes, coffee-makers, hair dryers, cable TV, refrigerators, minibars, fresh flowers, continental breakfasts, and access to the indoor/outdoor pool, sauna, and whirlpool tubs. A few of the rooms have king-size beds, and most have fire-places. The Inn at the Tides' restaurant, the **Bay View**, is open for dinner only. It offers ocean views and has a romantic, somewhat formal ambience, though it suffers from a so-so reputation. The owners, to their credit, have recently poured a bundle of money into revitalizing it and have hired two new chefs. Call for details about the monthly gourmet winemaker dinners (advance reservations are required). *On Hwy 1 across from the Tides Wharf; (707)875-2751 or (800)541-7788; 800 Hwy 1, PO Box 640, Bodega Bay, CA 94923; iatt@monitor.net; www.innatthe-tides.com; full bar; AE, DIS, MC, V; checks OK; dinner Wed–Sun; $$$.* ♿

BODEGA HARBOR INN ☆

A homey old-timer in a town of mostly modern accom-modations, the Bodega Harbor Inn consists of four clap-board buildings (with a total of 14 guest rooms) set on a large lawn overlooking the harbor. The rooms are small but tidy, with private baths, cable TV, double beds, and access to a private yard where you can kick back in lawn chairs. If you're willing to shell out a few extra dollars, request a room with a partial ocean view and a small deck. The inn also has two reasonably priced two-bed-room suites and rents out seven houses and cottages, including the three-bedroom, two-bath Spyglass home, located on the Bodega Harbour Golf Links and overlooking the ocean. Guests at the inn are treated to a complimentary continental breakfast. *Off Hwy 1 at the N end of Bodega Bay; (707)875-3594; 1345 Bodega Ave, Bodega Bay, PO Box 161, Bodega Bay, CA 94923; MC, V; checks OK; $–$$$.* &

JENNER

Story has it John Sutter of Gold Rush fame agreed to purchase Fort Ross from the Russians for $30,000. He stripped it of equipment and furnishings to improve his own fort in Sacramento, yet never paid a nickel toward the balance.

About 16 miles north of Bodega Bay on Highway 1 is what seems to be every Northern Californian's "secret" getaway spot: Jenner. Built on a bluff rising from the mouth of the Russian River, the tiny seaside town consists of little more than a gas station, three restaurants, two inns, and a deli, which means the only thing to do in town is eat, sleep, and lie on the beach—not a bad vacation plan. Perhaps Jenner's best attraction, however, is its location: two hours closer than Mendocino to the Bay Area, yet with the same spectacular coastal scenery and a far better selection of beaches.

ACTIVITIES

About 3 miles north of Fort Ross is one of Ansel Adams' favorite places to photograph, Timber Cove.

Seal Watching. One of the major highlights of the Jenner area is beautiful Goat Rock Beach, a popular breeding ground for harbor seals. Pupping season begins in March and lasts until June, and orange-vested volunteers are usually on hand to protect the seals (which give birth on land) from dogs, answer questions about the playful animals, and even lend out binoculars for a closer look.

Russian Fort. A sinuous 12-mile drive north of Jenner on Highway 1 takes you to the mildly interesting Fort Ross State Historic Park, a semirestored redwood fortress built by Russian fur traders in 1812. If you decide to cough up the $6 parking fee, plan to spend about an hour here and start with a short history lesson in the Fort Compound (offered at 11:30am, 1:30pm, and 3:30pm in the summer, and noon and 2pm in the winter). End your visit with a walk down to the cove and beach; (707)847-3286.

GETTING THERE

The most direct route to Jenner is via Highway 116, from the 116 turnoff on Highway 101 between Petaluma and Santa Rosa. A far, far more enjoyable route, however, starts in Petaluma, passes through Bodega Bay, and winds along a gorgeous stretch of Highway 1 before crossing the Russian River into Jenner (see "Getting There" in the Bodega Bay section).

 Salt Point State Park. A great day trip from Jenner is the scenic drive along Highway 101 to Salt Point State Park. There are all kinds of things to do here, including skin diving and tidepooling off rocky beaches, hiking through coastal woodlands' wildflower meadows, and poking around the 3,500-acre park for wild berries and mushrooms—simply pull the car over anywhere along Highway 1 and start walking. At the north end of the park on Kruse Ranch Road is the 317-acre Kruse Rhododendron Preserve, a forested grove of wild pink and purple flowers that grow up to 18 feet tall in the shade of a vast canopy of redwoods. Peak blooming time varies from year to year, but April is usually the best time to see the world's tallest *Rhododendron californicum*; (707)847-3221.

RESTAURANTS

RIVER'S END ☆

 Ever since owner/chef Wolfgang Gramatzki passed away, this oceanside institution has been on rocky soil (read: It may not be open by the time you read this). It's worth giving a call, however, because other than the Sizzling Tandoor (see below), this is the only restaurant in town. True to Gramatzki form, the menu is still decidedly eclectic, with entrees ranging from Indian curries to beef Wellington, seafood, and steaks. Lunch is more down to earth, with reasonably priced burgers and sandwiches. Most tables have a wonderful view of the ocean, as does the small outside deck—the perfect spot for a glass of Sonoma County wine. *On Hwy 1 in Jenner; (707)865-2484;*

As you head north from Jenner on Highway 1, keep an eye open for the new wheelchair-accessible Sonoma Coast State Beach Vista Trail, a paved 1-mile loop trail on a bluff overlooking the ocean. On a clear day you can see all the way to Point Reyes.

The entire coastal community contributed funds and materials to help sculptor Benny Bufano create the North Coast's towering monument to peace. Erected in 1969 and completed shortly before his death, the 8-story totem-like statue is located a short walk seaward from the Timber Cove Lodge parking lot on Highway 1.

1104A Hwy 1, Jenner; full bar; MC, V; no checks; lunch, dinner Fri–Sun (hours may vary, so call ahead); $$. &

SIZZLING TANDOOR ☆

 When the weather is warm and sunny, Sizzling Tandoor is the best place on the Sonoma coast to have lunch. This Indian restaurant is perched high above the placid Russian River, and the view, particularly from the outside patio, is fantastic. Equally great are the inexpensive lunch specials: huge portions of curries and kebabs served with vegetables, soup, *pullao* rice, and superb naan (Indian bread). Even if you don't have time for a meal, drop by and order some warm naan to go. *At the S end of the Russian River Bridge, S of Jenner; (707)865-0625; 9960 Hwy 1, Jenner; beer and wine; AE, DIS, MC, V; no checks; lunch, dinner every day (closed Mon in the winter); $.* &

LODGINGS

SEA RANCH ☆☆☆

 A ritual among upper-middle-class Northern California families and friends is to rent a vacation home along the 9-mile coastal stretch of the ritzy residential development called Sea Ranch. Begun in the 1960s by the land-hungry Castle and Cooke Company of Hawaii, Sea Ranch is undoubtedly one of the most beautiful seaside communities in the nation, due mostly to rigid adherence to environmentally harmonious (or "organic") architectural standards for its extravagant homes. Approximately 300 homes are available as vacation rentals, managed by eight or nine rental companies, with prices ranging from as low as $165 to as high as $550 for two nights. There's also a lodge and restaurant within Sea Ranch, but your best bet is to rent your own house and full kitchen for only a few dollars more. *On Hwy 1, between Stewarts Point and Gualala; contact Sea Ranch Rentals at (707)785-2579; Sea Ranch Rentals, PO Box 88, Sea Ranch, CA 95497; no credit cards; checks OK; $$–$$$.*

JENNER INN & COTTAGES ⭐⭐

 When people say they stayed at the cutest little place in Jenner, they're talking about Jenner Inn & Cottages. There are 16 guest rooms here, each dispersed within a cluster of cottages and houses perched above the Russian River or the ocean. The houses are subdivided into separate suites that are rented out individually, and all have private baths, separate entrances, and antique and wicker furnishings; many units also have kitchens, fireplaces, hot tubs, and private decks or porches. The rose-covered Rosewater Cottage, a honeymooners' favorite, sits right beside the Russian River estuary and is warmed by a stone fireplace (as well as the king-size bed and hot tub). The adorable Pelican Suite, also popular with newlyweds, has big bay windows overlooking the water. An extended continental breakfast, served in the main lodge, is included in the room rate. In addition to the bed-and-breakfast accommodations, the inn rents out six private vacation homes located along the river, within Jenner Canyon or overlooking the ocean. Note: Don't expect the Ritz if you opt for the lower-priced rooms, which are far from fancy but still a great deal for oceanfront property. *On Hwy 1 in the middle of Jenner, 1 mile N of the Hwy 116/Hwy 1 junction; (707)865-2377 or (800)732-2377; 10400 Hwy 1, PO Box 69, Jenner, CA 95450; innkeeper@jennerinn.com; www.jennerinn.com; AE, MC, V; checks OK; $$.*

THE MENDOCINO COAST

A south-to-north sweep of the Mendocino County coastline, beginning at Gualala and ending at Westport.

There are four things first-time visitors should know before heading to the Mendocino coast. First, be prepared for a long, beautiful drive; there are no quick and easy routes to this part of the California coast, and there's no public transportation, so traveling by car is your only option. Second, make your hotel and restaurant reservations as far in advance as possible because everything involving tourism books up solid during summers and holidays. Third, bring warm clothing. You might as well forget about packing only shorts and T-shirts—regardless of how broiling it is everywhere else—because a windless, sunny, 80° day on the Mendocino coast is about as rare as affordable real estate. Fourth and finally, bring lotsa money and your checkbook. Cheap sleeps, eats, and even banks are few and far between along this stretch of shoreline, and many places don't take credit cards (though personal checks are widely accepted).

For up-to-date information about the Mendocino coast, including upcoming events, visit the area's Web site at www.mendocino coast.com.

So where exactly is the Mendocino coast? Well, it starts at the county line in the town of Gualala and ends a hundred or so miles north at the sparsely populated stretch known as the Lost Coast. The focal point is, of course, the town of Mendocino, but the main center of commerce—and the region's only McDonald's, if you can believe it—is in Fort Bragg, 15 miles up the coast. Compared to these two towns, every other part of the Mendocino coast is relatively deserted—something to consider if you're looking to escape the masses.

Spring is the best time to visit, when the wildflowers are in full bloom and the crowds are still sparse. Then again, nothing on this planet is more romantic than cuddling next to the fireplace on a winter night, listening to the rain and thunder pound against your little cottage as you watch the waves crash against the cliffs, so don't rule out a trip in the colder months, either. Actually, when you get down to it, any time you have a few days off is a good enough excuse to pack your bags, head for the coast, and remind yourself why you don't live in Iowa.

GETTING THERE

Since Greyhound has shut down all routes to the Mendocino coast and the closest Amtrak route is 40 miles inland, the only way to get here is by car or by chartering a private plane. There are six routes into Mendocino from Highway 101; the most popular and scenic is the freshly paved stretch of Highway 128 starting from Cloverdale, which passes through a gorgeous redwood forest before dumping you onto Highway 1 a few miles south of Mendocino. Slightly faster but far less stimulating is the Highway 20 link between Willits and Fort Bragg. A somewhat secret, rarely used route starts at the north end of Ukiah at Orr Springs Road and ends as the Comptche-Ukiah Road right outside Mendocino, a sneaky alternative if you're bored of Highway 128 or 20. The last two options—entering via Highway 1 from the north at Leggett or from the south at Jenner (via 116)—should be considered all-day adventures.

GUALALA

The southernmost town in Mendocino County, Gualala also happens to have the most mispronounced name in Mendocino County. Keep the G soft and you end up with "wah-LAL-ah," the Spanish version of *walali*, which is Pomo Indian patois for "water coming down place." The water in question is the nearby Gualala River, a placid year-round playground for kayakers, canoers, and swimmers.

Once an industrious, lively logging town, Gualala has tamed considerably since the days when loggers would literally climb the saloon walls with their spiked boots. Though a few real-life suspender-wearing lumberjacks still end their day at the Gualala Hotel's saloon, the coastal town's main function these days is providing gas, groceries, and hardware for area residents. On the outskirts, however, are several excellent parks, beaches, and hiking trails; combine this with the region's glorious seascapes, and suddenly poor little mispronounced Gualala emerges as a serious contender among the better vacation spots on the North Coast.

Story has it Gualala's original spelling was Walalla until the federal postal bureau decided to dephoneticize the town's moniker to its proper Spanish version.

ACTIVITIES

Sea Kayaking. One of the most enjoyable, healthy, and rewarding activities on the California coast is river and sea kayaking. It's the ultimate form of escapism, effortlessly paddling your safe, silent, and unsinkable craft anywhere you please, sneaking up on river otters and great blue herons. The placid Gualala River is ideal for beginner kayakers, and the friendly staff at Adventure Rents, (888)881-4386, in downtown Gualala will transport single and two-person kayaks to and from the river and provide all the necessary gear and instruction. (Adventure Rents also carries canoes, rafts, inflatable kayaks, and on- or off-road and tandem bicycles.) You don't need any experience for river kayaking, and all ages are encouraged, so why not give it a try?

Scottish-style Links. Open to the public is the award-winning Sea Ranch Golf Links, a challenging Scottish-style 18-hole course designed by Robert Muir Graves. It's located along Sea Ranch's northern boundary at the entrance to Gualala Point Regional Park. Open daily; (707)785-2468.

Best Beach Access. Of the six public beach access points along Highway 1 between the south end of Sea Ranch and Gualala, the one that offers the most bang for the $3 parking fee is the 195-acre Gualala Point Regional Park. The park has 10 miles of trails through coastal grasslands, redwood forests, and river canyons, as well as picnic sites, camping areas, and excellent bird- and whale-watching along the mostly deserted beaches; (707)785-2377.

RESTAURANTS

ST. ORRES RESTAURANT ☆☆☆

The restaurant at St. Orres Inn is one of Gualala's star attractions, and one of the main reasons people keep coming back to this region. The constantly changing prix-fixe dinner menu focuses on wild game: dishes range from wild turkey tamales to tequila-marinated quail or sautéed medallions of venison. Self-taught chef Rosemary Campiformio's dark and fruity sauces and sublime soups are perfectly suited to the flavorful game, a distinctly

Northern California rendition of French country cuisine. St. Orres' wine cellar stores a sizable selection of California wines. *2 miles N of Gualala on the E side of Hwy 1; (707)884-3335; 36601 Hwy 1, Gualala; www.saintorres.com; beer and wine; MC, V for hotel guests only, otherwise no credit cards; checks OK; breakfast (guests only) every day, dinner every day; $$$.* ⅃

THE OLD MILANO HOTEL RESTAURANT ☆☆

If you can get over the odd feeling that you're dining in somebody's former living room (which you are), you're bound to enjoy a candlelight dinner in the Old Milano's small, wood-paneled, Victorian dining room. Chef Brian Knutson serves his guests such tantalizing entrees as spice-crusted rack of Sonoma spring lamb, seared sea scallops in a ruby red vinaigrette, and a wonderful puff pastry appetizer filled with sautéed wild mushrooms. The menu changes weekly, but always includes fresh seafood, thick steaks, and fancy fowl. Come early and spend some time basking on the sun porch overlooking the ocean, and be sure to request a table by the fireplace. *Just N of the Food Company, ¾ mile N of town; (707)884-3256; 38300 Hwy 1, Gualala; beer and wine; MC, V for hotel guests only, otherwise no credit cards; checks OK; breakfast (guests only) every day, dinner every day (reservations requested); $$$.*

THE FOOD COMPANY ☆

For fine dining in Gualala, go to the St. Orres or the Old Milano. For every other kind of dining, come here. Open all day, every day, the Food Company is a cross between a deli, bakery, and cafe, serving fresh-baked breads, pastries, and sandwiches alongside an ever-changing menu of meat pies, pastas, quiches, tarts, meat loaf, stuffed bell peppers, moussaka, enchiladas, and Lord knows what else. It's sort of like coming home from school for dinner—you never know what's going to be on the table, but you know it's probably going to be good. On sunny afternoons, the cafe's garden doubles as a picnic area; throw in a bottle of wine from the modest rack, and you have the makings for a romantic—and inexpensive—lunch. *½ mile N of Gualala at the corner of Hwy 1 and Robinsons Reef Rd; (707)884-1800; 38411 Hwy 1, Gualala; beer and wine; MC, V; checks OK; breakfast, lunch, dinner every day; $.*

LODGINGS

THE OLD MILANO HOTEL ☆☆☆

 Overlooking the sea above Castle Rock Cove, this picturesque Victorian bed and breakfast, built by the Lucchinetti family in 1905, is featured on the National Register of Historic Places. If you can drag yourself away from the veranda with the knockout ocean view and through the front door, you'll find six small yet elegant bedrooms upstairs (all with shared baths) and a downstairs suite replete with antique furnishings and a private bath. All but one of the rooms (the Garden View Room) feature fantastic views of the sea. Elsewhere on the 3-acre estate are the Vine Cottage, located in the gardens and furnished with a brass bed, reading loft, wood-burning stove, and private bath; the Caboose, a genuine railroad caboose converted into the quaintest, coziest, and most private room at the inn (if not on the coast) with its wood-burning stove and small deck; four new cottages with fireplaces, ocean views, and hot tubs or showers for two; and a cliff-side whirlpool tub reserved for only two at a time. A full breakfast, included in the room rate, may be served in your room, on the garden patio, or by the fire in the parlor. *Just N of the Food Company, ¾ mile N of Gualala; (707)884-3256; 38300 Hwy 1, Gualala, CA 95445; MC, V for hotel guests only, otherwise no credit cards; checks OK; breakfast (guests only) every day; $$$.*

ST. ORRES ☆☆☆

In the early '70s, a group of young architects and builders, inspired by the Russian architecture of the early Northern California settlers, took their back-to-the-land dreams to Gualala and created this dazzling copper-domed inn from redwood timbers scrounged from old logging mills and dilapidated bridges. Located just off Highway 1 and within walking distance of a sheltered, sandy cove, St. Orres consists of eight small, inexpensive rooms in the main lodge (two with great ocean views and all with shared baths) and 11 private cottages scattered throughout the 42 acres of wooded grounds. The best cottage is the ultra-rustic and surprisingly affordable Wild Flower Cabin, a former logging-crew shelter furnished with a cozy sleeping loft, a wood-burning stove (topped with cast-iron skillets), an adorable outside shower overlooking the woods, and even a gaggle of wild turkeys waiting for handouts at your doorstep. Another top choice: the gorgeous Sequoia Cottage, a solid-timbered charmer tucked into the edge of the forest. It has an elevated king-size bed, skylight, soaking tub, wet bar, private deck, and wood-burning fireplace. Start the day with a complimentary full breakfast (delivered to the cottages in baskets), spend the next few hours lolling around the nearby beaches, and have dinner at St. Orres' superb restaurant (see Restaurants, above). End the day at your private dacha, snuggled in front of the fireplace and listening to the distant roar of the ocean. Reserve a table for dinner when you make your room reservation; breakfast comes with the room, but dinner doesn't, and the restaurant is almost always booked. *2 miles N of Gualala on the E side of Hwy 1; (707)884-3335; 36601 Hwy 1, PO Box 523, Gualala, CA 95445; www.saintorres.com; MC, V for hotel only; checks OK; breakfast (guests only) every day, dinner every day; $$ (lodge), $$$ (cottages).*

The venerable Gualala Hotel saloon, built in 1903, was said to be one of Jack London's favorite watering holes.

POINT ARENA

Fifteen miles north of Gualala is one of the smallest incorporated cities in California, Point Arena. Once a bustling shipping port, the 3-block-long city is now home to only 400 or so people, mostly transplants from larger cities who have set up shop along Main Street with neither the desire nor the intention of making much money. They're just here to enjoy the quiet small-town life.

Locals know that Point Arena has some of the best surfing waves on the North Coast.

Since there is no direct inland road to Point Arena, few tourists pass through, ensuring that the city will never become as overloaded as Mendocino. Yet this ain't no cow town either. It has one of the hottest restaurants on the North Coast, artistic (and historic) lodgings, and pristine beaches. So if you're tired of the crowded Mendocino scene yet want to spend a relaxing weekend on the coast, there's no better alternative than little Point Arena.

ACTIVITIES

Lighthouse Tour. Oh boy, yet another historic lighthouse and museum. Ho hum, right? Not this one. Even people who loathe tourist attractions end up enjoying a tour of the Point Arena Lighthouse. Built in 1870 after 10 ships ran aground here on a single stormy night, the fully operational lighthouse had to be rebuilt after the 1906 earthquake, but now it's solid enough for visitors to trudge up the 6-story tower's 145 steps for a standout view of the coast (that is, if the fog has lifted). The dazzling 6-foot-wide, lead-crystal lens is worth the hike alone. The lighthouse is open 11am to 3:30pm weekdays, 10am to 3:30pm weekends in the summer (11am to 2:30pm daily in the winter), and is located at the end of scenic Lighthouse Road, about 5 miles northwest of downtown Point Arena off Highway 1. Parking/tour/museum fee is only a few bucks; (707)882-2777.

A Pier for All Ages. In 1983, a mother of a storm wiped out Point Arena's century-old city wharf. Seven years and $2.2 million dollars later, the old pier was replaced by a 330-foot bullet-proof cement pier. Though it ain't pretty, it's still worth a stroll to watch the fishermen unload their catch or, if you're lucky, spy a gray whale migrating along the coast. Access to the pier is free, and no license is required for fishing. Take the Iversen Avenue turnoff west off Highway 1 at the south end of town.

Beach Bliss. Virtually isolated is the 5-mile sweep of shore, dunes, and meadows that comprise Manchester State Beach. Though several access roads off Highway 1 lead to the shore, the closest one to Point Arena also happens to be the best—the 10- to 15-minute walk across the dunes from the parking lot is a leg-burner, but it's a small price to pay for your own private beach. Take the Stoneboro Road exit west off

Highway 1, 2 miles north of the turnoff to Point Arena Lighthouse; (707)882-2463 or (707)937-5804.

RESTAURANTS

PANGAEA ☆☆☆

After stints as the exalted chef of the local St. Orres and the Old Milano Hotel Restaurants, Shannon Hughes opened her own place in tiny Point Arena to the relief of every innkeeper in the city ("finally, a restaurant in town I can recommend," says one). Although it's a relative newcomer to the area, Pangaea is already the talk of the North Coast, particularly when Hughes goes off on one of her international tangents and astounds patrons with exotic menu items à la Indonesia, Nigeria, and other far-reaching latitudes. Not that she's above chicken and dumplings (i.e., the free-range Rocky Range chicken stewed in savory sage gravy) or even a good ol' American burger (beef from Marin County's hormone-free Niman-Schell Farms, fresh-baked buns, Thai chile sauce, organic greens, and house-made ketchup). Even the restaurant's neo-bronze decor and hand-blown Mexican glassware are dazzling works of art. Go Shannon. *In downtown Point Arena; (707)882-3001; 250 Main St, Point Arena; beer and wine; no credit cards; checks OK; dinner Wed–Sun (winter hours may vary); $$.*

LODGINGS

COAST GUARD HOUSE ☆☆

 Poised high above Arena Cove, this historic Cape Cod–style cottage was originally built by the Life-Saving Service in 1901 to lodge crew members. Beacon lamps, anchors, and a sea captain's hat tossed haphazardly on a table evoke memories of Point Arena's seafaring past, but the inn's Arts and Crafts interiors remain simple and uncluttered. The six guest rooms have all-cotton linens and fluffy down comforters, and are stocked with organic soaps, shampoo, conditioner, and body lotion. The Surfman Cove Room, with windows on three sides, has a

*"It was either have
another child . . .
or open an inn."*
—Coast Guard
House innkeeper
Merita Whatley

beautiful view of the ocean and cove, a wood-burning stove, and a sunken Japanese tub. Top choice is the separate Boathouse Cottage, a replica of the original Generator House (except for the spa tub for two, Swedish wood-burning stove, and private patio overlooking the cove). An ocean-view hot tub is available for guests. Breakfast, served by amiable innkeepers Mia and Kevin Gallagher, is included in the room rate. *Off Iversen Ave, 1 mile W of downtown Point Arena; (707)882-2442 or (800)524-9320; 695 Arena Cove; PO Box 117, Point Arena, CA 95468; coast@mcn.org; www.coastguardhouse.com; MC, V; checks OK; $$$.*

KOA KAMPING KABINS

Who would have guessed that Manchester Beach's Kampgrounds of America would make *Northern California Coast Best Places*? Well, KOA's Kamping Kabins are just too adorable to pass up. Inside each of the little one- or two-room log cabins are a log-frame double bed and bunk beds with mattresses (cabins sleep four to six people), a heater, and a light bulb ("rustic" is the key word here). Outside are a small porch with log swing, a barbecue, and a picnic table. Basically all you need to bring are kitchen utensils, charcoal, and bedding. Hot showers, clean rest rooms, laundry facilities, and a small store and pool are nearby (as is the beach*). On Kinney Rd off Hwy 1, 6 miles north of Point Arena; (707)882-2375; 44300 Kinney Rd, PO Box 266, Manchester, CA 95459; AE, DIS, MC, V; no checks; $.* &

ELK

Once known as Greenwood, this tiny former logging town was renamed Elk by the postal service when someone realized there was another town in California called Greenwood. For a such a small community (population 250), it sure has a booming tourist trade: six inns, four restaurants, and one authentic Irish pub. Its close proximity to the big tourist town of Mendocino, a mere 30-minute drive up the coast, is one reason for its popularity. Elk's paramount appeal, however, is its dramatic shoreline; the series of immense sea stacks here create one of the most awesome seascapes on the California coast.

The curvaceous stretch of Highway 1 between Elk and Little River is locally known as Dramamine Drive.

RESTAURANTS

HARBOR HOUSE RESTAURANT ☆☆☆

 The four-course prix-fixe dinners served at the Harbor House Restaurant change nightly, but they always begin with a small, hot-from-the-oven loaf of bread that's perfect for sopping up the chef's delicious soups, such as the tomato-basil or Indian spice–spinach. The salad, made from homegrown vegetables, might be a combination of greens tossed with an herb vinaigrette or sprouts mixed with olives, water chestnuts, and a toasted sesame-seed dressing. The seafood is harvested from local waters, and the meats and cheeses come from nearby farms. Expect to find entrees such as ravioli stuffed with crab, fennel, and shiitakes in a Pernod cream sauce or seared sea scallops on roasted-yellow-pepper rouille with Spanish basmati pilaf. Many of the fine wines offered are locally produced. To take full advantage of the restaurant's spectacular view, beg for a window table (alas, you can't reserve a particular table). The only seating (which is very limited when the inn is full) is at 7pm, and reservations are required. *In the Harbor House Inn, at the N end of Elk; (707)877-3203; 5600 Hwy 1, Elk; beer and wine; no credit cards; checks OK; dinner every day; $$$.*

GREENWOOD PIER CAFE ☆

 Most of the herbs and vegetables served in this cafe come straight from the elaborate gardens behind the restaurant, and all of the breads and pastries are baked on site. Try the walnut-corn waffle for breakfast and the black bean chili with polenta for lunch. Dinner items on the daily changing menu range from baked salmon in puff pastry to fresh summer veggies with baked polenta. Prices are very reasonable, and the ambience is pleasantly informal and relaxed. *In the center of Elk; (707)877-9997; 5926 Hwy 1, Elk; www.elkcoast.com/greenwoodpier; beer and wine; AE, MC, V; local checks only; breakfast, lunch,*

dinner every day May 15 to Oct 31 (Fri–Mon Nov 1 to May 15); $$.

LODGINGS

GREENWOOD PIER INN ☆☆☆

 What separates this cliff-top wonder from the dozens of other precariously perched inns along Highway 1 are its rooms' fantastic interiors and the brilliant flower gardens gracing the property. The inn offers 11 guest rooms, including three detached cliff-hanging suites (Cliffhouse and the two Sea Castles) and the separate Garden Cottage. Most of the units have private decks with stunning views of Greenwood Cove, and all guests have access to a hot tub on the cliff's edge. The whimsical avant-garde decor and tile and marble detailing in most of the rooms are the work of proprietor/artist Kendrick Petty. Some

---

TICK TALK

After a walk through coastal forests or meadows, it's always a good idea to check for hitchhikers on your pant legs and socks. The western black-legged tick, bearer of the dreaded Lyme disease, awaits its prey at the tips of knee-high vegetation, then burrows its head into the victim's skin.

While there are dozens of old wives' tales on how to remove a tick (from dousing it in peanut butter to "unscrewing" it counterclockwise), the only real solution is to pull it straight out—without twisting or jerking—with tweezers. Grab the tick as close to the skin as possible and gently pull. If you have to use your fingers, be sure to use a tissue; afterward, wash your hands and the bite site with soap and water and apply an antiseptic.

Symptoms of Lyme disease include a bull's-eye marking or other rash around the bite, often accompanied by a fever or flu-like feeling anywhere from a week to months after the encounter. Since Lyme disease can be fatal, it's important to call your doctor or the Infectious Diseases Branch of the California Department of Health Services in Berkeley, (510)540-2566, if symptoms start to occur.

---

units also feature Kendrick's colorful airbrush collages, and all the rooms have private baths, fireplaces or wood-burning stoves, and stereos. The elegantly rustic Cliff-house is a favorite, with its expansive deck, marble fireplace, whirlpool tub, and Oriental carpets. While the suites and castles are rather expensive, the rooms in the main house are moderately priced. Room rates include a continental breakfast delivered to your doorstep, and you can even have dinner from the cafe (see Restaurants, above) brought to your room. *In the center of Elk; (707)877-9997; 5926 Hwy 1, PO Box 336, Elk, CA 95432; www.elkcoast.com/greenwoodpier; AE, MC, V; local checks only; $$–$$$.*

HARBOR HOUSE INN

 In 1985, Helen and Dean Turner converted this palatial redwood house—perched on a bluff above Greenwood Landing—into the Harbor House Inn, adding six guest rooms, four cottages, and an exceptional restaurant (see Restaurants, above). Top picks are the Harbor Room, a romantic boudoir with a fireplace and a breathtaking view of the cliffs and surf, and the Lookout Room, a smaller, less expensive unit with a small private balcony that overlooks Greenwood Landing. Any old room will do, however, since you will probably want to spend most of your time relaxing in the fabulous garden or down at the private beach. Breakfast and dinner are included in the room rates. *At the N end of Elk; (707)877-3203; 5600 Hwy 1, PO Box 369, Elk, CA 95432; beer and wine; no credit cards; checks OK; dinner every day; $$$.*

ALBION

A renowned haven for pot growers until an increase in police surveillance and property taxes drove most of them away, Albion is more a free-spirited ideal community than an actual town. You'll know you're there when you cross a white wooden bridge; it was built in 1944 (steel and reinforced concrete were unavailable during World War II) and it's the last of its kind on Highway 1.

Albion was named in 1853 by Captain W. A. Richardson—builder of the first lumber mill at the mouth of the Albion River—after the high, pale cliffs of his British homeland.

RESTAURANTS

ALBION RIVER INN RESTAURANT

 Chef Stephen Smith presides over the Albion River Inn's ocean-view dining room, where fresh local produce complements such dishes as braised Sonoma rabbit, grilled sea bass, and rock shrimp pasta. The extensive wine list has a good selection of hard-to-find North Coast labels. Arrive before nightfall to ooh and aah over the view. *On the NW side of the Albion bridge; (707)937-1919 or (800)479-7944; 3790 Hwy 1, Albion; ari@mcn.org; www.albionriverinn.com; full bar; AE, MC, V; checks OK; dinner every day; $$$.*&

THE LEDFORD HOUSE RESTAURANT

 It's rare when an ocean-view restaurant's food is as good as the view, but owners Lisa and Tony Geer manage to pull it off, serving Provençal-style cuisine in a wonderfully romantic cliff-top setting. The menu, which changes monthly, offers a choice of bistro dishes, such as Antoine's Cassoulet (lamb, pork, garlic sausage, and duck confit slowly cooked with white beans), rack of lamb, and roast duckling. Vegetarian entrees and soups are always featured as well. With a view like this, a window table at sunset is a must. After dinner, sidle up to the bar and listen to the live music, featured nightly. *Take the Spring Grove Rd exit W off Hwy 1; (707)937-0282; 3000 Hwy 1, Albion; full bar; AE, DC, MC, V; checks OK; dinner Wed–Sun; $$$.* &

LODGINGS

ALBION RIVER INN

 After a long period of ups and downs, this modern seaside inn, poised high above Albion Cove where the Albion River meets the sea, is now one of the finest on the California coast. All 20 of the individually decorated New England–style cottages are equipped with antique and contemporary furnishings, private baths, queen- and king-size beds, fireplaces, and a bodacious array of potted plants. The clincher, though, is the private spa tub for two that overlooks the headlands and ocean. (All rooms have the same ocean view, but all do not have the spa tubs, so be sure to ask for one—it's well worth the added expense.) Breakfast, served in the restaurant (see Restaurants, above), is included in the rates. *On the NW side of the Albion bridge on Hwy 1; (707)937-1919 or (800)479-7944; 3790 Hwy 1, PO Box 100, Albion, CA 95410; ari@mcn.org; www.albionriverinn.com; AE, MC, V; checks OK; $$$.* ᶘ

LITTLE RIVER

Once a bustling logging and shipbuilding community, Little River is now more like a precious suburb of Mendocino. The town does a brisk business handling the tourist overflow from its neighbor two miles up the coast, and is centered around Van Damme State Park, one of the finest state parks on the Mendocino coast. Vacationers in the know reserve a room in serene Little River and make forays into Mendocino only for dining and shopping.

ACTIVITIES

Little River's Secret Sinkhole. Known by locals as the Little River Cemetery Sinkhole, this almost perfectly circular sinkhole is simply amazing. At low tide you can walk through the wave-cut tunnel located at the sinkhole's base to the nearby tide pools; at high tide, you can sit on the tiny sandy beach and look at the tunnel as the waves blast through. Either way, the feeling of being within this natural phenomenon is borderline sacred. To get here, park across from the Little River Cemetery on Highway 1, walk to the southwest corner of the cemetery, and look for a small opening in the chain-link fence. The sinkhole is only a few dozen yards down the trail, but be prepared to enter and exit the sinkhole on all fours or you might end up buried alongside it.

Van Damme State Park. A few miles south of Mendocino off Highway 1 is Van Damme State Park, a 2,337-acre preserve blanketed with ferns and second-growth

Budget lunch tip: The Little River Market, located across from the Little River Inn on Highway 1, has a great little deli serving inexpensive sandwiches, bagels, tamales, and even an assortment of just-baked breads from the famed Mendocino eatery Cafe Beaujolais. Three small tables in the back overlook a gorgeous view of the bay. Open 8am to 7pm daily; (707)937-5133.

redwoods. The park has a small beach, a visitors center, and a campground, but its main attraction is the 15 miles of spectacularly lush trails—ideal for a stroll or a jog—that start at the beach and wind through the redwood-covered hills. Fern Canyon Trail is the park's most popular, an easy and incredibly scenic 2½-mile hiking and bicycling path that crosses over the Little River. You can also hike or drive (most of the way) to Van Damme's peculiar Pygmy Forest, an eerie scrub forest of waist-high stunted trees. To reach the Pygmy Forest by car, follow Highway 1 south of the park and turn up Little River Airport Road, then head uphill 2¾ miles; (707)937-5804.

Plane Rides. For the ultimate romantic vacation—or if you can't stand the long drive to the coast—charter a Coast Flyers pilot to pick you up at the Northern California airport of your choice and fly you directly to Mendocino. Sure, it's big bucks, but for a group it just might be worth it. Coast Flyers also provides coastal tours, whale-watching trips, introductory student pilot flights, and even car rentals from the Little River Airport; (707)937-1224.

LODGINGS

GLENDEVEN INN   ☆☆☆

A few years ago Glendeven was named one of the 12 best inns in America by *Country Inns* magazine, and rightly so. This stately 19th-century farmhouse resides among 2½ acres of well-tended gardens and heather-covered headlands that extend all the way to the blue Pacific. The 10 spacious rooms and suites feature an uncluttered mix of country antiques and contemporary art. For the ultimate in luxury, stay in the Pinewood or Bayloft Suites in the Stevenscroft Annex—each has a sitting parlor, a fireplace, and a partial view of the ocean. The cozy East Farmington Room, with its private garden deck and fireplace, is another good choice. Above the Glendeven Gallery, the inn's fine-arts boutique, sits the fabulous Barn House Suite, a two-story, redwood-paneled house ideal for families or two couples. After breakfast, which is included with your room, walk to the beautiful fern-rimmed canyon trails in nearby Van Damme State Park. *2 miles S of Mendocino on Hwy 1; (707)937-0083 or (800)822-4536; 8221 Hwy 1, Little River, CA 95456; www.innaccess.com/gdi/; AE, MC, V; checks OK; $$$.*

HERITAGE HOUSE ✯✯✯

 Immortalized as the ultimate bed-and-breakfast lodge in the movie *Same Time, Next Year*, Heritage House has a history well suited to Hollywood melodrama: Its secluded farmhouse was used as a safe house for smugglers of Chinese laborers during the 19th century, for rumrunners during Prohibition, and for the notorious bandit "Baby Face" Nelson during the '30s. Since 1949, however, the hotel has catered to a considerably tamer crowd. The inn is situated on a bluff overlooking a rocky cove and is surrounded by 37 acres of cypress trees, bountiful flower and vegetable gardens, and expansive green lawns. Lodging consists of three guest rooms in the main building, 63 cottages, and a detached 1877 farmhouse. The best rooms are the cliff-hanging Same Time and Next Year Cottages with their king-size beds, fireplaces, and extraordinary ocean views (the Next Year Cottage also has a whirlpool tub). Room rates used to include breakfast and dinner at the restaurant, but the management has since dropped this requirement.

The Heritage House Restaurant offers high-quality cuisine served in several dining rooms, including alfresco seating for breakfast and brunch on sunny days. The menu changes seasonally, but may include such appetizers as local cod cakes and griddled polenta with wild mushroom ragout. Main-course selections vary from braised lamb shank with Basque white beans to pan-roasted pork chops, grilled salmon, and roast Peking duck breast. The extensive wine list ranks among the highest-rated in the country. Reservations are required for dinner. *Just S of Van Damme State Park on Hwy 1; (707)937-5885 or (800)235-5885; 5200 Hwy 1, Little River, CA 95456; www.innaccess.com/hhi/; full bar; MC, V; checks OK; breakfast Mon–Fri, brunch Sat–Sun, dinner every day (closed briefly in Dec, and from Jan 2nd to Feb 14th); $$$.* ♿

"Although it is difficult to ascertain the boundary between public and private lands, a general rule to follow is that visitors have the right to walk on a wet beach."
—Excerpt from the California Coastal Commission's California Coastal Access Guide

STEVENSWOOD LODGE   ★★★

Stevenswood Lodge is for people who want the comforts of a modern hotel—cable television, telephone, refrigerator, honor bar—without feeling like they're staying at a Holiday Inn. As it works out, not many Holiday Inns are surrounded on three sides by a verdant 2,400-acre forest, or located just a quarter of a mile from the Mendocino shoreline, or embellished with sculpture gardens and contemporary-art displays throughout the grounds. Built in 1988, the lodge's one wheelchair-accessible room and nine suites are outfitted with handcrafted burl-maple furniture, large windows with striking vistas (some with a partial ocean view), private bathrooms, and access to several shared decks. The Pullen Room has a particularly pleasant view of the forest and gardens. Recent additions to the lodge include a restaurant offering gourmet breakfasts to guests and the public, as well as two spas set within the forest canyon (one spa is available to all guests and the other is private and may be reserved by guests on an hourly basis). *On Hwy 1, 2 miles S of Mendocino; (707)937-2810 or (800)421-2810; 8211 Hwy 1, Little River, PO Box 170, Mendocino, CA 95460; info@stevenswood.com; www.stevenswood.com; AE, DIS, MC, V; checks OK, breakfast every day; $$$.*

THE INN AT SCHOOLHOUSE CREEK   ★★

 Whereas most small inns located along the Mendocino coast have to make do with an acre or less, the Inn at Schoolhouse Creek has the luxury of spreading its nine private, immaculate cottages amidst 10 acres of beautiful flower gardens, lush meadows, and cypress groves. As a result, the instant you pull into the driveway you feel like you've gotten away from it all and have entered a more tranquil environment. Most of Schoolhouse Creek's cottages sleep two, though a few can fit small families. The turn-of-the-century cottages are quaint and lovely, particularly the Cypress Cottage with its own private yard graced by an inviting pair of Adirondack chairs. *On Hwy 1, just S of Little River; (707)937-5525 or (800)731-5525;*

7051 N Hwy 1, Little River, CA 95456; www.innatschool-housecreek.com; MC, V; checks OK; $$. &

LITTLE RIVER INN AND RESTAURANT ☆☆

 Set on a 225-acre parcel of ocean-front land, the Little River Inn is an ideal retreat for those North Coast travelers who simply can't leave their golf clubs or tennis rackets at home; it's often jokingly referred to as the poor man's Pebble Beach. Susan McKinney, her husband, Mel, and brother Danny own and operate the inn and restaurant (as well as the nine-hole golf course, driving range, putting green, and two lighted championship tennis courts). All of the estate's 65 rooms and cottages offer spectacular ocean views, many feature fireplaces, and some also have whirlpool tubs (and if you prefer to relax indoors, check out the inn's extensive video library). The antique-filled rooms in the main Victorian house are preferable to the north wing's motel-style units, which suffer from uninspired decor.

The Little River Inn Restaurant is a casual place for breakfast or dinner but, oddly enough, is the only room at the inn without an ocean view. Chef Silver Canul maintains the house tradition of using mostly local products: fresh fish from nearby Noyo Harbor; lamb, beef, and potatoes from the town of Comptche; and greens and vegetables from local gardens. For breakfast try the popular Ole's Swedish Pancakes. *Across from the Little River Market and Post Office, S of Mendocino; (707)937-5942 or (888)466-5683; 7750 Hwy 1, Little River, CA 95456; lri@mcn.org; www.littleriverinn.com; full bar; MC, V; checks OK; breakfast, dinner every day; $$$.* &

RACHEL'S INN ☆☆

Strategically sandwiched between Van Damme State Park and the Mendocino headlands is Rachel Binah's 1860s Victorian farmhouse, one of the best bed and breakfasts on the Mendocino coast. Each of the six rooms and three suites has a queen-size bed with a fluffy comforter, a private bath, and original artwork (including some by Rachel); six rooms also have fireplaces. The

Parlor Suite is the most luxurious and spacious of the lot, although it's subject to highway noise and the hubbub of people eating breakfast on the other side of its French doors (not a good combo for late sleepers). A quieter unit is the Blue Room, with a balcony overlooking the back garden, meadow, and trees, or the Mezzanine Suite, which comes with a private sitting room, balcony, fireplace, and views of the park meadows. The inn's main attraction is Rachel, a vivacious innkeeper who spends her time campaigning to protect our nation's coastline from offshore oil drilling when she's not busy welcoming guests or preparing one of her grand breakfasts. *On Hwy 1, 2 miles S of Mendocino; (707)937-0088 or (800)347-9252; 8200 N Hwy 1, Little River; PO Box 134, Mendocino, CA 95460; www.rachelsinn.com; MC, V; checks OK; $$$.* &

MENDOCINO

The grande dame of Northern California's coastal tourist towns, this refurbished replica of a New England–style fishing village—complete with white-spired church—has managed to retain more of its appealing village-esqe allure than most North Coast vacation spots. Motels, fast-food chains, and anything hinting of development are strictly verboten here (even the town's only automated teller is subtly recessed into the historic Masonic Building), resulting in the almost-passable illusion that Mendocino is just another quaint little coastal community.

Founded in 1852, Mendocino is still home to a few fishermen and loggers, although writers, artists, actors, and other urban transplants now far outnumber the natives. In fact, Mendocino County is rumored to have the highest percentage of Ph.D.s of any rural county in the country. Spring is best time to visit, when parking spaces are plentiful and the climbing tea roses and wisteria are in full bloom. Start with a casual tour of the town, end with a stroll around Mendocino's celebrated headlands, and suddenly the long drive and inflated room rates seem a trivial price to pay for visiting one of the most beautiful places on earth.

The Chevron station in Mendocino is one of the last totally full-service gas stations in Northern California.

ACTIVITIES

Shop & Eat. To tour Mendocino proper, lose the car and head out on foot to the Tote Fête Bakery, (707)937-3383, located in the back of the large building on the northwest corner of Albion and Lansing Streets (don't confuse it with the Tote Fête deli in the same building). Fuel up with a double capp and cinnamon bun, throw away your map of the town, and start walking—the shopping district of Mendocino is so small it can be covered in under an hour, so why bother planning your attack? One must-see shop is the Gallery Bookshop & Bookwinkle's Children's Books, one of the best independent bookstores in Northern California, with a wonderful selection of books for kids, cooks, and local-history buffs; it's located at Main and Kasten Streets; (707)937-BOOK. Another is Mendocino Jams & Preserves, a town landmark at 440 Main Street that offers free tastings—with the help of little bread chips—of its luscious marmalades, dessert toppings, mustards, chutneys, and other spreads; (707) 937-1037 or (800)708-1196.

Arts & Crafts. The Mendocino Art Center offers various art classes and workshops—storytelling, sculpture, ceramics, gardening, textiles, jewelry, crafts, and more—to the public, including annoying tourists. Either call for a free brochure of future classes, or drop by 45200 Little Lake Street at Williams Street and crash a class already in session. The center also has multiple art exhibits on display and a retail art shop; (707)937-5818.

To rent mountain
bikes for exploring
nearby Van Damme
and Russian Gulch
State Parks, or to
rent a kayak,
canoe, or outrigger
for a leisurely
paddle up the Big
River, head to
Catch a Canoe &
Bicycles, Too!, a
rental shop located
at Stanford Inn by
the Sea. On
Highway 1 at
Comptche-Ukiah
Road, 1/2 mile
south of Mendo-
cino; (707)937-
0273.

THE SECRET GORDON?

*Here's a little-known walk for people who love to sit alone for
hours and watch the waves pound against stone. About a mile
south of Mendocino along Highway 1, look for the Gordon
Lane turnoff heading inland. Park on the raised dirt shoulder
across from the Gordon Lane turnoff and look for a small
opening in the barbed-wire fence. The unmarked half-mile
trail through Chapman Point's meadows ends at an enormous
rocky outcropping with a letter-box view of Mendocino far
across the bay.*

Headlands & Parks. As with many towns that hug
the Northern California coast, Mendocino's premier attractions are provided by Mother Nature and the Department of Parks and Recreation, which means they're free (or
nearly free). Mendocino Headlands State Park, the small grassy
stretch of land between the village of Mendocino and the ocean,
is one of the town's most popular attractions. The park's flat, 3-
mile-long trail winds along the edge of a heather-covered bluff,
providing spectacular sunset views and good lookout points for
seabirds and California gray whales. The Headlands' main access
point is at the west end of Main Street, or skip the footwork altogether and take the scenic motorist's route along Heeser Drive
off Lansing Street.

About two miles north of Mendocino off Highway 1 is the
worst-kept secret on the coast: Russian Gulch State Park, a veritable paradise for campers, hikers, and abalone divers. After
paying a $5 entrance fee, pick up a trail map at the park entrance
and find the path to Devil's Punch Bowl—a 200-foot-long, sea-
carved tunnel that has partially collapsed in the center, creating
an immense blowhole that's particularly spectacular during a
storm. Even better is the 5½-mile round-trip hike along Falls
Loop Trail to the Russian Gulch Falls, a misty 35-foot waterfall
secluded in the deep old-growth forest; (707)937-5804.

Botanical Gardens. If you have a passion for plants and
flowers, it's worth the $5 admission fee to peruse the Men-
docino Coast Botanical Gardens, located 2 miles south of Fort
Bragg at 18220 Highway 1; (707)964-4352. The nonprofit gar-

dens feature 47 acres of plants—ranging from azaleas and rhododendrons to dwarf conifers, ferns, fuchsia, dahlias, and more—as well as a picnic area, retail nursery, gift store, and the popular Gardens Grill restaurant (see review under Fort Bragg). It's open 9am to 5pm in the summer and 9am to 4pm in the winter.

Coastal Trail. The black sheep of Mendocino's hiking trails is Jug Handle State Reserve's Ecological Staircase Trail. Perhaps people think it's not worth the effort because it's free and "educational," but this 5-mile round-trip trail is a wonderful hike and gets surprisingly little traffic. The attraction is a series of naturally formed, staircase-like bluffs—each about 100 feet higher and 100,000 years older than the one below it—that differ dramatically in ecological formation: from beaches to headlands to an amazing pygmy forest filled with waist-high, century-old trees. The trail entrance is located on Highway 1, 1½ miles north of the town of Caspar, between Mendocino and Fort Bragg; (707)937-5804.

Golf & Tennis. The North Coast has never been famous for its golf courses or tennis courts, but if you get the urge to smack a ball across the range or over the net, the only show in town is the Little River Inn Golf and Tennis Club. Located a few miles south of Mendocino on Highway 1, the club has a

Docent-led tours of the Point Cabrillo Light Station, built in 1908 to protect schooners hauling lumber to San Francisco, are offered on summer Sundays at 11am from May through September. The tour starts at the light station's main gate, located on Point Cabrillo Drive, 1⅕ miles north of the Russian Gulch State Park entrance. Call to confirm before you go; (707)937-0816.

MENDOCINO'S SECRET BEACH

There couldn't possibly be a cuter, more secluded little beach on the California coast than this one. Naturally there are no signs pointing the way and it requires a little effort to get there, but my-oh-my is it worth the walk. First you need to find the Pine Beach Inn along Highway 1 between Fort Bragg and Mendocino. Take the Ocean Drive turnoff next to the hotel's giant sign, park in the small dirt parking lot near the tennis courts, walk toward the ocean, and you'll see the trailhead leading into a small forest. A five-minute walk through scrub pines and meadows rewards you with a billion-dollar view of the coast. At the bluff's edge, head south toward the green-roofed house, and you'll come to a small creek that provides easy access to the beach.

regulation nine-hole course, driving range, lighted tennis courts, and a pro shop, all open to the public; 7750 Highway 1, Little River; (707)937-5667.

Drinks & Dancing. After a full day of adventuring, why not top off the evening with a little nightcap and music? If you appreciate classical tunes and warm snifters of brandy, take a stroll down Mendocino's Main Street to the elegant bar and lounge at the Mendocino Hotel and Restaurant (see Restaurants, below) at 45080 Main Street; (707)937-0511. If blue jeans and baseball caps are more your style, hang out with the guys at Dick's Place, which has the cheapest drinks in town and the sort of jukebox-'n'-jiggers atmosphere you'd expect from this former logging town's oldest bar; 45080 Main Street, next to the Mendocino Hotel; (707)937-5643. For a rowdy night of dancing and drinking, head a few miles up Highway 1 to Caspar Inn, the last true roadhouse in California where everything from rock and jazz to reggae and blues is played live Thursday through Saturday nights starting at 9:30pm. Take the Caspar Road exit off Highway 1, 4 miles north of Mendocino and 4 miles south of Fort Bragg; (707)964-5565.

A Walk on the Edge. This has to be one of the most beautiful seaside trails on the California coast. The trailhead starts $3/10$ of a mile down road 500D, the first left turn off Highway 1 north of the Lansing Street exit in Mendocino (park across from the red-and-white "No Parking 10pm–6am" sign). Veer left at the trailhead to see an enormous sinkhole linked by a wave-cut tunnel, then backtrack and veer right to start the coastal trail. When the trail loops back to the road, turn left, walk up the road (away from your car) to the dead end, and start the second half of the trail, which is even better than the first. The total walk is about one hour.

RESTAURANTS

CAFE BEAUJOLAIS ☆☆☆

Cafe Beaujolais started out as the finest little breakfast and lunch place in Mendocino. Then, over the years, owner Margaret Fox (author of two best-selling cookbooks, *Cafe Beaujolais* and *Morning Food*) and her hus-

If the house on the corner of Little Lake and Ford Streets in Mendocino looks strangely familiar, that's because it was the set for the hit TV show Murder, She Wrote, starring Angela Lansbury.

WHERE EVERY DAY IS SUN-DAY

When the fog refuses to lift for days—even weeks—at a time during Mendocino summers, locals are sure to be found a few miles inland at the perpetually sunny "3.66 Beach" on the Navarro River. The small golden-sand beach fronts a placid pool of cool green river water that's ideal for swimming. To get here, head south from Mendocino on Highway 1, turn inland at the Highway 128 junction, and look for the 3.66 mile marker. Park along the road and take the short, well-worn path down to the beach.

band, Chris Kump, managed to turn this modest Victorian house into one of the most celebrated restaurants in Northern California. Unfortunately, now that Margaret and Chris spend half their time in Austria running their recently inherited castle-cum-bed-and-breakfast inn (not to mention tending to their newly adopted baby), the kitchen doesn't always turn out such stellar four-star fare as it once did, but the food is still quite good. When chef Kump is in town he usually takes charge of the kitchen, where his weekly changing dinner menu might feature entrees such as roast free-range chicken with kumquat sauce and chickpea pancakes; salt cod bouillabaisse with local rockfish, mussels, and shrimp; or Niman-Schell steak served with yellow mashed potatoes and green beans. Listed under "Of Course" are a sinful array of desserts such as the chocolate hazelnut fragilité—a soft nut meringue layered with ganache (a rich semisweet chocolate icing) and served with Frangelico whipped cream. Try to avoid sitting in the bustling bench section, which has itsy-bitsy tables; opt for the enclosed atrium overlooking the garden instead. *At Ukiah and Evergreen Sts, on the E end of town; (707)937-5614; 961 Ukiah St, Mendocino; www.cafebeaujolais.com; beer and wine; DIS, MC, V; checks OK; dinner every day; $$$.*

Cafe Beaujolais' renowned "brickery breads" are sold daily from 11am till around 5pm at its bakery on Ukiah Street, just east of the restaurant.

MACCALLUM HOUSE RESTAURANT ★★★

Using the freshest ingredients—seafood straight from the coast, organic meats and produce from neighboring farms and ranches—chef/owner Alan Kantor whips up some wonderful North Coast cuisine. Entrees on the seasonally changing menu may range from roasted Pacific salmon with saffron-pistachio risotto and arugula pesto to pan-seared duck confit with huckleberry-honey vinegar sauce. Lighter and less expensive fare, such as the delicious pan-charred rock-cod tacos with handmade corn tortillas, are served at the adjoining Grey Whale Bar & Cafe, a nice alternative for those who wish to forgo a formal dinner in the elegant dining room. MacCallum House also hosts a weekend brunch, offering such treats as Grand Marnier French toast with pistachio butter and organic maple syrup. *On Albion St Between Kasten and Lansing Sts; (707)937-5763; 45020 Albion St, Mendocino; www.maccallumhousedining.com; full bar; MC, V; checks OK; brunch Sat–Sun, dinner every day (closed Jan to mid-Feb); $$$.*

955 UKIAH STREET RESTAURANT ★★★

This relatively unknown Mendocino restaurant is described by local epicureans as "the sleeper restaurant on the coast." The powers behind the restaurant's doors are Jamie and Peggy Griffith, who have managed to turn 995 Ukiah into a serious (and slightly less expensive) rival to its more famous neighbor, Cafe Beaujolais. The dramatic interior, with its split-level dining room, 20-foot ceilings, rustic wood-trimmed walls, and elegant table settings, sets the mood for the haute cuisine, which might include seared pork loin stuffed with prosciutto, crispy duck served with ginger–apple brandy sauce, and a thick swordfish steak resting in a red chile–tomatillo sauce. The upstairs section can get cramped and a little noisy, so try to sit downstairs—preferably at the corner window table—where the vaulted ceiling imparts a comfortable sense of space. *At Ukiah and Evergreen Sts, on the E end of town; (707)937-1955; 955 Ukiah St, Mendocino; beer and wine; MC, V; checks OK; dinner Wed–Sun; $$$.* ⅃

Mendocino's only automated cash cow is at the northwest corner of Lansing and Ukiah Streets.

One of the best burger-and-fries combos in California is at Mendo Burgers, located behind the Mendocino Bakery & Cafe at 10483 Lansing Street in Mendocino; (707)937-1111. Open daily 11am to 7pm (Sundays till 5pm).

STANFORD INN BY THE SEA RESTAURANT ☆☆☆

 To complement their environmentally friendly lodge (see below), Joan and Jeff Stanford have taken a huge gamble and opened the region's only vegetarian/vegan restaurant. Aside from the occasional disgruntled patron ("a few older gentlemen took one look at the menu and walked out," says Joan), the gambit worked, and now the Stanfords are enjoying that most relished of patrons, the repeat customer. The menu varies monthly to take advantage of seasonal organic produce, some of which derives from the lodge's own gardens. Dishes range from lighter fare—herbed asiago polenta cakes sauteed in a roasted garlic–Chardonnay sauce with local organic shiitake mushrooms (fantastic)—to hearty entrees such as tarragon roasted acorn squash filled with wild rice, shiitake mushrooms, roasted garlic, and caramelized apples. Truly, these are masterfully crafted dishes that implode the myth that it takes meat to make a meal. Though the dining room exudes a rustic elegance, dining attire is anything but formal. *1 mile S of Mendocino at Hwy 1 and Comptche-Ukiah Rd; (707)937-5615 or (800)331-8884; full bar; AE, DC, DIS, MC, V; brunch Sun, breakfast, lunch Mon–Sat, dinner every day; checks OK; $$.*

THE MOOSSE CAFE ☆☆

Rising triumphantly from its ashes—literally—this small, popular cafe has made an amazing comeback after burning to the ground a few years back. Formerly known as the haunt for Mendocino's confessed chocoholics, the Moosse has switched to a more substantial (read healthier) menu that makes the most of local and organic meats, herbs, and vegetables (the caesar salad, fashioned with a perfect balance of Parmesan and a robust smack of garlic, is particularly good). Popular entrees are the fresh mixed seafood cakes served over basmati rice with a roasted red pepper remoulade and the lavender-smoked double-thick pork chop served with roasted yam and apple puree. The result? Make a reservation, because there's usually a waiting list for dinner. Of course, dessert (especially the wicked Blackout Cake) is as good as it ever

Budget lunch tip: Tote Fête Bakery has a divine little carry-out deli located on the corner of Albion and Lansing Streets in Mendocino; (707)937-3383. Choose from inexpensive items such as pesto pizza by the slice, twice-baked potatoes, house-made focaccia bread, and foil-wrapped barbecued-chicken sandwiches, then take your loot to the bakery's garden patio around the corner or head to the headlands for an impromptu picnic.

For a quick, healthy bite to eat while touring Mendocino, keep an eye peeled for Lu's Kitchen on Ukiah Street between Lansing and Ford Streets (look for a small shack with a few plastic tables around it). The mostly Mexican menu—burritos, tacos, salads, and quesadillas—is all vegetarian, organically grown, and a real deal at under $7; (707)937-4939.

was. *At the corner of Kasten and Albion Sts; (707)937-4323; 390 Kasten St, Mendocino; beer and wine; no credit cards; checks OK; brunch Sun, lunch Mon–Sat, dinner every day (closed in Jan); $$.*

MENDOCINO CAFE ☆

The Mendocino Cafe is one of the last vestiges of the Mendocino of the '60s. Everyone from nursing mothers to tie-dyed teenagers to Gap-clad couples queues up for the cafe's eclectic mix of Asian and Mexican specialties, served fresh and fast. The hands-down winner is the Thai burrito, a steamed flour tortilla filled with brown rice, sautéed vegetables, a healthy dash of the cafe's fresh chile sauce, and a choice of smoked chicken, pork, or beef. The hot Thai salad, spicy nachos, and barbecued half chicken are also good bets. Xenophobes needn't worry: There's also good ol' American food like salads, steaks, and fresh fish, as well as macaroni and cheese for the kids. If the weather's mild, grab a table on the deck. *At the corner of Lansing and Albion Sts, 10451 Lansing St, Mendocino; (707)937-2422; beer and wine; DC, DIS, MC, V; checks OK; brunch Sat–Sun, lunch Mon–Fri, dinner every day; $.*

LODGINGS

THE STANFORD INN BY THE SEA ■ BIG RIVER LODGE ☆☆☆☆

 Hats off to Joan and Jeff Stanford, the environmentally conscious couple who turned this parcel of prime coastal property and the former Big River Lodge into something more than a magnificent resort. It's a true ecosystem, a place where plants, animals, and people coexist in one of the most unforgettable lodging experiences in California. Upon entering the estate you'll see several tiers of raised garden beds, where a wide variety of vegetables, herbs, spices, and edible flowers are organically grown for local grocers and restaurants. Watching your every move as you proceed up the driveway are the Stanfords' extended family of 14 curious llamas, which, besides providing an endless source of entertainment, do their part in fertilizing the gardens. Guests may also bring along their own menagerie of critters, be they pet dogs, cats, parrots, or iguanas—it's all part of the Stanfords' commitment to animal equality. Also on the grounds is a gigantic, plant-filled greenhouse that encloses a grand swimming pool, sauna, and spa. And if all this doesn't provide you with enough diversions, there's also a mountain-bike and canoe shop on the property; you can borrow a bike and pedal along several tree-lined trails or slip into a canoe and paddle through the Big River's pristine estuaries.

The Comptche in Comptche-Ukiah Road is pronounced Comp-chee.

The inn's 23 rooms and 10 suites display a mixture of styles, from units with dark wood walls, deep burgundy furnishings, and four-poster beds to sun-streaked suites with pine-wood interiors, country antiques, and sleigh beds topped with down comforters. All of the rooms feature decks with ocean views, fireplaces or Waterford stoves, TVs with VCRs, telephones, and sitting areas. The isolated, utterly romantic River Cottage sits right on the water's edge—an ideal honeymooners' hideaway. A cooked-to-order full breakfast, served in the restaurant (see Restaurants, above), afternoon snacks, and evening wine and hors d'oeuvres are included in the price. *¾ mile S of Mendocino at Hwy 1 and Comptche-Ukiah Rd; (707)937-5615 or (800)331-8884; PO Box 487, Mendocino, CA 95460; stanford@stanfordinn.com; www.stanfordinn. com; AE, DC, DIS, MC, V; checks OK; $$$.*

AGATE COVE INN ✩✩✩

 Completely renovated in 1995 with light pine furnishings and "casual country" decor, the cottages at Agate Cove offer seclusion, privacy, and views that in-town B&Bs just can't match. All but one of the 10 cottages have good views of the ocean, king- or queen-size beds, down comforters, CD players, TVs with VCRs (and a free video and CD library), wood-burning stoves or gas fireplaces, and private decks. In the morning you'll find the *San Francisco Chronicle* on your doorstep, and you can peruse the paper at your leisure over a bountiful country breakfast in the main house's enclosed porch. *½ mile N of downtown; (707)937-0551 or (800)527-3111; 11201 N Lansing St, PO*

Geologists speculate
that within the next
50 to 150 years, a
sudden shift in the
Pacific Northwest's
offshore subduction
zone could cause
an earthquake any-
where between
Mendocino and
Vancouver Island
that would far sur-
pass the strongest
ever recorded in the
mainland United
States.

Box 1150, Mendocino, CA 95460; www.agatecove.com; AE,
MC, V; checks OK; $$$.

CYPRESS COVE ☆☆☆

 Hidden among the cypress trees that encircle the bluff
across the bay from Mendocino is Suzanne and Jim Hay's
Cypress Cove, a pair of bright, modern suites stacked
atop each other in a fashion that results in one of the best
views of the Mendocino Coast. Each abode is lavishly
appointed with a wood-burning fireplace, fully equipped
kitchen, spa tub, separate shower, stereo, and TV with a
VCR, but it's the stellar view from the large bay windows
and private deck that will make you fall instantly in love
with this place. Trust us: If you're looking for a romantic
weekend retreat, this is where you want to be. *On
Chapman Dr off Hwy 1 at the S end of Mendocino Bay
(call for directions); (707)937-1456 or (800)942-6300;
PO Box 303, Mendocino, CA 95460; jimbay@mcn.org;
www.cypresscove.com; MC, V; checks OK; $$$.*

JOSHUA GRINDLE INN ☆☆☆

The most authentic of Mendocino's many New England–style B&Bs, this masterpiece was built in 1879 by
the town's banker, Joshua Grindle. Startlingly white
against a backdrop of wind-whipped cypress trees, the
two-story beauty has lovely bay windows and a wraparound front porch trimmed with gingerbread arches.
There are five Early American rooms in the clapboard
house (including one with a whirlpool tub and fireplace),
two in the cottage, and three in an old-fashioned water
tower set back in the trees. Top picks are any of the cute
water-tower rooms or the Library Room with its country-
pine furnishings, four-poster bed, and 19th-century hand-
decorated tiles encircling the fireplace. All of the rooms
have sitting areas and private baths. The large front lawn
and garden, equipped with a pair of Adirondack chairs
and a redwood picnic table, is an ideal place to relax in
the sun. *At the E end of Little Lake Rd; (707)937-4143
or (800)GRINDLE; 44800 Little Lake Rd, PO Box 647,*

Mendocino, CA 95460; stay@joshgrin.com; www.joshgrin.com; MC, V; no checks; $$$.

JOHN DOUGHERTY HOUSE ★★

This classic saltbox is a wonderful example of why so many movies supposedly set in New England (*The Russians Are Coming, Summer of '42*) are actually filmed in Mendocino. The John Dougherty House features authentic Early Americana throughout: stenciled walls, Early American furniture, and all-cotton linens on the beds. Innkeepers Marion and David Wells have given each of the six rooms touches of individual charm, but your first choice should be one of the spacious two-room suites: the Starboard Cottage, Port Cottage, or everyone's favorite, Kit's Cabin—a small private cottage hidden in the flower garden. All of the rooms have a private bath, and most have a TV, a small refrigerator, and a wood-burning stove. An expansive breakfast including home-made bread and scones is served next to a crackling fire. *On Ukiah St just W of Kasten St; (707)937-5266 or (800)486-2104; 571 Ukiah St, PO Box 817, Mendocino, CA 95460; jdhbmw@mcn.org; www.innaccess.com/jdh/; MC, V; checks OK; $$$.*

MENDOCINO FARMHOUSE ★★

Once you emerge from deep within the redwood forest surrounding Marge and Bud Kamb's secluded estate, you know you're going to be very happy here. First to greet you is one of the Kambs' friendly farm dogs, followed by their can't-pet-me-enough cats, and finally the instantly likable Kambs themselves. All five rooms—filled with antique furnishings and fresh flowers from the surrounding English gardens—have private baths, queen- and king-size beds, and, if you listen carefully, echoes of the nearby ocean; all but one have fireplaces as well. A real country breakfast (straight from the chicken coop) is served each morning at tables-for-two in the sitting room, after which the dogs give free lessons in the meadow on how to loll around in the sunshine. *From Hwy 1 just S of Mendocino, turn E on Comptche–Ukiah Rd, drive*

1½ miles to Olson Lane, and turn left; (707)937-0241 or (800)475-1536; 43410 Comptche–Ukiah Rd, PO Box 247, Mendocino, CA 95460; mkamb@mcn.org; www.innaccess.com/ mfh/; MC, V; checks OK; $$.

MENDOCINO HOTEL AND RESTAURANT ☆☆

 The Mendocino Hotel, built in 1878, combines modern amenities—telephones, full bathrooms, room service—with turn-of-the-century Victorian furnishings to create a romantic yesteryear setting with today's creature comforts. The hotel's 51 rooms—all decorated with quality antiques, patterned wallpapers, and old prints and photos—range from inexpensive European-style rooms with shared baths to elaborate garden suites with fireplaces, king-size beds, balconies, and parlors. Suites 225A and 225B, on the hotel's third floor, have wonderful views of Mendocino Bay from their private balconies. Other favorites are the deluxe rooms with private baths, particularly rooms 213 and 224, which face the water. Breakfast and lunch are served downstairs in the verdant **Garden Cafe**. For dinner, chef Colleen Murphy's California-style cuisine, which might include pan-seared ahi tuna, double-baked pork chops, and prime rib au jus, is offered in the adjacent **Mendocino Hotel Restaurant**'s Victorian dining room. Budding sommeliers should inquire about the hotel's Winemaker Dinners, featured one Sunday a month from October through May. *On Main St between Lansing and Kasten Sts; (707)937-0511 or (800)548-0513; 45080 Main St, PO Box 587, Mendocino, CA 95460; mdohotel@mcn.org; full bar; AE, MC, V; checks OK; breakfast, lunch, dinner every day; $$$.*

JUG HANDLE CREEK FARM AND NATURE CENTER

Getting next to nature has never been more fun and financially feasible. For a mere $12 to $25 per night per person, you can afford to put up the whole family in this glorious old 1860 Victorian farmhouse. This isn't a hostel, so there's no sharing a room with strangers. Instead, you can opt for one of the private rooms in the farmhouse or the ultra-rustic cabins. In the morning you're welcome to make your own breakfast in the huge, fully equipped kitchen, then trek around the center's 39 wild acres or venture into the adjacent 1,000-acre State Reserve with its Ecological Staircase trail. Though the three bathrooms are shared, and pitching in for an hour of chores—chopping wood, weeding the garden, etc.—is part of the deal, most guests come to feel that all the money in the world couldn't buy such a positive communal experience. *Off Hwy 1 across from the Jug Handle State Reserve exit (look for a small white sign across from the N Caspar St exit); (707)964-4630; PO Box 17, Caspar, CA 95420; no credit cards; checks OK; $.* &

FORT BRAGG

Even Fort Bragg, a poetically proletarian neighbor of bourgeois Mendocino, hasn't been able to escape the relentless approach of gentrification. Originally built in 1855 as a military outpost to supervise the Pomo Indian Reservation, it's still primarily a logging and fishing town proud of its century-old timber-and-trawler heritage. But not a year goes by in Fort Bragg without yet another commercial fishing vessel being converted into a whale-watching boat (the ultimate insult), or an unemployed logger trading his chain saw for a set of carving knives.

On the first Friday of each month, Fort Bragg has an open house of sorts in all its downtown galleries. The free wine starts flowing around 6:30pm and has been known to keep flowing all night long.

Fort Bragg's two largest festivals best exemplify the sociological split: Paul Bunyan Days on Labor Day weekend feature a big Labor Day parade and log-cutting races, while the annual Whale Festival, held the third Saturday of March, includes ranger-led talks about the cetaceans, a Whale Run, and a beer and chowder tasting. Whether this is progress or not is debatable, but hey, at least you have a choice.

ACTIVITIES

Theater. Before the Warehouse Repertory Theatre opened its performance loft at the corner of Redwood and Harrison Streets in Fort Bragg, there was little in the way of quality evening entertainment in Mendocino County. What possessed this gaggle of professional actors and producers—most of whom came from much bigger cities with much bigger salaries—to make the pilgrimage to the Mendocino coast? Ashland II: If a stupid little town on the Oregon border can become world-renowned, they figured, surely Mendocino can. The result has been one of the hottest new theater groups in Northern California. Visit their Web site at www.theatre@warerep.org, or call the 24-hour reservation and information line at (707)961-2940 for a listing of performances ranging from modern comedies to Shakespearean classics. It's $10 well spenteth.

Seal Watching. One of the prettiest—and largest—public beaches on the Mendocino coast is MacKerricher State Park, located 3 miles north of Fort Bragg off Highway 1. The 8-mile shoreline is the perfect place to while away an afternoon, and it's free admission to boot. The highlight of the park is the Laguna Point Seal Watching Station, a fancy name for a small wood deck overlooking a gaggle of harbor seals sunning themselves on the rocks below; (707)937-5804.

Shopping. If you've visited all of Mendocino's boutiques and still haven't shrugged the shopping bug, head over to downtown Fort Bragg, which has enough shops and galleries—all within walking distance of each other—to keep you entertained for hours. Two dangerous places for a credit card are the Union Lumber Company Store, a work of redwood art housing several shops as well (corner of Main and Redwood Streets), and the numerous antique shops along Franklin Street between Laurel and Redwood (aka "Antiques Row").

Lettuce Rejoice. Long before "pesticide free" became the mantra of California growers, organic gardening was the modus operandi of local Mendocino farmers, who for years have catered to the desires of health- and quality-conscious clients such as Mendocino's Cafe Beaujolais. Although the produce is pricey, you can pay less for your luscious pesticide-free strawberries, asparagus, melons, and other goodies if you skip the middleman and buy directly from the growers. From May through October, they sell their wares to the public at the Mendocino Farmers Market on Fridays, noon to 2pm (Howard Street, between Main and Ukiah Streets), and at the Fort Bragg Farmers Market on Wednesdays, 3:30pm to 5:30pm (Laurel Street, between Franklin and McPherson Streets). Mendocino, (707)937-3322; Fort Bragg, (707)964-0536.

📷 **Train Ride.** If you've dragged your feet up and down too many coastal trails this vacation, give your tired dogs an extended rest aboard Fort Bragg's popular Skunk Train (so named because the odoriferous mix of diesel fuel and gasoline once used to power the train allowed you to smell it before you could see it). Depending on which day you depart, a steam-, diesel-, or electric-engine train will take you on a scenic 6- to 7-hour round-trip journey through the magnificent redwoods to the city of Willits and back again (or you can take the 3½-hour round-trip excursion to Northspur). Reservations are recommended, especially in summer. At 100 Laurel Street Depot, Fort Bragg; (707)964-6371.

Ricochet Ridge Ranch near Fort Bragg offers guided horseback rides (English- and Western-style) along the beach and into the redwoods. Call (707)964-PONY for more information.

🐟 🔭 **Whale Watching & Deep Sea Fishing.** If you're passing through between December and April, be sure to watch the migrating California gray whales and humpback whales make their annual appearances along the North Coast. Although they're visible from the bluffs, you can practically meet the 40-ton cetaceans face to face by boarding one of the whale-watching boats in Fort Bragg. The *Tally Ho II* charter offers two-hour tours for about $20 per adult, departing from the Old Fish House on North Harbor Drive in Fort Bragg; (707)964-2079. Another great way to get out on the ocean is to book a trip on one of the numerous fishing charters that depart from Noyo Harbor. For approximately $45 per person, which includes pole and bait, Telstar Charters will take you on a five-hour salmon- or rock-cod-fishing trip (whale-watching excursions are also available January through March). No experience is necessary, and gear, instruction, and fish-cleaning services are provided; (707)964-8770.

RESTAURANTS

NORTH COAST BREWING COMPANY ★★

If Norm Peterson of Cheers died and went to heaven, he'd end up here, permanently hunched over the bar within easy reach of his own ever-flowing tap of the North Coast Brewing Company's Scrimshaw Pilsner (a Gold Medal winner at the Great American Beer Fest, the Super Bowl of beer tastings). To his right would be a bowl of the

Fort Bragg's North
Coast Brewing Com-
pany, (707)964-
2739, offers free
tours of its brewery
at 455 N Main
Street. Register at
the brewery gift
shop in advance of
the daily 1:30pm
tour.

brewery's tangy Route 66 Chili, on his left a hearty plate of beef Romanov (made with braised sirloin tips, fresh mushrooms, and Russian Imperial Stout), and in front of his brewski would be a big platter of fresh Pacific oysters. This homey brew pub is the most happening place in town, especially at happy hour, when the bar and dark wood tables are occupied by boisterous locals. The pub is housed in a dignified, century-old redwood structure, which in previous lives has functioned as a mortuary, an annex to the local Presbyterian Church, an art studio, and administration offices for the College of the Redwoods. Beer is brewed on the premises, in large copper vats displayed behind plate glass. A pale ale, wheat beer, stout, pilsner, and a seasonal brew are always available, though first-timers should opt for the inexpensive four-beer sampler—or, heck, why not indulge in the eight-beer sampler?—to learn the ropes. You'll like the menu, too, which offers above-average pub grub as well as more exotic fare ranging from Mayan roast pork to seafood crêpes. *At the north end of Main St; (707)964-3400; 444 N Main St, Fort Bragg; beer and wine; DIS, MC, V; checks OK; lunch, dinner Tues–Sun; $$.* &

GARDENS GRILL ☆

The perpetually packed parking lot is a dead giveaway to the popularity of this relatively new restaurant, located in the Mendocino Coast Botanical Gardens (for information on the gardens, see Mendocino, above). The romantic alfresco seating on the elevated deck overlooking the flower gardens is the main attraction. Though the lengthy lunch menu leans heavily toward salads and sandwiches, it's the grill's fajitas that take first prize. Dinner entrees range from fresh local fish, such as pan-seared salmon with fennel ragout, to vegetarian dishes and applewood-grilled New York steak served with mashed potatoes. *In the Mendocino Coast Botanical Gardens, on Hwy 1 S of Fort Bragg; (707)964-7474; 18220 Hwy 1, Fort Bragg; beer and wine; MC, V; checks OK; brunch Sun, lunch Mon–Sat, dinner Thurs–Sat; $$.* &

PURPLE ROSE ☆

Three miles north of Fort Bragg in the small town of Cleone is a low flagstone building that isn't much to look at, but inside is some of the best Mexican food on the Mendocino coast. Although the Purple Rose is owned by gringos, the Latino sous chefs are wholly responsible for the traditional Mexican dishes—burritos, chimichangas, enchiladas, machacas, and tostadas, all packed with plenty of fresh chiles and cilantro. Everything here comes in huge portions, including the menudo (spicy tripe soup), the succulent chiles rellenos, and the tasty tomato-based Baja chowder with fresh swordfish and clams. The dark, tiny bar in the back, decorated with sombreros and velvet (what else?) paintings, serves the best margaritas in town. *On Hwy 1, 2 miles N of Fort Bragg; (707)964-6507; 24300 Hwy 1, Cleone; full bar; no credit cards; checks OK; dinner Wed–Sun; $.*

Bored and hungry? Chew on some tasty cod cheeks-'n'-chips from the deep fryers of Eureka Fisheries Inc. at Fort Bragg's Noyo Harbor while watching the sea lions vie for dock space. Open daily 11am–5:30pm; (707)964-1600.

THE RESTAURANT ☆

One of the oldest family-run restaurants on the coast, this small, unpretentious Fort Bragg landmark is known for its good dinners and Sunday brunches. The eclectic menu offers dishes from just about every corner of the planet: blackened New York strip steak, sweet-and-sour stir-fry, Livorno-style shellfish stew, and even scampi-style crab cakes. The comfortable booth section is the best place to sit if you want to keep an eye on the entertainment—courtesy of ebullient chef Jim Larsen—in the kitchen. *On Main St, 1 block N of Laurel St; (707)964-9800; 418 N Main St, Fort Bragg; beer and wine; MC, V; checks OK; brunch Sun, lunch Thurs–Fri, dinner Thurs–Tues; $$.*

VIRAPORN'S THAI CAFE ☆

When Viraporn Lobell opened this tiny Thai cafe in 1991, Asian-food aficionados on the North Coast breathed a communal sigh of relief. Born in northern Thailand, Viraporn attended cooking school and apprenticed in restaurants there before coming to the United States. After moving to the North Coast with her husband, Paul, she worked for a while at Mendocino's most popular restaurant, Cafe Beaujolais. A master at balancing the five traditional Thai flavors of hot, bitter, tart, sweet, and salty, Viraporn works wonders with refreshing Thai classics such as spring rolls, satays, phad Thai, lemongrass soup, and a wide range of curry dishes. *Off Hwy 1, across from PayLess; (707)964-7931; 500 S Main St, Fort Bragg; beer and wine; no credit cards; checks OK; lunch Mon, Wed–Fri, dinner Wed–Mon; $.*

LODGINGS

GREY WHALE INN ☆☆

Wide doorways and sloped halls are the only vestiges of this popular inn's previous life as the town hospital. Owners Colette and John Bailey have successfully transformed this stately four-story building into one of the more comfortable and distinctive inns on the coast. Decorated with quilts, heirlooms, and antiques, the 14 large guest rooms have private baths and wonderful views of the town or sea. Reserve one of the two penthouse rooms: Sunrise offers a view of the town, pretty wicker furniture, and a double whirlpool bath, while Sunset opens onto a private deck overlooking the ocean. Another good choice is the spacious Campbell Suite, which comes with a marble gas-log fireplace, a TV with a VCR, a microwave oven, and a refrigerator. There's also a large rec room with a pool table and a TV. The full buffet breakfast (with trays for carrying your food back to bed, if you prefer) is

COMFORT CAMPING

Do you like to camp along the coast but hate the hassle of pitching tents, lighting lanterns, and picking grains of sand out of your food? Here's the solution: Call Adventure in Camping at (800)417-7771 and ask them to set up one of their self-contained, fully equipped trailers for you and your friends. You select the seaside campground (it must be in the Fort Bragg–Mendocino area), and they take care of the rest. There's a two-night minimum rental requirement, and prices start at about $73 a night—a real deal for beachfront property.

included in the rates. *At the corner of Main and 1st Sts; (707)964-0640 or (800)382-7244; 615 N Main St, Fort Bragg, CA 95437; gwhale@mcn.org; www.innaccess.com/gwi; AE, DIS, MC, V; checks OK; $$.* ₺

BEACHCOMBER MOTEL

 If all those fancy B&Bs in Mendocino are way out of your price range, the Beachcomber Motel has just what you're looking for. Okay, so the rooms aren't exactly reeking with ambience, but they are certainly spacious, comfortable, and equipped with the basic necessities such as cable TV and private bathrooms. Not that it matters much, since you'll be spending most of your time on the huge back deck that overlooks the cool blue Pacific (at sunset it's a veritable postcard view). Directly across from the motel is MacKerricher State Park's miles of beaches and dunes. Those in the know get a room with a kitchenette, stock up on groceries, and make use of the barbecue area. Rates range from $59 for a standard room with no ocean view to $195 for the deluxe suite with king bed, hot tub, fireplace, and ocean view. Pets are welcome, but will cost you an extra $10. A huge 49-room expansion is scheduled to open in 1999. *On Hwy 1 at the far N end of Fort Bragg; (800)400-7873 or (707)964-2402; 1111 N Main St, Fort Bragg, CA 95437; AE, DIS, MC, V; checks OK; $$.* ₺

WESTPORT

If you've made it this far north, you're either lost or determined to drive the full length of Highway 1. If it's the latter, then you'd best stock up on a sandwich or two at the Westport Community Store & Deli, at 37001 North Highway 1, Westport, (707)964-2872, because you still have a loooong way to go.

LODGINGS

DEHAVEN VALLEY FARM AND RESTAURANT ★★★

This remote 1875 Victorian farmhouse, with its sublime rural setting and access to a secluded beach, comes complete with a barnyard menagerie of horses, sheep (including one that thinks it's a horse), goats, and donkeys. If the animals aren't enough to keep you amused, try a game of croquet or horseshoes, do a little bird-watching or horseback riding, or take a meditative soak in the hot tub set high on a hill overlooking the ocean. The inviting parlor has deep, comfortable couches, while the five guest rooms in the house and the three nearby cottages are decorated with colorful comforters and rustic antiques; some even have fireplaces. In the morning, you'll wake to such treats as apple pancakes or potato-artichoke frittata. The small *DeHaven Valley Farm Restaurant* offers a commendable prix-fixe four-course menu that might include entrees like roasted pork tenderloin with apple horseradish or seafood baked in filo dough with roasted pepper aioli, and a killer apple strudel for dessert. *On Hwy 1, 1.7 miles N of Westport; (707)961-1660; 39247 Hwy 1, Westport, CA 95488; www.dehaven-valley-farm.com; beer and wine; MC, V; checks OK; dinner every Sat and any day 6 or more people make a reservation; $$.*

HOWARD CREEK RANCH ☆☆☆

Located off a remote stretch of Highway 1 near the tiny town of Westport, this isolated 40-acre ranch appeals to travelers who really want to get away from it all. You'll revel in the peace and quiet of this rustic retreat, which Mendocino County has designated a historic site. For more than two decades, proprietors Sally and Charles Grigg have been renting out three cabins, four guest rooms in the farmhouse, and four rooms in the renovated carriage barn. Set back just a few hundred yards from an ocean beach, the farmhouse and barn are on opposite sides of Howard Creek, connected by (among other routes) a 75-foot-long swinging footbridge. The rooms in the farmhouse feature separate sitting areas, antiques, and homemade quilts, while the barn units—each one handcrafted by Charles Grigg, a master builder with a penchant for skylights—have curly-grain redwood walls and Early American collectibles. The separate Beach House, with its freestanding fireplace, skylights, king-size bed, large deck, and whirlpool tub, is a great romantic getaway. A hot tub and sauna are perched on the side of a hill, as are Sally's guardian cows, sheep, llama, and horses. In the morning, Sally rings the breakfast bell to alert her guests that it's eatin' time—and the fare is definitely worth getting out of bed for. Note: Pet dogs are welcome with prior approval. *On Hwy 1, 3 miles N of Westport; (707)964-6725; PO Box 121, Westport, CA 95488; www.HowardCreekRanch.com; AE, MC, V; checks OK; $$.*

THE REDWOOD COAST

Considering that California's Redwood Coast contains the most spectacular coastal forests in the world—including the world's tallest tree—it's surprising how few tourists venture north of Mendocino to get there. Perhaps it's the myth that the upper coast is permanently socked in with rain and fog, and that the only places to eat or sleep are greasy diners and cheap motels.

Like most myths, of course, this isn't true (at least it's no longer true). Granted, the coastal weather can be a bit soggy at times, but the fog usually burns off by the afternoon, and the rain—well, bring an umbrella; it's the price you pay for vacationing among the thirsty redwood giants.

And while there are no Hyatts or Hiltons this far north, the Redwood Coast offers something even better: a wealth of small, personable inns and bed and breakfasts run by proprietors who bend over backwards to make your stay as enjoyable as possible. The food? Include the northern region's penchant for organic gardening with a year-round supply of just-off-the-boat seafood, and you have the ingredients for remarkably fresh—and healthy—gourmet cuisine.

All this, combined with the region's beautiful scenery and absence of crowds, has made the Redwood Coast one of the premier—and relatively unknown—tourist destinations in California.

THE LOST COAST

The Lost Coast is proof that if you don't build it, they won't come. What wasn't built between Ferndale and Rockport was a coastal road: the geography of the 90-mile stretch—steep mountain ranges abutting rocky shore—wouldn't allow it. The result is the last untamed and undeveloped region of the California coast, a place where two cars following each other are considered a convoy and there are more cows lying on the beach than people (seriously). Popular with campers, backpackers, and fishers, the Lost Coast is beginning to see a hint of gentrification at its only seaside town, Shelter Cove. Otherwise, the land is mainly inhabited by ranchers, retirees, and alternative lifestylers (aka hippies), the latter of which have made the Lost Coast one of the most productive pot-growing regions in the world.

ACTIVITIES

 Scenic Drive. The Lost Coast makes for a fantastic day trip by car. Of the three entrance points into the region— Garberville, Humboldt Redwoods State Park, and Ferndale—the most scenic route is through the state park. Take the State Park turnoff on Highway 101 and follow the Mattole Road all the way to Ferndale and back onto Highway 101. The three- to four-hour, 75-mile drive is incredible, transporting you through lush redwood forests, across golden meadows, and along miles of deserted beaches (well, if you don't count the cows). Be sure to start with a full tank, and bring a jacket if you plan to venture anywhere on foot.

Avenue of the Giants. Touristy to no end but always worth the detour is the 31-mile stretch of old Highway 101 known as the Avenue of the Giants. The narrow, paved road—which runs parallel to Highway 101 between Phillipsville and Pepperwood—winds through the world's largest concentration of coastal redwoods. Described by John Steinbeck as "ambassadors from another time," some of these trees have been around for 1,500 years, growing to heights of 350 feet. The best roadside attraction along the Avenue is Founders Grove, 4 miles north of the Humboldt Redwood State Park Visitors Center in Burlington; (707)946-2263. Take the half-mile, self-guided loop trail that passes by the Dyerville Giant, which, before it fell on March 24, 1991, was considered the "champion" coastal redwood at 364 feet tall, 53 feet in circumference, and weighing in at nearly a million pounds. That's one big tree.

RESTAURANTS

COVE RESTAURANT ★★

 At the north end of a small runway for private planes, this rather remote restaurant—selected by Private Pilot magazine as one of the nation's premier fly-in lunch spots—is situated in an A-frame beach house with two-story-high picture windows, an outdoor dining area, and a spectacular view of this untamed region of California known as the Lost Coast. The menu's offerings are wide

"What the. . . ?" is usually the initial response from tourists when they get a load of the 50-foot, 30,000-pound statue of Paul Bunyan and his azure sidekick, Babe. Welcome to Trees of Mystery, folks, the roadside freak show of the redwoods. Enter at your own risk. On the Redwood Highway, off Highway 101. Open daily 9am to 6pm; (800)638-3389.

A seed taken from the Dyerville Giant the day it fell was nurtured in a greenhouse and planted where the Giant now lies. It is hoped that the genes that created the champion of coastal redwoods will create yet another.

ranging and well prepared: charbroiled steak cut to order, Cajun-style fish (we're talking right out of the water), grilled chicken, juicy hamburgers, and piles of fresh shellfish. All meals are served with a creamy clam chowder, a shrimp or green salad, and house-made bread. Desserts range from fresh fruit pies (snatch a slice of the wonderfully tart wild huckleberry if it's available) to chocolate mousse and a cheesecake. *On Wave Dr off Lower Pacific Dr; (707)986-1197; 210 Wave Dr, Shelter Cove; full bar; MC, V; local checks only; lunch, dinner Thurs–Sun; $$.*

LODGINGS

SHELTER COVE OCEAN INN ⭐⭐

 Snoozing seals, grazing deer, and migrating whales are just some of the sights you'll see in Shelter Cove, the Lost Coast's only oceanside community. Once you leave Highway 101 in Garberville, prepare to navigate along 24 miles of steep, twisting tarmac that passes through rocky grasslands and patches of forest before reaching the cove (good brakes are a must). At the end of the journey you'll reach the Shelter Cove Ocean Inn, a handsome Victorian-style facility built smack-dab on the shoreline. The inn, which is popular with recreational pilots who can park their planes within walking distance, offers two spacious suites with sitting rooms and whirlpool tubs. Two smaller rooms upstairs have private baths and balconies. All rooms have an ocean view, but the panorama from the suites is definitely worth the extra expense. Since the B&B is in such a remote location, a home-cooked breakfast, lunch, and dinner may be delivered to your room upon request. Serious R&R is the theme here: Lie on the sun deck overlooking the ocean, play a round of golf across the street, or walk to the nearby black sand beach, 'cause there ain't nothin' to do around here except relax. *From Shelter Cove Rd, turn right on Upper Pacific Dr, left on Lower Pacific Dr, then right on Dolphin Dr; (707)986-7161; 148 Dolphin Dr, Shelter Cove, CA 95589; AE, MC, V; checks OK; $$.* ♿

LOST INN BED AND BREAKFAST ☆

As you wind along Old Mattole Road through the sleepy hamlet of Petrolia, keep a lookout for an old green tractor with a hand-painted sign that reads, "Welcome! You have just found the Lost Inn." Once you've spotted it, drive up the circular driveway lined with flowers, fruit trees, and rustic antiques, and prepare to be greeted by a friendly entourage of cats, dogs, and chickens. They belong to Gail and Phil Franklin, the friendly keepers of this remote country inn, the only B&B in the Mattole Valley. There are just two guest rooms here: a large two-room suite with a queen bed, glassed-in porch, and private entrance (parties of three or four also may rent an adjoining suite), and a much smaller room with a queen bed and couch. Breakfast, including eggs from the Franklins' chickens and organic fruit from their trees, is served either in your room or on the porch. Solitude is this inn's selling point (you can't get any more away-from-it-all without a backpack) and it comes at a very reasonable price. You can even bring your pooch, and the Pacific Ocean is only 5 miles away. *On Old Mattole Rd, 1 block from the Petrolia General Store; (707)629-3394; PO Box 161, Petrolia, CA 95558; no credit cards; checks OK; $.*

"Grow pot, mostly. And collect welfare. I'll deliver four, five checks to a single address."
—Petrolia postman, when asked what people do around here for a living

Two of the best-selling items at Lost Coast hardware stores are plastic piping and camouflage netting.

The Lost Coast community of Petrolia was named for California's first commercial oil well, drilled 3 miles east of town in the 1860s.

FERNDALE

Even if Ferndale isn't on your itinerary, it's worth a detour off Highway 101 to stroll for an hour or two down its colorful Main Street, browsing through the art galleries, gift shops, and cafes that are strangely reminiscent of Disneyland's "old town." Ferndale, however, is for real, and hasn't changed much since it was the agricultural center of Northern California in the late 1800s. In fact, the entire town is a National Historic Landmark because of its abundance of well-preserved Victorian storefronts, farmhouses, and homes. What really distinguishes Ferndale from the likes of Eureka and Crescent City, however, is the fact that Highway 101 doesn't pass through it; the difference—no cheesy motels, liquor stores, or fast-food chains—is remarkable.

One of the largest abalones ever recorded was harvested at Shelter Cove. The shell is on display in a sporting goods store in Garberville.

For information on
Ferndale's
upcoming event
and activities, visit
the town's Web site
at www.victorian-
ferndale.org/
chamber.

ACTIVITIES

The Way It Was. For a trip back in time, view the village's interesting memorabilia—working crank phones, logging equipment, a blacksmith shop—at the Ferndale Museum, 515 Shaw Street at Third Street; (707)786-4466. Not officially a museum but close enough is the Golden Gate Mercantile at 421 Main Street. Part of the general store hasn't been remodeled (or restocked) in 50 years, giving you the feeling that you're walking through some sort of time capsule or movie set. Far less historic but equally engrossing are the previous pedal-powered entries in the World Championship Great Arcata to Ferndale Cross-Country Kinetic Sculpture Race on display at the Kinetic Sculpture Museum, 780 Main Street at Shaw Street. The dusty, funky museum is unlike anything you've ever seen.

Ferndale's own
little forest, Russ
Park, has miles of
nature trails
leading through
groves of fir and
Sitka spruce. From
the southwest end
of Main Street, take
Ocean Avenue
southeast half a
mile to the gravel
trailhead parking
area; a few yards
up the trail is a
map of the park.

Coastal Drive. Reserve an hour of your day in Ferndale for a leisurely drive along scenic Centerville Road. The 5-mile excursion starts at the west end of Main Street downtown and passes through several ranches and dairy farms on the way to the Centerville Beach County Park. If you continue beyond the park and past the retired Naval Facility, you'll be rewarded with an incredible view of the Lost Coast to the south. On the way back, keep an eye out for Fern Cottage, a restored 1865 Victorian farmhouse built by the late state senator Joseph Russ, one of the first Ferndale settlers. Tours of the farmhouse are by appointment only; call caretaker Greg Martin (who's also an accomplished organic gardener) at (707)786-4835.

Show Time. In keeping with its National Historic Landmark status, Ferndale has no movie theaters. Rather, it has something better: the Ferndale Repertory Theatre. Converted in 1972 from a movie theater, the 267-seat house—located at 447 Main Street downtown—hosts live performances by actors from all over Humboldt County. The revolving performances run pretty much year-round and range from musicals to comedies, dramas, and mysteries. Tickets are reasonably priced and, due to the popularity of the shows, reservations are advised; (707)786-5483.

RESTAURANTS

CURLEY'S GRILL

Longtime restaurateur and Ferndale resident Curley Tait decided it was finally time to open his own business, so in April 1995 he filled the 460 Main Street vacancy (former home of the Bibo and Bear Restaurant) with Curley's Grill, and it's been a hit ever since. The reason? Curley doesn't fool around: The prices are fair, the servings are generous, the food is good, and the atmosphere is bright and cheerful. Sure bets are the roast pork loin with rosemary honey glaze; the grilled polenta with Italian sausage, fresh mushrooms, and sage-laden tomato sauce; or the barbecued baby-back ribs—all in the $16 to $17 range. Vegetarians and penny-pinchers can opt for the $6 garden burger. Indulge in Curley's house-made breads and desserts, too. On sunny afternoons, request a seat on the shaded back patio. *On Main St between Washington and Brown Sts; (707)786-9696; 460 Main St, Ferndale; beer and wine; DIS, MC, V; checks OK; lunch, dinner every day; $.* &

STAGE DOOR CAFE   ☆

Ferndale's top soup-and-sandwich shop is the tiny Stage Door Cafe, run by Barbara and Jerry Murry. Barbara does most of the cooking, while Jerry—a real character—takes the orders and directs the foot traffic. Daily specials are posted in the front window; if one of them happens to be Orange Wonder soup, the Ferndale tradition requires that you order a bowl of this puréed concoction, made from a secret recipe (hint: carrots are the key ingredient). Other top picks are the Cloverjack Melt (locally made Jack cheese, bacon, and a fried or poached egg layered on sourdough toast), Ferndale scramble, and honey-almond granola topped with fresh fruit. If you can't find a seat inside, order your food to go and dine alfresco at an outside table or on one of the many benches lining the town's main drag. *On Main St next to the Ferndale Theatre; (707)786-4675; 451 Main St, Ferndale; no alcohol; no credit cards; checks OK; breakfast, lunch Thurs–Mon; $.*

The owner of Ferndale Books at 405 Main Street leaves an assortment of used books in front of the store each night for after-hours browsers. Her customers pay the old-fashioned way: on the honor system, by leaving their money outside the door.

LODGINGS

THE GINGERBREAD MANSION ✦✦✦

The awe-inspiring grande dame of Ferndale, this peach-and-yellow Queen Anne inn is a lavish blowout for Victoriana buffs. Gables, turrets, English gardens, and architectural gingerbread galore have made it one of the most-photographed buildings in Northern California. The mansion has been through several reincarnations since 1899, including stints as a private residence, a hospital, a rest home, an apartment building, and even an American Legion hall before Ken Torbert converted it into a B&B in 1983. All 10 guest rooms have queen- or king-size beds and private baths. The Fountain Suite boasts a grand view of Ferndale and the garden, twin claw-footed tubs for side-by-side bubble baths, a canopied bed, a fireplace, and a fainting couch. The corner Rose Suite has a wonderful view of Ferndale village through a cutout gingerbread veranda, stained-glass windows, two fireplaces, hanging plants, and a vast, mirrored bathroom that's as big as the bedroom. For the ultimate in luxury, though, reserve the new Empire Suite, an orgy of marble and columns with twin fireplaces and a lavish bathing area. In the morning all guests are treated to a sumptuous breakfast in the formal dining room that overlooks the garden. An extravagant afternoon tea is served in one of five parlors, each handsomely furnished with Queen Anne, Eastlake, and Renaissance Revival antiques. *On Berding St at Brown St, 1 block S of Main St; (707)786-4000 or (800)952-4136; 400 Berding St, PO Box 40, Ferndale, CA 95536; kenn@humboldt1.com; www.gingerbread-mansion.com; AE, MC, V; checks OK; $$$.*

THE SHAW HOUSE BED AND BREAKFAST INN ✦✦✦

This Carpenter Gothic beauty, the oldest house in Ferndale, is modeled after the titular manse of Nathaniel Hawthorne's *House of the Seven Gables*. It was built in 1854 by Ferndale founder Seth Louis Shaw and is listed on the National Register of Historic Places. Owners Norma and Ken Bessingpas meticulously restored the house and filled it with books, photographs, baskets, antiques, and all manner of memorabilia; the couple also added a gazebo and a fish pond to the inn's well-tended acre. Each of the six guest rooms has its own bath (although three of the bathrooms are down the hall), and most have bathtubs and showers. Three units—the Honeymoon Suite, the Garden Room, and the Wisteria Room—have balconies overlooking the garden, and the Shaw Room, under the central gable, features the original bed Shaw and his bride slept in during their honeymoon (though the mattress is new, of course!). In the morning, guests feast on Norma's homemade breakfast fare, which may include oven-baked Dutch babies and cheddar French toast served with dried-fruit syrup specked with apricots and currants. After breakfast, ride around town on a vintage bicycle from Ken's collection. *On Main St, just E of downtown Ferndale; (707)786-9958 or (800)557-SHAW; 703 Main St, PO Box 1125, Ferndale, CA 95536; AE, MC, V; checks OK; $$$.*

EUREKA

One can only wonder what the city's founders were thinking of when they named this town after the popular gold-mining expression "Eureka!" (Greek for "I have found it!"). They certainly never found any gold in these parts. Perhaps the Eureka of yesteryear offered more to get excited about, but nowadays the North Coast's largest city has little to offer the visitor except a slew of cheap (and mostly dingy) motels, fast-food restaurants, gas stations, and a somewhat entertaining Old Town garnished with stately Victorian homes and storefronts. Most travelers take advantage of Eureka's budget prices and bunk down for the night, then head north to Arcata and the Lost Coast for more stimulating explorations. There are, however, a handful of exceptional hotels, restaurants, and shops here, particularly the Carter Hotel and its restaurant. Otherwise, you're better off spending your time up the road in Arcata, which is about half the size of Eureka but has twice the appeal.

One of the finest examples of Victorian architecture anywhere is the gabled and turreted Carson Mansion, built in 1885 for lumber baron William Carson, and now the home of a snooty private club. Mere commoners, however, are allowed to gawk from the sidewalk at the most-photographed Victorian house in America. At the corner of 2nd and M Streets in Old Town Eureka.

ACTIVITIES

 Native American Art. History buffs will want to stroll through the Clarke Memorial Museum, which has one of the top Native American displays in the state; more than 1,200 examples of Hupa, Yurok, and Karuk basketry, dance regalia, and stonework are showcased (240 E Street at 3rd Street; (707)443-1947). A block up the street there's more Native American artwork—including quality silver jewelry—at the Indian Art & Gift Shop, which sells much of its wares at surprisingly reasonable prices; 241 F Street at 3rd Street; (707)445-8451.

Beet of a Different Grower. If purple potatoes, cylindrical beets, and other fancy foods are on your shopping list, then you're in luck, because you'll find them at the farmer's markets held weekly May through October in Eureka and Arcata. Most of the produce is grown along the local Eel and Trinity Rivers, and it's sold at bargain prices at Arcata Plaza on Saturday from 9am to 1pm, at Eureka Mall (on Highway 101 at the south end of Eureka) on Thursday from 10am to 1pm, and at Eureka's Old Town on Tuesday from 10am to 1pm.

Better yet, why not beet them to the punch and spend the day picking produce directly from the North Coast's small farms. Call the North Coast Growers Association at (707)441-9699 for a free copy of the *Farmers Market Directory & Farm Trails Guide*, a map and listing of 13 local family-run farms that encourage visitors to drop by and purchase their products—vegetables, fruit, herbs, teas, flowers, plants, etc.—directly from the dirt.

Bay Cruise. For a surprisingly interesting and amusing perspective on the history of Humboldt Bay, take a bay cruise on skipper Leroy Zerlang's *Madaket*, the oldest passenger vessel on the Pacific coast. The 75-minute narrated tour departs daily from the foot of C Street in Eureka, and gets progressively better after your second or third cocktail. For more information, call Humboldt Bay Harbor Cruise at (707)445-1910.

Wildlife Refuge. More than 200 species of birds feed, rest, or nest in the Humboldt Bay National Wildlife Refuge, a bird-watcher's paradise that is open to the public year-round for hiking, bird-watching, boating, and fishing. The 2,200 acres of wetlands, marshes, mud flats, and open bay are accessible by two short, easy foot trails. To get there, take the Hookton Road exit off Highway 101 south of Eureka and turn west on Ranch Road. A free guide to the refuge is available at the Ranch Road entrance. For more information, call (707)733-5406.

RESTAURANTS

RESTAURANT 301

The highly acclaimed Restaurant 301, located on the first floor of Hotel Carter, is easily the finest restaurant north of Mendocino, and a must-visit if you're venturing this far north. It's the combination of first-rate cuisine, service, and a phenomenal wine list—owner Mark Carter recently won *Wine Spectator*'s Grand Award, bestowed annually to only four recipients in the world—that garner a four-star status. Executive Chef Christi Carter takes great pride in using ultra-fresh ingredients, including herbs and edible flowers from the hotel's gardens and seafood direct from local fisheries. Diners, seated in the large, airy, and warmly lit dining room, may order either à la carte or via the Discovery Menu, a highly recommended prix-fixe five-course dinner menu paired with suggested wines by the glass for each course. Dinner might begin with an artichoke, green lentil, and fennel salad followed by a warm chèvre cake appetizer, then on to a roasted chanterelle tian, followed by a main entree of grilled duck breast served with a seasonal fruit and zinfandel sauce. Finish the evening with outstanding passion fruit crème *chiboust*, and you'll understand why most of the clientele are repeat customers. *At the corner of 3rd and L Sts in Old Town; (707)444-8062 or (800)404-1390; 301 L St, Eureka; full bar; AE, DC, DIS, MC, V; checks OK; breakfast (by reservation only for nonguests), dinner every day; $$$.* &

LOS BAGELS

Simply put, this is Eureka's best bagel shop. For more details, see the review of the Los Bagels branch in Arcata. *2nd St at E St in Old Town Eureka; (707)442-8525; 403 2nd*

If you need a good book at a great price, stop by the Booklegger, a marvelous Old Town bookstore where thousands of used paperbacks (especially mysteries, westerns, and science fiction) are stocked, as well as children's books and cookbooks; 402 2nd Street, Eureka; (707)445-1344.

St, Eureka; no alcohol; no credit cards; local checks only; breakfast, lunch Wed–Mon; $. &

TOMASO'S TOMATO PIES ✩

This family-style Italian pizza parlor reeks so divinely of baked garlic and olive oil that you can smell it a block away. Top of the list of Tomaso's favored fare are the calzone and the spinach pies, both guaranteed to make garlic lovers (and their dining partners) swoon. Be prepared for a 30-minute wait—it's the price you pay for such fresh ingredients. Other popular plates include the chicken cannelloni and the square pizza with a wholewheat crust. For a proper Italian finale, order a cremosa: a blend of milk, soda water, and whipped cream infused with a fruity Torani Italian syrup. *On E St between 2nd and 3rd Sts in Old Town; (707)445-0100; 216 E St, Eureka; beer and wine; AE, DIS, MC, V; local checks only; lunch Mon–Sat, dinner every day; $. &*

SAMOA COOKHOUSE ✩

Visiting the Eureka area without a stop at the Samoa Cookhouse is like visiting Paris without seeing the Eiffel Tower. This venerable dining spot is the last surviving cookhouse in the West (it's been in operation for more than a century) and a Humboldt County institution, where guests are served lumber-camp–style in an enormous barnlike building at long tables covered with checkered cloths. Few decisions are required—just sit down, and the food will come until you say uncle. Breakfast typically features sausages, biscuits, scrambled eggs, and potatoes as well as a choice of French toast, hash browns, or pancakes (not to mention all the coffee and OJ you can drink). Lunch and dinner include potatoes and the meat of the day, which might be ham, fried chicken, pork chops, roast beef, barbecued chicken, or fish. Mind you, the food isn't great (except for the delicious bread, which is baked on the premises), but there's plenty of it. And just when you think you're about to burst, along comes the fresh-baked pie. After your meal, spend a few minutes waddling through the adjoining logging museum.

From Hwy 101 take the Samoa exit (R St) in downtown Eureka, cross the Samoa Bridge, turn left on Samoa Rd, then left on Cookhouse Rd; (707)442-1659; Cookhouse Rd, Samoa; no alcohol; AE, DIS, MC, V; checks OK; breakfast, lunch, dinner every day; $.

LODGINGS

HOTEL CARTER ■ CARTER HOUSE ■ THE CARTER COTTAGE ■ THE BELL COTTAGE ☆☆☆☆

What is now one of the finest accommodation-and-restaurant complexes on the upper North Coast started serendipitously in 1982, the year Eureka residents Mark and Christi Carter converted their newly built dream home—a four-story, five-bedroom Victorian reproduction—into an inn. Not only did they turn out to be some of the area's best hosts, but the Carters actually reveled in their newfound innkeeper roles. Once word got around that the Carter House was the place to vacation, they were flooded with folks who wanted a room. In 1986, Mark, a former carpenter, added the 23-room Hotel Carter across the street (its design is based on the blueprints of a historic 19th-century Eureka hotel), and four years later he refurbished the Bell Cottage, an adjacent turn-of-the-century Victorian mansion built in 1890. The crème de la crème, however, is the new Carter Cottage, a small home that has been converted—at considerable expense—into one of the most sumptuous lodgings in Northern California, a mini-mansion replete with two fireplaces, a chef's kitchen, a large bathroom with a whirlpool tub for two, a private deck, and even an honor wine cellar.

The quartet of inn, hotel, and two cottages offers a contrasting array of luxury accommodations, ranging from rooms with classic Victorian dark-wood antique furnishings in the Carter House and Bell Cottage to a softer, brighter, more contemporary decor in the hotel and Carter Cottage. The decor varies from guest room to guest room, but some boast marble fireplaces, imported antiques, two-person whirlpool bathtubs with views of

Thirsty? Stroll over to the always lively Lost Coast Brewery for a fresh pint of Alleycat Amber Ale and a fresh rock cod taco. At 617 4th Street, between F and G Streets, in downtown Eureka; (707)445-4480.

Guests and nonguests are invited to tour the Hotel Carter's 10,000-square-foot organic garden, where more than 300 varieties of herbs, vegetables, fruits, and edible flowers are grown exclusively for the hotel restaurant. Tours are generally from 4pm to 6pm daily and advance notice is required; call (707)444-8062.

the marina, immense four-poster beds, double-headed showers, entertainment centers, and kitchens. Amenities include baskets filled with wine and specialty foods, concierge services, overnight dry cleaning and shoe shining, a videotape and CD library, tea-and-cookie bedtime service, and wine and hors d'oeuvres in the evening. Also included in the room rate is an outstanding full breakfast featuring fresh-baked tarts, muffins, cinnamon buns, breads, fresh fruit, an ever-changing array of entrees, juices, and strong coffee. The highly acclaimed Restaurant 301 (see Restaurants, above), is located on the first floor of Hotel Carter and is widely regarded as one of the North Coast's top restaurants. *At the corner of L and 3rd Sts in Old Town Eureka; (707)444-8062 or (800)404-1390; 301 L St, Eureka, CA 95501; carter52@ carterhouse.com; www.carterhouse.com; full bar; AE, DC, DIS, MC, V; checks OK; breakfast (by reservation only for nonguests), dinner every day; $$$.* &

AN ELEGANT VICTORIAN MANSION ☆☆☆

This inn is a jewel—a National Historic Landmark lovingly maintained by owners Doug "Jeeves" Vieyra and Lily Vieyra. If you're a fan of Victoriana, be prepared for a mind-blowing experience. Each of the four guest rooms upstairs has furnishings reflecting a different period, place, or personage. The light-filled Lillie Langtry Room, named for the famed 19th-century chanteuse who once sang at the local Ingomar Theatre, has an impressive four-poster oak bed and a private bath down the hall. The French country-style Governor's Suite sleeps up to three, has a private bath, and offers a distant view of the bay. The Vieyras have an incredible array of old (1905–1940) movies and a collection of popular music from the same era, which guests often enjoy in the common room. Then there's Doug's obsession with antique autos—he's frequently seen motoring (with guests on board) in his 1928 Model A Ford or one of his other two old Fords. Doug and Lily are incredibly attentive hosts; they'll lend you bicycles, show you the way to their Finnish sauna and Victorian flower garden, pore over road maps with you, and make your dinner reservations. Lily, trained as a French chef (and Swedish masseuse), prepares a morning feast. *At the corner of C and 14th Sts; (707)444-3144; 1406 C St, Eureka, CA 95501; www.bnbcity.com/inns/20016; MC, V; no checks; $$.*

BAYVIEW MOTEL ☆

The Bayview Motel is Eureka's top budget motel and so squeaky-clean you could eat off the floor. Perched on a knoll high above noisy Highway 101, the Bayview *does* have a view of the bay, but you have to look real hard past the industrial park to see it. Each of the 17 "mini-suites" has a private bath, remote-control TV, and queen-size bed. The motel's best views are actually of the lovely, meticulously manicured lawn and garden. If you feel like splurging, request a room with a whirlpool tub or fireplace. Family units are also available. *From Hwy 101, take the Henderson St exit at the S end of town and follow the signs; (707)442-1673; 2844 Fairfield St, Eureka, CA 95501; AE, DIS, MC, V; no checks; $.*

ARCATA

Home to the California State University at Humboldt, a liberal arts school, Arcata is like most college towns in that everyone tends to lean towards the left. Environmentalism, artistry, and good beads and bagels are indispensable elements of the Arcatan philosophy, as is a cordial disposition towards tourists, making Arcata one of the most interesting and visitor-friendly towns along the North Coast. The heart of this oceanside community is Arcata Plaza, where a statue of President McKinley stands guard over the numerous shops and cafes housed in Arcata's historic buildings. It's been said that a walk around the plaza—with its perfectly manicured lawns, ubiquitous hot dog vendor, and well-dressed retirees sitting on spotless benches—is enough to restore anyone's faith in small-town America.

ACTIVITIES

 Community Forest. A two-minute drive east of downtown Arcata on 11th Street will take

"The Arcata Marsh and Wildlife sanctuary is a must-see. It's a great place to go for a walk or jog, particularly during sunset or for some early-morning bird-watching."
—Arcata's former mayor, Sam Pennisi

You can see (and touch!) 3-billion-year-old fossils and view various California flora and fauna exhibits at Humboldt State University's Natural History Museum at 13th and G Streets in downtown Arcata; (707)826-4479.

you to Arcata's beloved Redwood Park, a beautiful grass expanse—ideal for a picnic—complemented by a fantastic new playground that's guaranteed to entertain the tots. Surrounding the park is the Arcata Community Forest—600 acres of lush second-growth redwoods favored by hikers, mountain bikers, and equestrians. Before you go, pick up a free guide to the forest's mountain-biking or hiking trails at the Arcata Chamber of Commerce, 1062 G Street at 11th Street in downtown Arcata; (707)822-3619.

Bird-watching. On the south side of town is the Arcata Marsh and Wildlife Preserve, a 154-acre sanctuary for hundreds of egrets, marsh wrens, and other waterfowl. A free self-guided walking tour of the preserve, which doubles as Arcata's integrated wetland wastewater treatment plant, is available at the Chamber of Commerce. Each Saturday at 8:30am the Audubon Society gives free one-hour guided tours at the cul-de-sac at the foot of South I Street; (707)826-7031.

Baseball. The best way to spend a summer Sunday afternoon in Arcata is at the Arcata Ballpark, where only a few bucks buys you nine innings of America's favorite pastime hosted by the Humboldt Crabs semipro team. With the band blasting and the fans cheering, you'd swear you were back in high school. Most games are played Wednesday, Friday, and Saturday evenings June through July, with an occasional doubleheader thrown in. The ballpark is located at 9th and F Streets in downtown Arcata, but don't park your car anywhere near foulball territory. Visit the Arcata Chamber of Commerce for schedule information at 1062 G Street at 11th Street, or call (707)822-3619.

Movies. For first-run and classic college flicks, queue up at the Arcata or the Minor Theatre, both of which offer a wide range of films at starving-student prices (the daily matinees are particularly cheap). Arcata Theatre: 1036 G Street at 10th Street; (707)822-5171. Minor Theatre: 1013 H Street at 10th Street; (707)822-5171.

Kinetic Kontraptions. Arcata is a festival-happy town, and its wackiest event of the year is the World Championship

Great Arcata to Ferndale Cross-Country Kinetic Sculpture Race. The three-day event, held every Memorial Day weekend, draws more than 10,000 spectators who come to watch about 50 crazy competitors try to slog through 38 grueling miles of sand, swamp, and salt water in their custom-made, people-powered amphibious crafts. Contestants start in Arcata Plaza, pass though Eureka, and finish (if they're lucky) in the town of Ferndale. Cheating and bribery are part of the rules, provided they're done with "proper style and panache." The zaniest "sculptures" are showcased in the Kinetic Sculpture Museum at 780 Main Street in Ferndale. For more information about the race, call the Arcata Chamber of Commerce at (707)822-3619.

That handsome 1857 brick building at the southwest corner of Arcata Plaza is Jacoby's Storehouse, a fully restored California State Landmark that houses several shops, offices, and restaurants.

RESTAURANTS

ABRUZZI ★★

Named after a region on the Italian Adriatic, Abruzzi is located on the bottom floor of the 140-year-old Jacoby Storehouse, an old brick complex that's been converted into the historic Arcata Plaza shopping mall. If you have trouble finding the place, just follow your nose: The smell of garlic and fresh bread will soon steer you to Chris Smith and Bill Chino's friendly spot, where you'll be served an ample amount of artfully arranged food. Meals begin with a basket of warm bread sticks, focaccia, and a baguette, followed by such highly recommended dishes as pasta carbonara, linguine *pescara* (prawns, calamari, and clams tossed in a light Sicilian tomato sauce), or any of the fresh seafood specials. The standout dessert is the chocolate *paradiso*—a dense chocolate cake set in a pool of champagne mousseline. Smith and Chino also own the **Plaza Grill** on the third floor of the same building—a great place to finish off the evening by sipping a glass of wine in front of the fireplace. *At the corner of 8th and H Sts at Arcata Plaza; (707)826-2345; 791 8th St, Arcata; full bar; AE, DIS, MC, V; checks OK; dinner every day; $$.* &

FOLIE DOUCE ★★

To say Folie Douce just serves pizza is like saying Tiffany's just sells jewelry. Designer pizza is more like it. Try the

"Baseball's a big tradition in Arcata; it's been around for 50 years. It's a really neat family activity . . . something to get the whole family out, young and old."
—Shandra Grobey, Arcata Ballpark ticket seller

Heaven is a full
pitcher of Red
Nectar Ale at the
Humboldt Brewing
Company in down-
town Arcata. For
tour information,
call (707)826-BREW
or just show up at
the corner of 10th
and G Streets.

Thai chicken pizza—marinated bits of breast topped with fontina, ginger, and peanuts, cooked in a wood-fired oven. Other toppings you won't find in your standard Pizza Hut include house-smoked salmon, chèvre, Brie, and wild mushrooms. If pizza doesn't set your heart aflutter, indulge in macadamia-encrusted scallops served in a light cream sauce or the moist Monk's Chicken, a full boneless breast sautéed in butter, flambéed in brandy, and simmered in white wine, mustard, and cream. The artichoke heart cheesecake appetizer is wonderful as well. Locals love this festive, brightly painted place, so reservations—even for early birds—are strongly recommended. *On G St between 15th and 16th Sts; (707)822-1042; 1551 G St, Arcata; beer and wine; DIS, MC, V; checks OK; dinner Tues–Sat; $$.* &

LOS BAGELS ☆

In 1987 bagel companies all over the country sent their doughy products to NBC's *Today Show* to vie for the title of Best Bagel. The verdict: The best bagel outside of New York City was made by Los Bagels in Arcata. This emporium is a popular town hangout, where you'll see lots of folks scanning the morning paper while they munch on bagels layered with smoked salmon, smoked albacore, or lox. Try some fresh-baked challah or, if you're feeling particularly adventurous, a poppyseed bagel topped with jalapeno jam and cream cheese, or a multigrain bagel smeared with hummus or guacamole. Owing to Los Bagels' brisk business, the owners opened a second location in Eureka. *On I St between 10th and 11th Sts; (707)822-3150; 1061 I St, Arcata; no alcohol; no credit cards; local checks only; breakfast, lunch Wed–Mon; $.* &

At TJ's Classic Cafe
on H Street at 11th
you can start your
morning off with a
big three-course
breakfast for under
$5. Darn good
onion rings, too;
(707)822-4650.

LODGINGS
THE LADY ANNE ☆☆

Just a few blocks from Arcata Plaza in a quiet residential neighborhood, this exquisite example of Queen Anne architecture has been painstakingly restored by innkeepers Sharon Ferrett and Sam Pennisi (who, by the way, was once Arcata's mayor). Five large and airy guest rooms are each decorated with antiques, burnished woods, English stained glass, Oriental rugs, and lace curtains. Romantics should book the Lady Sarah Angela Room, which boasts a four-poster bed and a beautiful bay view. Families often request the Cinnamon Bear Room, which is chock-full of teddy bears and will sleep up to four with its king-size and trundle beds. The inn's two parlors are stocked with several games, as well as a grand piano and other musical instruments that you're welcome to play. When the weather is warm, relax on Lady Anne's veranda or head out to the lawn for a game of croquet. Breakfast (beg for the Belgian waffles) is served in the grand dining room, which is warmed by a roaring fire in the winter. *At the corner of 14th and I Sts; (707)822-2797; 902 14th St, Arcata, CA 95521; MC, V; checks OK; $$.*

HOTEL ARCATA ☆

Located at the northeast corner of Arcata's winsome town plaza, this handsome turn-of-the-century hotel has been carefully restored to its original state, evoking an ambience of Arcata's halcyon days (it wouldn't take much to imagine Humphrey Bogart or Grace Kelly strolling down the lobby). If you're not inclined to stay at the more sumptuous Lady Anne B&B (see above), this is definitely the next-best choice. The individually decorated rooms range from small singles starting at a modest $66 to twice that amount for a large Executive Suite that overlooks the plaza. The mini-suites, a bargain at $88, are the quietest. A few requisite modern amenities include cable TV and shuttle service to the airport. Continental breakfast is complimentary, and there's also a Japanese restaurant, Tomo, on the premises (under different management). The hotel offers its guests free passes to the health club and indoor pool just a few blocks down the street. *At the corner of 9th and G Sts; (800)344-1221 or (707)826-0217; 708 9th St, Arcata, CA 95521; AE, CB, DC, DIS, MC, V; no checks; $$.*

Held the Saturday before Father's Day is the Arcata Bay Oyster Festival, hosted by "Fred Oystair."

Need a new read? Tin Can Mailman, located at the corner of 10th and H Streets in downtown Arcata, is a terrific used-book store with more than 130,000 hard- and softcover titles, including a few collector's items. Open daily 10am–6pm; (707)822-1307.

FAIRWINDS MOTEL

The Fairwinds Motel—your classic American freeway-side AAA-rated motel, right down to the wall-to-wall carpeting and cheap framed prints—is the only budget motel in downtown Arcata. Located two blocks from Humboldt State University and a short walk from the town square, it has 27 plain-but-passable rooms, all with direct-dial phones, cable TV, and double-, queen-, or king-size beds. Although the hotel has been around for a few decades and its age lines are showing, the interiors have been completely remodeled with new beds and modern furnishings. *At the corner of 17th and G Sts; (707)822-4824; 1674 G St, Arcata, CA 95521; AE, DIS, MC, V; no checks; $.*

TRINIDAD

For a brief, scenic detour off Highway 101, take the West-haven Drive exit on northbound 101, cross under the freeway, and turn right on Scenic Drive. The narrow shoreline drive passes two public beaches—Moonstone and Luffe-holtz—before ending in downtown Trinidad.

In the early 1850s Trinidad was a booming supply town with a population of 3,000; now it's one of the smallest incorporated cities in California, a small rocky bluff that a handful of fishers, artists, retirees, and shopkeepers call home. A sort of Mendocino in miniature, cute-as-a-button Trinidad is known mainly as a sportfishing town: Trawlers and skiffs sit patiently in the bay, awaiting tourists willing to part with a $50 bill for an afternoon of salmon fishing. Scenery and silence, however, are the town's most desirable commodities; if all you're after is a little R&R on the coast, Trinidad is among the most peaceful and beautiful areas you'll find in California.

ACTIVITIES

Oceanside Park. Five miles north of Trinidad, off Patrick's Point Drive, is Patrick's Point State Park, a 640-acre ocean-side peninsula laden with lush, fern-lined trails that wind through foggy forests of cedar, pine, and spruce. The park was once a seasonal fishing village of the Yurok Indians. Nowadays it's overrun with campers in the summer, but it's still worth a visit to stroll down Agate Beach (keep an eye out for the semiprecious stones), climb the stone stairway up to the house-size Ceremonial Rock, and admire the vistas from Rim

Trail—a 2-mile path along the cliffs where you can sometimes spot sea lions, harbor seals, and gray whales. In 1990 descendants of the original Indian settlers reconstructed an authentic Yurok village—open to the public—within the park. A map and guide to all the park's attractions is included in the $5-per-vehicle day-use fee (which you can skip by parking outside the entrance and walking in); (707)677-3570.

Forest Trail. If the long drive on Highway 101 has you feeling cramped, unwind for a spell at Trinidad's Demonstration Forest. The self-guided trail—virtually unknown and almost always deserted—leads through a lush, peaceful redwood forest and takes about 20 minutes to complete. A picnic area hidden near the parking lot is the perfect spot for a leisurely lunch in the cool shade. Take the Trinidad exit off Highway 101 and head north on Patrick's Point Drive for about a mile.

Sinker Swim. A day spent sportfishing off Trinidad's bounteous coast is both fun and easier than you think. Simply drop your prerigged line, reel in when something's tugging on the other end, and throw it in the burlap sack at your feet. For a small fee, the crew does all the dirty work of cleaning and cutting your catch, and Katy's Smokehouse (see sidebar) will take care of the rest. Trinidad's two sportfishing charter boats are the 36-foot *Jumpin' Jack*, (707)839-4743 or (800)839-4744, and the 45-foot *Shenandoah*, (707)677-3625. Both charters offer morning and afternoon trips daily from Trinidad Pier, and walk-ons are welcome. The five-hour salmon and rockfish hunt runs about $60 per person, which includes all fishing gear. One-day fishing licenses can be purchased on board.

If you're lucky enough to reel in a lunker salmon, haul it up to Katy's Smokehouse, located just up the road from the pier at 740 Edwards Street in Trinidad; (707)677-0151. Katy herself will smoke 'er up and wrap it to go, or even send it via UPS to your home. Her salmon jerky ain't bad, either.

RESTAURANTS

LARRUPIN' CAFE ★★★

Trinidad's finest restaurant—looking very chic with its candlelit tables and colorful urns full of exotic flowers—draws a major crowd nightly with its creative seafood dishes and fantastic pork ribs served with a side of sweet and spicy barbecue sauce. Oysters, mussels, and crab are often served the same day they're plucked from Humboldt Bay. Every meal comes with a red- and green-leaf

The Humboldt State University Marine Laboratory, located at Edwards and Ewing Streets in downtown Trinidad, is open to the public daily from 9am to 5pm. The lab features various live marine life displays, including a touch tank and tide pool; (707)826-3671.

salad tossed with a Gorgonzola vinaigrette and an appetizer board stocked with gravlax, pâté, dark pumpernickel, apple slices, and the house mustard sauce. For your choice of a starch, order the tasty twice-baked potato stuffed with locally made cheese, sour cream, and scallions. Finish off your feast with a slice of pecan-chocolate pie topped with hot buttered rum sauce or the wickedly good triple layer chocolate cake layered with caramel and whipped cream. When making your reservation (highly recommended), ask for a table on the attic-like second floor; its arched ceiling and wicker chairs make it slightly more intimate than the main dining room. *From Hwy 101, take the Trinidad exit and head N on Patrick's Point Dr; (707)677-0230; 1658 Patrick's Point Dr, Trinidad; beer and wine; no credit cards; checks OK; dinner every day in the summer (Thurs–Sun only from Labor Day to Memorial Day); $$.* &

If you have a little time to kill in Trinidad, take the drive along Stagecoach Road, which starts on Main Street and ends a few miles later at Larrupin' Cafe on Patrick's Point Drive. The winding, fern-lined road is well worth the trip.

LODGINGS

THE LOST WHALE BED AND BREAKFAST INN ☆☆☆

 The Lost Whale isn't just a place to stay overnight, it's a destination in itself—particularly for families with small children. The traditional Cape Cod–style building, constructed in 1989, stands alone on a 4-acre grassy cliff overlooking the sea, with a private stairway leading down to miles of deserted rocky beach. Proprietors Susanne Lakin and Lee Miller manage to give romancing couples lots of space and solitude, yet they have also created one of the most family-friendly inns on the California coast. Five of the inn's eight soundproof rooms have private balconies or sitting alcoves with views of the Pacific, two rooms have separate sleeping lofts, and all have private baths and queen-size beds. Lakin and Miller also rent out two furnished private homes that can accommodate up to six people each: a spectacular beach house that overlooks the ocean, and a charming farmhouse set on 5 acres that's equipped with a whirlpool tub, a fireplace, a kitchen, and a laundry room. After a day on the inn's beach or at neighboring Patrick's Point State Park, relax in the outdoor hot tub while listening to the distant bark of sea lions or looking out for whales. Kids can romp around on the playground—which has a small playhouse with its own loft—or play with the menagerie of pygmy goats and rabbits roaming the inn's 1½-acre plot up the street. Lakin and Miller take great pride in their huge breakfasts—casseroles, quiches, home-baked muffins, fresh fruit, locally smoked salmon served with vegetables from the garden—and provide plenty of snacks throughout the day and evening. *From Hwy 101, take the Seawood Dr exit and head N for 1¾ miles on Patrick's Point Dr; (707)677-3425 or (800)677-7859; 3452 Patrick's Point Dr, Trinidad, CA 95570; lmiller@northcoast.com; www.lostwhale-inn.com; AE, DIS, MC, V; checks OK; $$$.*

A great way to start your day in Trinidad is with a hefty omelet at the Seascape Restaurant, (707)677-3762, followed by a shoreline stroll along Trinidad Head Trail. You'll find the restaurant at the foot of Trinidad Pier and the trailhead at the southeast corner of the pier's dirt parking lot.

TRINIDAD BAY BED AND BREAKFAST

 Perched on a bluff overlooking Trinidad's quaint fishing harbor and the rugged California coast, this Cape Cod–style inn is the dream house of innkeepers Carol and Paul Kirk, Southern California transplants who fell in love with the area while visiting Arcata more than a decade ago. They offer four guest rooms and two great suites. Both suites have private entrances, comfortable sitting rooms, spectacular views of Trinidad Bay, and breakfast-in-bed service. The Mauve Suite has a large brick fireplace, wraparound windows, and a king-size bed; the Blue Bay View Suite upstairs offers more privacy (its entrance is outside the inn), a telescope for whale watching, a king-size bed, and the best bay view in town. The Kirks' expanded continental breakfast features fresh and baked fruit, homemade breads served with lemon-honey and molasses butter, muffins (pear-ginger, cranberry-orange, fruit-bran), and locally made cheeses. *From Hwy 101, take the Trinidad exit to Main St, and turn left on Trinity St; (707)677-0840; 560 Edwards St, PO Box 849, Trinidad, CA 95570; www.visitormags.com/trinidadbay; MC, V; checks OK; $$$.*

Redwood National Park, which stretches for 44 miles along the coast from Orick to Crescent City, was created in 1968 to protect 76,000 of the then-remaining 93,000 acres of old-growth forest—a forest that once covered a whopping 2 million acres of California and Oregon.

TRINIDAD INN ☆

It's always exciting to discover a lodging that offers so much for so little, and the Trinidad Inn is exactly that sort of place. Located 2 miles north of Trinidad on a quiet stretch of road ensconced by groves of aromatic redwoods, this 10-room motel trimmed in white and blue is impeccably maintained. Each room is unique: some are family units that hold up to four persons, while others offer a comfortable queen bed, large TV, and private bath for as little as $65 per night. The best room for couples is number 10, an adorably quaint cottage complete with a full kitchen, living room, private bath, bedroom, and small patio (a steal at $100). Each morning Pearl, the manager, serves fresh coffee, tea, and homemade raspberry scones and muffins under the gazebo in the flower-filled garden. Guests are free to use the picnic table and barbecue, or wander through the adjacent forest to the beaches a short stroll away. *From Hwy 101, take the Trinidad exit and head 2 miles N on Patrick's Point Dr; (707)677-3349; 1170 Patrick's Point Dr, Trinidad, CA 95570; AE, MC, V; checks OK; $$.* ㅎ

ORICK

For more information about the Redwood National and State Parks, visit the Web site at www.nps.gov/redw.

The burl capital of the world, Orick resembles more of a huge outdoor gift shop than a town. What's a burl, you ask? Well, take a sizable chunk of redwood, do a little carving here and there with a small chain saw, and when it resembles some sort of mammal or rodent, you have yourself a burl (actually, it's still not a burl; a real burl is a growth on the side of a redwood's trunk). There are thousands of burls to choose from here, ranging from the Abominable Burlman to Sasquatch and the Seven Dwarfs. Several roadside stands have viewing booths where mesmerized tourists watch the redwood chips fly. Orick is also regarded as the southern entrance to Redwood National and State Park; 1 mile south of town off Highway 101 is the Redwood Information Center, where visitors can pick up a free map of Redwood National and State Park and browse through the geologic, wildlife, and Native American exhibits. Open daily 9am to 5pm; (707)464-6101, ext. 5265.

ACTIVITIES

Fern Canyon Trail. Up there with the natural wonders of the world is the spectacular Fern Canyon Trail in Prairie Creek Redwoods State Park. The half-mile trail winds through a narrow canyon whose 50-foot-high vertical walls are blanketed with lady, deer, chain, and five-finger ferns. In the summer several footbridges allow you to cross the small stream that runs down the middle. One of the highlights of a trip to Fern Canyon, Gold Bluffs Beach, and Prairie Creek are the hundreds of wild Roosevelt Elk that wander and graze next to the road. From Highway 101, take the Davison Road exit (at Rolf's Park Cafe), which follows along Gold Bluffs Beach to the Fern Canyon parking lot. Day-use fee is $5. No motor homes or trailers more than 24 feet long.

Is that a big deer in that meadow? Nope. Roosevelt elk. Around 2,000 of Redwood National Park's largest mammals live in northwestern California; many of them can often be spotted at the Elk Prairie campground off the Newton B. Drury Scenic Parkway or along Gold Bluffs Beach.

Chief Tenderfeet. Love nature but hate to hike? Then the Big Tree Trail is just for you. It's short (a quarter of a mile), paved, and has a big finish; take the Big Tree turnoff along the Newton B. Drury Scenic Parkway. Even more popular among hill-haters is the Lady Bird Johnson Grove Trail, an easy self-guided tour that loops 1 mile around a glorious grove of mature redwoods; take the Bald Hills Road exit off Highway 101, half a mile north of Orick. Then again, why leave your car at all? Cal-Barrel Road, a narrow, packed-gravel road located just north of the Prairie Creek Visitor Center off the Newton B. Drury Scenic Parkway, offers a spectacular 3-mile tour through an old-growth redwood forest (no trailers or motor homes).

Fall is rutting season for Roosevelt elks, when the 1,000-pound bulls claim their harem of cows by charging at anything that stands in their way. Story has it that one particularly irate bull broke nearly every window at Prairie Creek State Park's information center, and soon became part of the center's stuffed wildlife exhibit. That'll teach him.

Tallest Tree. To see the world's tallest tree—we're talkin' 368 feet tall and 14 feet in diameter—you'll first have to go to the Redwood Information Center near Orick (see above) to obtain a free map and permit—only 50 issued per day—to drive to the trailhead of Tall Trees Grove. Of course, you still have to walk a steep 1⅓ miles from the trailhead to the grove, but then you can tell your friends at home that, hey, you saw the tallest tree in the world. For more information, call the center at (707)464-6101.

The average time
spent gawking at
the world's largest
tree is 1 minute 40
seconds.

Prairie Creek Red-
woods State Park
has a fantastic 19-
mile mountain-bike
trail through dense
forest, elk-filled
meadows, and glo-
rious mud holes.
Parts of it are a
real thigh burner,
though, so begin-
ners should sit this
one out. Pick up a
$1 trail map at the
Elk Prairie camp-
ground ranger
station.

"For elk informa-
tion tune to
1610AM."
—A roadside sign
in Prairie Creek
Redwoods State
Park

RESTAURANTS

ROLF'S PARK CAFE ☆

After decades of working as a chef in Switzerland, Austria, San Francisco, and even aboard the presidential ship
SS Roosevelt, the trilingual Rolf Rheinschmidt decided it
was time to semi-retire. He wanted to move to a small
town to cook, and towns don't get much smaller than
Orick—population 650. So here among the redwoods
Rheinschmidt serves good bratwurst, wiener schnitzel,
and crêpes Suzette. His specialty is the marinated rack of
spring lamb, and he has some unusual offerings such as
wild boar, buffalo, and elk steak (the truly adventurous
should get the combo platter featuring all three). Each
dinner entree includes lots of extras: hors d'oeuvres, a
salad, vegetables, farm-style potatoes, and bread. And
ever since the debut of Rheinschmidt's German Farmer
Omelet—an open-faced concoction of ham, bacon,
sausage, mushrooms, cheese, potatoes, and pasta, topped
with sour cream and salsa and garnished with a strawberry
crêpe—breakfast in Orick has never been the same. *On
Hwy 101 about 2 miles N of Orick; (707)488-3841; beer and
wine; MC, V; local checks only; breakfast, lunch, dinner every
day in the summer (typically open Mar through Nov); $$.* &

KLAMATH

From the looks of it, the town of Klamath apparently hasn't
recovered since it was washed away in 1964, when 40 inches of
rain fell within 24 hours. All that remains are a few cheap
motels, trailer parks, tackle shops, and boat rentals, which are
kept in business solely by the gaggles of fishermen who line the
mighty Klamath River, one of the finest salmon and steelhead
streams in the world. The scenery around Klamath, however, is
extraordinary; smack in the middle of the Redwood National
and State Parks, the area has some incredible coastal drives and
trails that even the timid and out-of-shape can handle with
aplomb.

ACTIVITIES

The Klamath is California's second-largest river, a 263-mile-long waterway fed by more than 300 tributaries.

Yurok Loop Nature Trail. A great way to spend an hour of your day is walking the Yurok Loop Nature Trail at Lagoon Creek, located 6½ miles north of the Klamath River bridge on Highway 101. The 1-mile self-guided trail gradually climbs to the top of rugged sea bluffs—with wonderful panoramic views of the Pacific—and loops back to the parking lot. If your partner's up to it, have him or her meet you at the Requa Trailhead (see below) and take the 4-mile coastal trail to the mouth of the Klamath. Dress warmly, and bring some water and sunscreen.

Coastal Overlook. As good a place to stretch your legs as any is the lofty Klamath Overlook, which stands some 600 feet above an estuary at the mouth of the Klamath River. A short but steep trail leads down to a second overlook that is ideal for whale watching and photo ops. The coastal trail continues 4 miles north to the Yurok Loop trail at Lagoon Creek (see above). To get here, take the Requa Road turnoff from Highway 101, north of the Klamath River bridge, and keep heading west.

Forest & Coastal Drive. One of the premier coastal drives on the Redwood Coast starts at the mouth of the Klamath River and runs 8 miles south toward Prairie Creek Redwoods State Park. The narrow, partially paved drive winds through stands of redwoods, with spectacular views of the Pacific and numerous pull-offs for picture-taking (sea lions and pelicans abound) and short hikes. Keep an eye out for the World War II radar station, disguised as a farmhouse and barn. If you're heading south on Highway 101, take the Klamath Beach Road exit just south of the Klamath River bridge and follow the signs to the Mouth of Klamath. Northbound travelers should take the Redwood National and State Parks Coastal Drive exit off the Newton B. Drury Scenic Parkway. Campers and cars with trailers are not advised.

Kid-Friendly Kayaking. For a mere six bucks, thrill-seekers can shoot the Smith River's wimpier rapids in an inflatable kayak. The 4-hour ranger-led outings

A must-do detour along Highway 101 is the Newton B. Drury Scenic Parkway, which passes through dazzling groves of redwoods and elk-filled meadows before leading back onto the highway 8 miles later.

include educational highlights covering local flora and fauna. Participants must be at least 10 years old, sign up at least two days in advance, weigh under 220 pounds, and be able to swim. The tour, which takes place in the summer (and only if the park budget permits) is limited to 12 kayakers, and spaces—as you would imagine—fill up fast, so reserve a spot (in person) as far in advance as possible. For more information, call the Redwood National Park Information Center at(707)464-6101, ext 5265.

Jet Boating the Klamath River. If you've never been on a giant jet boat on the river, you're missing out on one heck of a thrill ride. Tours aboard these incredibly powerful and fast boats take visitors upriver from the estuary to view bear, deer, elk, osprey hawks, otters, and other wildlife along the river banks. Rates for the 30-mile scenic trip are $20 for adults, $10 for children ages 4 to 11, and free for kids under 4. Open May 1 to October 30. For more information and reservations, contact Klamath River Jet Boat Tours at (800)887-JETS or (707)482-7775.

RESTAURANTS

KLAMATH INN RESTAURANT ☆

Besides being the only decent lodge in the greater Klamath area, the Klamath Inn also has the only decent restaurant. The inn's dining area is simple yet dignified, with views overlooking the Klamath River and a wonderful parlor for sipping an after-dinner sherry by the fireplace. The no-nonsense double-digit menu of steak, chicken, and fresh seafood obviously caters to Klamath's more well-heeled fishermen. On Friday and Saturday summer nights, go with the seasoned prime rib and baked potato; the grilled salmon and halibut are also safe bets. Be sure to leave room for the fresh-baked blackberry cobbler and a side of vanilla ice cream. *From Hwy 101 take the Requa Rd exit and follow the signs; (707)482-8205; 451 Requa Rd, Klamath; beer and wine; DIS, MC, V; checks OK; breakfast (for guests only) every day, lunch Mon–Fri (in the summer only), dinner every day; $$.* &

LODGINGS
KLAMATH INN ☆

The Klamath Inn was established in 1885, and since then it has gone through several owners, four name changes, one relocation, and a major fire that burned it to the ground in 1913 (it was rebuilt the same year). But this venerable riverside inn is still going strong. The 10 spacious guest rooms are modestly decorated with antique furnishings and have private baths with showers or claw-footed tubs; 4 offer views of the lower Klamath River. The inn's highlight is the cozy parlor downstairs, where guests bury themselves in plump armchairs and read beside the wood-burning stove. If you're the outdoorsy type, there are plenty of enticements just outside: sandy riverside beaches, myriad hiking trails in nearby Redwood National and State Parks, and, of course, fishing in the mighty Klamath. If you'd rather luxuriate indoors, make an appointment for the tender ministrations of the inn's massage therapist. *From Hwy 101 take the Requa Rd exit and follow the signs; (707)482-1425; 451 Requa Rd, Klamath, CA 95548; DIS, MC, V; checks OK; $$.*

REDWOOD AYH HOSTEL ▪ DEMARTIN HOUSE

 This turn-of-the-century logger's mansion was remodeled in 1987 to accommodate 30 guests dormitory style (i.e., bunks and shared baths). What it lacks in creature comforts it makes up for in location—a mere 100 yards from the beach, and surrounded by hiking trails leading along the Redwood Coast. A few rooms are reserved for families or couples with advance notice, and the hostel even takes reservations by credit card—strongly recommended in the summer. Showers, country kitchen, dining room, common room, wood stove, redwood deck, and bicycle storage are included in the $12 nightly rate. *Off Hwy 101 on Wilson Creek Road across from Wilson Creek Beach, about 7 miles north of Klamath; (707)482-8265; 14480 Hwy 101, Klamath, CA 95548; MC, V; checks OK; $.* ♿

If you're bringing the family or traveling in a group along the Redwood Coast, then ixnay on the motelay and rent a fully furnished home on the ocean or river's edge for as little as $80 a night. Call Redwood Coast Vacation Rentals for a free brochure at (707)465-0150.

For more information about motels, hotels, campgrounds, and attractions in Klamath, Crescent City, and Del Norte County, log on to www.delnorte.org.

CRESCENT CITY

Because it's the northern gateway to the popular Redwood National Park, one might assume Crescent City would be a major tourist mecca, rife with fine restaurants and hotels. Unfortunately, it's not. Cheap motels, fast-food chains, and mini-malls are the main attractions along this stretch of Highway 101, as if Crescent City exists only to serve travelers on their way someplace else. The city is trying to enhance its image, however, and if you know where to go (which is anywhere off Highway 101), there are actually numerous sites worth visiting in the area and several outdoor-activity options that are refreshingly nontouristy. You won't want to make Crescent City your destination, mind you, but don't be reluctant to spend a day lolling around here, either; you'd be surprised what the town has to offer besides gas and groceries.

ACTIVITIES

Sea Life Under Glass. Crescent City's version of the Bay Area's popular Marine World–Africa USA is Ocean World, a painfully touristy attraction filled with sharks, eels, octopi, and various other caged creatures of the sea. Located on Highway 101 near the Crescent City Harbor (you can't miss it), it's best seen from the car window unless you have kids, who get a kick out of the petting pools and trained sea lion acts. Oh, and don't forget to pick up a tiny shrink-wrapped seashell for only $4 at the glittery gift store. Open daily 9am to 6pm, open later in summer; (707)464-4900.

GETTING THERE

There's only one route along the Redwood Coast—Highway 101—and only one way to get there: drive. Greyhound (800-231-2222) offers limited bus service to Eureka and Crescent City but is next to worthless for exploring the coast, and Amtrak only runs inland along Interstate 5. A popular option among groups of couples is to rent a small motor home for wheels and book a series of rooms for sleeping; look in the Yellow Pages under "Motor Home–Renting & Leasing" for the nearest dealer.

Pebble Beach Drive. To see the winsome side of Crescent City, take a shoreline cruise along Pebble Beach Drive from the west end of Sixth Street to Point St. George. Along the way you're bound to see a few seals and sea lions at the numerous pullouts. End the tour with a short walk though a sandy meadow to Point St. George, a relatively deserted bluff that's perfect for a picnic or beach stroll. On a clear day, look out on the ocean for the St. George Reef Lighthouse, thought to be the tallest (146 feet above sea level), deadliest (several light-keepers died in rough seas while trying to dock), and most expensive ($704,000) lighthouse ever built.

Wildlife Area. Crescent City's best-kept secret is the Lake Earl Wildlife Area, a gorgeous habitat replete with deer, rabbits, beavers, otters, red-tailed hawks, peregrine falcons, bald eagles, songbirds (some 80 species), shorebirds, and migratory waterfowl who share 5,000 acres of the area's pristine woodlands, grasslands, and ocean shore. Hiking and biking are permitted, but you'll want to make the trip on foot with binoculars in hand to get the full effect of this amazing patch of coastal land. To get here, take the Northcrest Drive exit off Highway 101 in downtown Crescent City and turn left on Old Mill Road. Proceed 1½ miles to the park headquarters at 2591 Old Mill Road (if it's open, ask for a map) and park in the gravel lot. Additional trails start at the end of Old Mill Road. For more information, call the Department of Fish and Game at (707)464-2523.

Picnic & Hiking. One of the prettiest picnic sites on the California coast is along Enderts Road at the south end of Crescent City. Pack a picnic lunch at Alias Jones Cafe (see Restaurants, below), stop by a liquor store for a few bottles of Chianti, drive 3 miles south on Highway 101 from downtown, and turn right on Enderts Road (across from the Ocean Way Motel). Continue 2⅓ miles, park at the Crescent Beach Overlook, lay your blanket on the grass, admire the ocean view atop your personal 500-foot bluff, and relax. Type A personalities can drive to the end of Enderts Road and take the short hiking trail to Enderts Beach. In the summer, free 1½- to 2-hour ranger-guided tide pool and seashore walks are offered when the tides are right,

Who says crime doesn't pay? Employing more than 1,500 people and pumping an annual $32 million into logging-starved Del Norte County's economy is Pelican Bay State Prison. The high-tech maximum-security facility, located 7 miles north of Crescent City on Lake Earl Drive, has become so profitable that a second prison is on the drawing board.

Don't disturb any abandoned baby seals or sea lions you may encounter on California's beaches. The mom is probably out getting lunch, and she won't come back until you leave; in fact, you may be fined up to $10,000 for your good intentions. However, if a pup looks injured or in danger, call the Marine Mammal Center at (707)465-MAML.

Before touring the Redwood National and State Parks, pick up a free guide at the Redwood National Park Headquarters and Information Center at 1111 2nd Street (at K Street) in Crescent City, open daily 9am–5pm; (707)464-6101, ext. 5265. For information about Crescent City, across the street is the County Visitors Center, open daily 9am to 6pm (Monday to Friday in winter); (800)343-8300.

Worth a gander is the vast fleet of stalwart fishing vessels docked in Crescent City Harbor off Highway 101. Watch the leathery crews unload their slimy catch and splay their massive nets in the public parking lot, and you'll soon understand why Crescent City ain't no wimpy tourist town.

starting at the beach parking lot. For specific tour times, call (707)464-6101, ext 5064.

📷 **Through the Redwood Forest.** For car-bound cruisers who want to take a journey through an unbelievably spectacular old-growth redwood forest—considered by many to be one of the most beautiful areas in the world—there's a hidden, well-maintained gravel road called Howland Hill Road that winds for about 12 miles through Jedediah Smith Redwoods State Park. To get there from Highway 101, keep an eye out for the 76 gas station at the south end of Crescent City; just before

WHAT TO DO IN CRESCENT CITY

Tennis: Lighted courts are available off Washington Boulevard near the Del Norte High School in Crescent City. Take Northcrest Drive off Highway 101 in downtown Crescent City and turn left on Washington Boulevard. Free.

Golf: Kings Valley Golf Course, a par-28 9-hole course, is at 3030 Lesina Road at the junction of Highway 101 and Highway 199, 3 miles northeast of Crescent City. Green fee under $7 for nine holes; (707)464-2886.

Swimming: Fred Endert Municipal Swimming Pool is at 1000 Play Street, directly behind the Crescent City Chamber of Commerce/Visitors Center. $2–$3 fee; (707)464-9503.

Horseshoes: Pits are located on Beach Front Park near the visitors Center (BYO shoes). Free.

Marine Mammal Center. Located at the north end of Crescent City Harbor at 424 Howe Drive in Beach Front Park is the North Coast Marine Mammal Center, a nonprofit organization established in 1989 to rescue and rehabilitate stranded or injured marine mammals. Staffed by local volunteers and funded by donations, the center is the only facility of its kind between the San Francisco area and Seattle, providing emergency response to environmental disasters and assisting marine researchers by collecting data on marine mammals. The center is open daily year-round to the public, who are welcome to watch the volunteers in action, make a donation, and buy a nature book or two at the gift shop; (707)465-MAML.

the station, turn right on Elk Valley Road, and follow it to Howland Hill Road, which will be on your right. After driving through the park, you'll end up at Highway 199 near the town of Hiouchi, and from there it's a short jaunt west to get back to Highway 101. Plan at least two to three hours for the 45-mile round-trip, or all day if you want to do some hiking or mountain biking in the park. Trailers and motor homes are not allowed.

Secret Beach. For your very own private beach, take the Mouth Smith River Road exit on Highway 101 near the Oregon border. At the Mouth Smith River parking lot, turn right on S Indian Road and park at the small, flower-filled cemetery. Take the footpath at the north end of the cemetery and—voilà!—you'll come upon a secluded little beach overlooking majestic Prince Island. On the way back to Crescent City, take the Lake Earl Drive turnoff for a brief, bucolic tour of the Smith River area before rejoining Highway 101 in town.

RESTAURANTS

BEACHCOMBER RESTAURANT ☆

View If you can get past the Beachcomber Restaurant's tired nautical theme and blue Naugahyde booths, you'll find that this Crescent City institution does a fair job of providing fresh seafood—halibut, red snapper, lingcod, chinook salmon—at reasonable prices. Set right on the beach, the Beachcomber also specializes in flame-broiled steaks, cooked to your specification on an open barbecue pit. Friday and Saturday are prime-rib nights. Ask for a booth by the window, and start the evening with the steamer-clam appetizer: 1½ pounds of the North Coast's finest. Note: The restaurant occasionally closes in the fall for a month, so be sure to call ahead. *2 miles S of downtown Crescent City on Hwy 101; (707)464-2205; 1400 Hwy 101, Crescent City; beer and wine; MC, V; local checks only; dinner Thurs–Tues; $$.* &

For a romantic beachside bonfire, drive to the west end of W 3rd Street, walk down the spiral staircase, gather a few logs from the enormous piles of driftwood, and light them in the provided fire ring. Maybe the best things in life are free.

The operational Battery Point Lighthouse, built in 1856, is on a small island off the foot of A Street in Crescent City; 20-minute guided tours of the lighthouse and the lightkeeper's living quarters are offered Wednesday through Sunday from 10am to 4pm, tide permitting (you have to cross a tide pool to get there), April through September; (707)464-3089.

If you brought along your camping supplies, be sure to check out the relatively unknown Clifford Kamph (pun intended?) Memorial Park, located 1 mile south of the Oregon border off Highway 101. It has several grassy campsites—with picnic tables and barbecues—perched on a bluff overlooking the ocean. At $5 per night for beachfront access, it's a steal.

On the morning of March 28, 1964, a series of tsunamis spawned by a massive Alaskan earthquake devastated Crescent City, destroying much of the downtown district and killing 14 people.

LODGINGS

CRESCENT BEACH MOTEL ☆

 Crescent City has the dubious distinction of being the only city along the coast without a swanky hotel. There is, however, an armada of cheap motels, the best of which is the Crescent Beach Motel. A new color scheme of brown, beige, and green has improved the interiors considerably, and all but 4 of the 27 rooms are within steps of the beach. Most units have queen-size beds and color TVs. The small lawn area and large sun decks overlooking the ocean are great venues for kicking back and enjoying some true R&R. Another perk: You can get a seafood dinner at the Beachcomber Restaurant (see the review above), which is right next door. *2 miles south of downtown on Hwy 101; (707)464-5436; 1455 Hwy 101, Crescent City, CA 95531; AE, DIS, MC, V; no checks; $.*

CURLY REDWOOD LODGE ☆

Built in 1959 with lumber from a single ancient redwood on grasslands across from the town's harbor, the Curly Redwood Lodge looks as if it's been preserved in a time capsule from the '60s, the kind of place where you might have stayed as a kid during one of those cross-country vacations in the family station wagon. Granted, it's not as fancy as the newer chain motels down the street, but it's loaded with character (as well as the requisite TVs and telephones) and lean on price. As an added bonus, both the beach and Beachcomber Restaurant (see Restaurants above) are right across the street. *2 miles S of downtown on Hwy 101; (707)464-2137; 701 Hwy 101, Crescent City, CA 95531. AE, CB, DC, MC, V; no checks; $.*

INDEX